BARRON'S BUSINESS LIBRARY

Computers and Business Tasks

Douglas Downing
School of Business and Economics
Seattle Pacific University

contributors:
Gregg Rosenberg
  University of Georgia
Mark Yoshimi
  Family Life Insurance
Marlys Downing
  mortgage loan processor

BARRON'S
New York • London • Toronto • Sydney

General editor for *Barron's Business Library* is George T. Friedlob, professor in the School of Accountancy at Clemson University.

Copyright © 1991 by Barron's Educational Series, Inc.

All rights reserved.

No part of this book may be reproduced in any form, by photostat, microfilm, xerography or any other means, or incorporated into any information retrieval system, electronic or mechanical, without the written permission of the copyright owner.

All inquiries should be addressed to:
Barron's Educational Series, Inc.
250 Wireless Boulevard
Hauppauge, New York 11788

Library of Congress Catalog Card No. 90-28811

International Standard Book No. 0-8120-4543-2

Library of Congress Cataloging in Publication Data
Downing, Douglas.
   Computers and business tasks / Douglas Downing : contributors, Gregg Rosenberg, Mark Yoshimi, Marlys Downing.
    p. cm.
  Includes index.
  ISBN 0-8120-4543-2
   1. Lotus 1-2-3 (Computer program)   2. Business—Computer programs. I. Title.
HF5548.4.L67D68   1991
650'.0285'5369—dc20   90-28811
                                                                                              CIP

PRINTED IN ITALY
1234 9929 987654321

Dedication

This book is dedicated to my father, Robert Downing, who worked with punched-card data processing equipment in the 1950s (and let his children visit his office to watch the machines punch and sort the cards), who worked with the early IBM 360s in the 1960s, who implemented microcomputer budgeting systems in the 1980s, and who reached a well-deserved retirement in the 1990s.

Acknowledgments

I am deeply indebted to my father, Robert Downing, for sharing his experience and carefully reading the manuscript. Three people contributed chapters: Gregg Rosenberg, of the University of Georgia artificial intelligence program, who wrote the chapter on expert systems; Mark Yoshimi, a data processing computer programmer, who wrote the chapter on purchase order maintenance systems; and my sister, Marlys Downing, who wrote chapters on collecting overdue accounts and mortgage loan processing. Several people helped with advice: Michael Covington of the University of Georgia; Dale Foreman, of the law firm of Foreman and Arch, Wenatchee, Washington; and Alec Hill, Professor of Business Law at Seattle Pacific University. Special thanks also to my mother, Peggy Downing, for reviewing the manuscript.

Contents

Introduction / vii
1. Business Tasks, Software, and Hardware / 1
2. Brief History of Information Processing / 21
3. Spreadsheets: Making Optimal Decisions / 42
4. Spreadsheets: Budget Development / 71
5. Macros / 87
6. Accounting / 96
7. Advanced 1-2-3 Macros for Accounting / 105
8. Budget Monitoring / 129
9. Data Base Management / 139
10. Investment Decisions / 156
11. Budget Information for Large Organizations / 177
12. Three-Dimensional Spreadsheets / 192
13. Networks and Electronic Data Interchange / 214
14. Expert Systems / 225
15. Problems / 237
16. Example: Collecting Past-due Accounts / 250
17. Example: Mortgage Loans / 254
18. Example: Purchase Order Maintenance System / 257
19. Example: Information Retrieval / 262

Appendices / 267

Glossary / 272

Index of Lotus 1-2-3 commands / 275

Index / 277

Introduction

This is a book about computers. It focuses not on the technical aspects of how to use computers, but on business and the types of business tasks for which computers can be helpful. In each case we focus first on the objective and then discuss how computers might be used to achieve that objective.

After you determine the tasks your business needs to accomplish, you need to determine which computer software can help you achieve them. We do not go into the details of how to use the many specialized software packages available; instead, we discuss the use of a computer spreadsheet program, since such programs are very versatile and should find a use in any business. Specifically, we focus on Lotus 1-2-3, which has become the most popular computer spreadsheet. In Chapters 3 to 10, we discuss the use of 1-2-3 Release 2; in Chapter 12 we discuss the power of the newer version, Release 3. (The appendix contains a brief discussion of Excel, another popular spreadsheet program.)

If you are not familiar with 1-2-3, this book will introduce you to its use. If you are familiar with the program, this book will help you learn how to create business application spreadsheets. In either case, you need to work out examples yourself on your own computer; you cannot learn how to operate a computer merely by reading about it.

The focus of most of the book is the use of microcomputers for small business. Your business may grow, however, so some of the later chapters include examples related to larger organizations.

Computers can be intimidating if you have no experience with them. However, if you concentrate on the tasks that need to be accomplished and view the computer as a servant to perform those tasks, you will discover many ways in which computers can make your business more successful.

Business Tasks, Software, and Hardware

CHAPTER 1

INTRODUCTION AND MAIN POINTS
Suppose you have come up with a brilliant idea for a new product to improve the world. You plan to start your own business, but you have nightmares about the mind-numbing paperwork that you fear will consume all your time. One question you will probably be asked by those helping you get your business started is: "Do you know how to use a computer?" This is actually a rather silly question. Computers are incredibly versatile; nobody knows how to use all of their capabilities. The important question is: "Do you know how a computer can help you perform the tasks that need to be performed in your business?"

In this book the focus is on the tasks you must accomplish to make your business run smoothly. Clearly there are plenty of business tasks, particularly those that require creativity, insight, and judgment, that cannot be turned over to machines. However, there are many others that are tedious and time-consuming. For these, it would help to have a dedicated servant who doesn't mind boring tasks. Think of computers that way: as dedicated servants who help take care of the boring tasks and leave you free to spend time on the exciting, interesting parts of your business.

After studying the material in this chapter:

— You will be familiar with some of the tasks for which computers can be helpful in business.

— You will know what types of software are available to accomplish those tasks.

— You will know how to shop for computer hardware to meet your needs.

TYPES OF TASKS FOR COMPUTERS
A computer is a machine capable of executing instructions much faster than humans can. However, the tasks need to be spelled out very precisely. Computers have no way to determine what

you really mean; they can do only precisely what you tell them to do. Even more annoying, computers need to have their commands translated into a very peculiar type of language that uses only two symbols: 1 and 0. A string of commands in this type of language, called machine language, might look like this: 1 0 1 1 0 1 1 1 1 0 0 1. If people had to speak to computers in language like this, before long people would decide that they would prefer to do the tasks themselves. Fortunately, you do not need to learn machine language to use computers, and we do not say much about machine language in this book.

Soon after the first computers were developed, people realized that it would be necessary to develop translators that could accept commands from the human operators and then translate them into machine language for the computer. Unfortunately, you cannot buy a translator that converts English into machine language, as you see on *Star Trek*. This is because human languages are very complicated, and nobody has been able to develop a computer program that allows a computer to understand a human language. Some progress has been made in this area, so as time passes you may see computers that are easier to talk to; in the meantime, you may obtain prewritten computer instructions (known as *programs*) designed to perform commonly needed tasks. Programs are known as *software,* to distinguish them from the physical components of the system, known as *hardware.* (Here is one way to think of the distinction: If you can drop it, it's hardware; if you can erase it, it's software.)

A computer is only part of an information-processing system. The complete system includes the people who work with the information and the other tools that they use. An information system must perform three tasks: obtaining information in the first place, processing it, and presenting it in meaningful form so that it can be used to achieve the purposes of the system. You should always focus on your information needs first and then figure out how the computer can meet those needs.

As a rule, computers are best suited for tasks that need to be repeated often. Because of the work involved in programming the computer, if the task needs to be done only once, it is often harder to use the computer than to do it by hand. However, once the program has been set up, you can use it every time the task has to be repeated, saving enormous amounts of time and effort.

A general list of the types of business tasks for which computers can be used includes:

- Maintaining accounting records. Your business needs a double-entry bookkeeping system to keep track of income and expenditures. Computers can perform many of the repetitive calculations of such an accounting system.
- Supporting a budget and planning system. You need not only to keep track of the past; you need to figure out where you are trying to get to. It's important to have a planning process to determine the goals of your organization and to figure out how to accomplish them. Computers are no help in the process of developing a vision for your organization—remember that they have no imagination—but they can help perform calculations and process information that can be used to support planning. Since there is a lot of uncertainty about the future, you have to ask many "what if" questions—for example, what will happen to your sales revenue if a new housing development is built in your neighborhood. Computer spreadsheets are particularly helpful with this type of calculation, since you can construct the spreadsheet so that a change in one of the variables (such as the interest rate) automatically causes appropriate changes in all of the other variables that depend on the first variable.

Computers spare you the drudgery of recalculating all the consequences whenever you change one assumption. However, you have to be sure that you do not become mesmerized by the results and assume that, because they came out of a computer, they must be right. Any results that come from a computer can be no better than the assumptions that went into their calculations. There is a saying in computer science that summarizes this principle: "Garbage in, garbage out."

The organization's budget—a plan for allocating the resources of your organization in order to achieve its goals—is a key part of the planning process. Computers can help in developing the budget and monitoring compliance with its guidelines.
- Word processing. Communication is crucial to any organization. Word processing systems have made it much easier to write almost anything. The initial process of typing a document on a word processor is almost as much work as typing it on a typewriter (after all, you do have to type every letter in both cases, although it is much easier to make corrections on the word-processing system). However, the big advantage of word processing systems is apparent when you must make revisions. In the old days, revising a document usually meant that complete pages, or the complete document, had to be retyped.

It is wasteful for trained typists to spend a lot of time retyping pages that are 95 percent correct in order to make changes in the remaining 5 percent. Word processors have made it possible to edit the document easily and have it letter-perfect before it is printed.

Word processing systems have rapidly improved over the last decade and have added many new capabilities. The lengthy manual for a word processing program can be very intimidating. Fortunately, you do not need to learn all of the complicated features of a word processing program in order to start using it. The best way to learn a word processing program is to start by typing simple documents as soon as possible. You will quickly become familiar with the basic commands. You can learn more advanced features as you need them.

Desktop publishing systems offer even greater capabilities. You shouldn't rush into obtaining a desktop publishing system if you don't have a use for it or if you use it so rarely that it would be more economical to hire an outside printing firm to handle your publishing needs. However, if you regularly publish a newsletter, a sales brochure, or other printed materials, you will probably find that a desktop publishing system can be of tremendous help. Desktop publishing programs allow you to lay out the page of your document; you can arrange the text of stories in whatever location you wish, include headlines of various sizes, and mix illustrations with the text.

— Maintaining the data bases. You no doubt have to keep track of data about your employees whether or not you use a computer; using a computer makes the task much easier. You may also need a data base of your customers, of your inventory of supplies, or of the maintenance record of your equipment.

The preceding tasks apply to nearly all businesses. Here are some tasks that may or may not apply to your business:

— Establishing on-line networks linking remote sites. For example, airlines need networks linking all of their ticket agents so that the agents can determine seating availability and then book customers on flights. Banks with a system of automated teller machines need to have them linked so that the bank can determine if customers have adequate funds in their accounts to cover their withdrawals.

— Using computers for CAD/CAM (computer-aided design and computer-aided manufacturing). The recent improvement in the graphics capabilities of small computers has led to a revolution in the way that architects are able to prepare drawings of buildings. CAD programs make it possible to design buildings on the screen where it is easy to make changes, increase or decrease the scale of the diagram, and add predrawn standard parts. Advanced programs let you keep track of the object in three dimensions and rotate it to view it from different directions or even pretend that you are walking from room to room and view it from different locations. As computers rapidly improve, they are changing the way that many engineers work; computers can now be used for tasks that range from designing airplanes to designing molecules.

- Searching for data in libraries. Suppose you need information on a particular topic. It can take a long time to search through the appropriate indexes of newspapers, periodicals, and books to find this information. Today, many libraries have access to computer search programs that automatically keep track of extensive indexes. You may also be able to find all the information from an encyclopedia accessed through your computer. This would not have been possible in the past because of limitations in storage capacity, but the development of CD-ROM (compact disk, read-only memory) technology in recent years has made it possible to store a huge quantity of information on a small disk.

- Performing statistical calculations. Suppose you are performing research on your customers or potential customers, perhaps by conducting a survey. You will obtain a lot of raw data in the form of survey responses, but then you need to analyze those responses to determine their meaning. That is where computers can be very helpful. There are several programs that are designed to perform statistical calculations.

- Projecting management and scheduling. Your business may involve the need to coordinate a large number of different tasks with varying priorities and resource requirements. Programs are available now to help you schedule these different tasks and to draw diagrams to help you visualize the sequence in which they will be carried out.

- Aiding communication and electronic mail. You may find it helpful to set up an electronic mail system so that people in your organization can type messages on their keyboards and then send them electronically to another person or group of people. The recipient receives the message when he or she logs onto the computer system. Electronic mail has several advantages: the messages are delivered faster; they arrive in a machine-readable form, making it easy to add notes and send the revised message along to someone else; and clutter is less than with paper notes. Of course, you can always print the notes if you are deeply attached to having paper all over your office.

Computer systems are also used to handle voice messages through a system known as voice mail. A voice mail system acts like an ordinary telephone answering machine for each person in the office, but it also has additional capabilities. For example, a person can record one message and then have it automatically sent to all people in a particular group.

— Mapping. Suppose you wanted to draw a map showing the locations of the homes of all your customers. Although such a map would be very helpful in planning your business, it would be very tedious to draw by hand. However, a computer that had the information about the street grid of your city, and the rules to determine the location of a particular address, could draw the map for you. Ideally, you could even adjust the scale of the map, zooming in for a more detailed view of a particular area or moving back for a wide-angle view of a larger area. This type of mapping system is becoming more commonly available. Again, one of the key ingredients necessary is your computer's storage capacity; storing the information needed to draw a map requires a lot of memory, so it would not have been feasible to attempt such a complex task with early microcomputers.

— Serving as an expert system. When you have a problem, often the best solution is to call in an expert if one is available. An expert is someone who has considerable knowledge and experience with your problem, who knows a lot of facts and the rules that determine how those facts can be used to reach a conclusion.

Suppose an expert is not available. Would you dare let a computer act as an expert and help you make decisions? For example, would you trust a computer to make a medical diagnosis? Clearly, you would be willing to do that only if the computer had stored a lot of information so that it would "know" as much as an expert doctor would know. Then the computer would need a set of rules that would allow it to read information about the patient's situation and consult its data base to determine what the possible diagnosis might be. The rules that the computer would follow could come only from the actual experts in the field. As you can imagine, it is a long and costly process to set up a computer system that can act as an expert decision maker. The development of this type of system, known as an *expert system,* requires teamwork from both the experts in the field and the computer programmers. Expert systems will likely become more common in the future.

You should be careful to avoid falling into the trap of believing that if something can be done on a computer, it must be done on a computer. There are some tasks that are not easily executed on computers. For example, consider the task of maintaining your personal appointment schedule. You could obtain a computer program that allows you to enter data on your appointments and then prints a schedule for each day. You might very well find such a program useful; however, you might also find that it is easier to keep a little calendar with you. For example, if you see a friend while you are on the sidewalk, you will probably not have your computer terminal handy to see if Tuesday is available for a get together. However, a computer scheduling program may be very helpful if you use it to keep track of the schedules of all members of a group. The computer can automatically examine each person's schedule, determine what time is available for the entire group to meet, and enter that meeting time into the schedule for each individual.

As another example, you are probably wondering if you should use a computer to file your tax return. You can use a computer spreadsheet to re-create the tax forms and then build in the different formulas that are used. Of course, the computer will not be much help in obtaining the original data, such as that from your W2 form. And you will probably find that it is more work to set up the spreadsheet than to do the calculations by hand. Remember that one of the key principles of computer tasks is: Computers are most efficient with repetitive tasks. If you have to file a hundred tax returns (for example, if you run a tax preparation business), then you will probably find that the computer tax calculation spreadsheet is a big help. If you must prepare only your own return, though, there is no repetition and you lose one of the points of computerizing the task. You may think that you can use the same spreadsheet for next year, and of course that is true—if ever Congress and the IRS decide to stop changing the rules every year.

In the future you will probably find more ways in which the computer can help with tax returns. It seems a bit primitive to use your computer spreadsheet program to calculate the results and then write the results on the tax return by hand. The next improvement will be for the computer to print out an exact copy of the form for you to mail in. However, even that approach is still relatively primitive compared to the next step—filing the return with the IRS electronically. Instead of using any paper at all, you will hook up your computer to the IRS computer over a telephone line and transmit the data that way. This approach is likely to become much more common in the future; the IRS will save a lot of work if the returns arrive in machine-readable form, so in the future it may well provide taxpayers with incentives to file their returns electronically.

CHOOSING SOFTWARE

Now that you have determined what tasks need to be done by your business, the next step is to determine what software is required to perform them. There is a tradeoff between programs aimed at specific tasks (such as managing an apple orchard or keeping track of legal cases for a law firm) and programs aimed at a general task (such as a word processing program, a spreadsheet program, or a data base program). A specific task program will be very helpful if you can find one for the task that you actually need; a general-purpose program is more versatile but usually requires more work to set it up to meet your specific tasks.

Some suggested types of software that you might need include:

- a word processing program, such as Word Perfect, Microsoft Word, or Wordstar. Each of these programs is constantly being improved, so in general a higher-version number indicates a program with more capabilities. You may also want to work with a desktop publishing program, such as PageMaker or Ventura.

- a spreadsheet program, such as Lotus 1-2-3, Excel, or Quattro. These programs can be used for a wide variety of calculations. They have some data base capabilities built-in, but you may want to obtain a specialized data base program such as dBASE, R-BASE, or Paradox.

- an accounting package, such as DACEASY or Peachtree Complete.

- a communications program that allows your computer to communicate with other computers through a modem and telephone line.

- a local area network (LAN) program that links several computers together so they can share both information and hardware resources.

- a CD-ROM information library.

- a project management program.

- a CAD program.
- a mapping program.

Before deciding what to buy, it's a good idea to discuss a program you are considering with someone who already has it. If that's not possible, you can usually find a dealer who will be glad to demonstrate a particular program, in the hopes of convincing you to buy it.

CHOOSING HARDWARE

Once you have determined the tasks you must accomplish and chosen the software to perform them, you need to choose the hardware that will run the software. The choice of hardware depends on the scale of your operation. Computers can be divided into four general classes:

- supercomputers, designed for research tasks that involve massive calculations.
- mainframes, the basic computers for large businesses. These were the only types of computers available during the 1950s and 1960s. You need a mainframe if you will have to process large volumes of information or support a large number of users connected to the computer at once, as at a bank. As you might imagine, mainframe computers are expensive and big, and require their own carefully controlled air-conditioned environment. Mainframe computers are often leased from a company such as IBM. If your business requires a mainframe computer, you will need a staff of professional operators and programmers to run it; if you are in an area of management other than data processing, you will have less need to learn the technical details of the computer system operation. In this book we do not go into details about how to shop for or operate a mainframe computer, although we provide some examples of how mainframe computers are used in business.
- minicomputers. A minicomputer is intermediate in size between a mainframe and a microcomputer. The line of VAX machines from Digital Equipment are examples. A minicomputer can support more than one user at a time, although not as many as a mainframe computer (there is not always a sharp line between the two).
- microcomputers, in which the central processing unit (CPU) has been placed on a single integrated circuit, or chip. The development of microcomputers in the mid-1970s, and the vast improvements in their capabilities and affordability during the 1980s, revolutionized the computer industry by allowing people

to have their own personal computers, both at the office and at home. Once computer operations were sufficiently simplified that experts were no longer required to run them, computer manufacturers had a strong incentive to make them easier for ordinary people to use. If you are running a relatively small business, you will probably find that microcomputers will handle your information needs. Microcomputers can be linked with other microcomputers in networks, allowing data to be shared by more than one machine, and they can be used as terminals connected by phone lines to mainframe computers.

When investigating the purchase of a microcomputer, you should look at:

▬ memory capacity. The main internal memory of a computer is called RAM (Random Access Memory), which means that the computer can obtain access to any part of the memory as quickly as any other part of the memory, on average. Memory is defined in terms of the number of characters the computer can store, measured in "bytes" (one byte is equal to one character). For convenience, the memory size is usually listed in a larger unit: one kilobyte, which is approximately one thousand bytes (2^{10} or 1,024, to be precise), or one megabyte, approximately one million bytes (2^{20} or 1,048,576). How much memory you need depends on the software you will be running. There has been a rapid progression in the last decade in two areas: the memory available for microcomputers has expanded, while at the same time the available software has become more powerful and therefore requires more memory. In the early 1980s, 64K (that is, 64 kilobytes) was a common size for a microcomputer memory. By the early 1990s, 640K had become the minimum size to consider if you are planning to run business software such as a spreadsheet program; you will need at least three or four megabytes of memory to use software based on the operating system OS/2.

▬ clock speed. A computer has a clock that "ticks" a few million times each second. The speed of the ticks is one of the factors that determines how fast the computer can perform operations. Speed is measured in units of megahertz; one megahertz equals one million cycles per second. As with memory capacity, there has been considerable improvement in the clock speed of microcomputers in the last few years; it is now common for business microcomputers to have clock speeds of 16 to 33 megahertz. If you are planning to use the computer largely for word processing, it is not as important to have it operate quickly;

if you will be working with large spreadsheets that must be frequently recalculated, it will be helpful if it can perform the calculations quickly. Also, extensive work with CAD programs requires a fast computer.

▄ microprocessor. Many of the big improvements in the capacities of microcomputers can come from the development of new microprocessors. As new microprocessors come into use, the prices of machines with older processors generally fall. This means that you have a choice between going for more economical but more out-of-date machines or buying the more expensive state-of-the-art machines. If you are in a business that requires a lot of intense number-crunching or uses very graphics-intensive processes such as CAD or mapping, or if you are in a business that you expect to grow rapidly, it is probably worth your while to invest in the newest machines available. If your computing needs center largely on word processing and relatively small-scale accounting transactions, it may be economical for you to look at some of the older machines.

The progression of microprocessors for the IBM PC family goes like this: 8086 and 8088 processors were used in PCs in the early 1980s; the 80286 was first used in the IBM AT, introduced in 1984; the 80386 was used in the IBM PS/2, introduced in 1987; and the 80486 became available in the 1990s. These chips are all produced by Intel. Macintosh computers have progressed from the Motorola 68000 microprocessor to the Motorola 68020 processor found in newer machines.

An optional feature is a math coprocessor, such as the Intel 80387. A co-processor is an additional processing chip designed to perform calculations efficiently. This is a good investment if your business will require a lot of calculations where speed is important, because the math coprocessor allows the computer to run faster than it would with its CPU alone.

You should consider the size of various microcomputers. Desktop computers need a desktop, of course, with adequate space for you to spread your work out, to run your mouse, and to store your printer. You also need to make sure that the computer will be at a comfortable height. Laptop computers are light (approximately 8 pounds) machines that are easier to move around than desktop models and that can run on batteries. They are very convenient, although they are not as easy to carry around as a pocket calculator; for one thing, there are certain minimum sizes for the screen and the keyboard that make it impossible to shrink them too much. However, there have been considerable improvements in the computing capability of laptops.

INPUT

The central processing unit of the computer is of no value to you unless you are able to communicate with it. So you also need to look at the hardware devices that provide interaction between you and the machine. These include:

■ keyboards. Keyboards will probably remain the dominant way to feed information into computers for the next few years. If you will be entering a lot of numerical data, a separate numerical keypad is very convenient. (Most newer computers have remedied a major inconvenience of the original IBM PC keyboard design, in which the cursor arrow keys were on the same keys as the numeric keypad.)

■ mouse. Keyboards are fine for entering text into the computer, but what if you want to draw a picture for the computer or point to a particular area of the screen? Efforts to develop screens that users could draw on or point to have not been successful, but the computer mouse was developed as a convenient substitute. A mouse is a small device that fits into your hand and can roll around the desktop beside your computer. A wire connects the mouse to the computer, which is able to sense the direction you are moving the mouse and moves a pointer around the screen in the same direction. Mice became widely used when the Apple Macintosh computer was introduced in 1984. If you do not have space for a mouse beside your computer (which might be the case if you are using a laptop computer), an alternative pointing device is a trackball (a stationary ball that you rotate in different directions to signal to the screen how you want the pointer to move). Another pointing device is a digitizer, which gives you more precise control.

A pointing device is essential if you will be using the computer for drawing purposes, such as CAD, or if you will be doing desktop publishing that involves moving blocks of text and pictures around the page. You may also find a mouse useful as a way to point to menu choices on the screen, although the arrow keys on the keyboard provide another way to do this.

■ voice recognizer. After seeing *Star Trek,* you will likely think that it would be nice to have a computer that you can talk to, instead of typing to. Voice recognition systems are becoming more widely available, but they are still very expensive and have limited capacity. Different people sound very different even when they are saying the same words, so it has proven difficult to program computers to recognize the words. The more commonly available voice processing systems have to be "tuned" to one particular voice, and they have a limited capability. This type of system has a long way to go before it will be possible for a person to just start talking into the computer and have the computer "understand" the words. However, this problem is difficult, not impossible; it is likely that during the 1990s improved voice recognition systems will become much more available.

■ devices for reading machine-readable code, such as magnetic ink readers, bar-code readers, and optical scanners. Banks, for example, must sort returned checks to see whose account they were drawn on, precisely the tedious type of task a machine can help perform. However, the machine needs to be able to read the account number and the identifying number for the bank, which are printed at the bottom of the check in a strange type of block lettering. These magnetic ink numbers can be read by the check-sorting machine at the check clearinghouse.

The bank cannot, however, print the amount on the check because it doesn't know in advance how much you will write the check for. There must be a person who looks at each check and then types the amount into a machine, which then writes the amount in magnetic ink on the check. (Look at a canceled check to see this.) Then the computer can read the amount as well as the account number. The next step will be for a machine to look at the handwritten amount and then decode it, although this is a difficult task. One program, of course, is that people often have trouble reading the illegible handwriting of other people (or even their own handwriting); a computer would not be able to do much better in those cases. We can expect that improved systems for interpreting handwriting will become available in the 1990s, but they may never be 100 percent reliable.

Bar-code readers can read a standardized code, called the Universal Product Code, which is now automatically encoded on many products when they are produced. Many grocery stores have built bar-code readers into their cash register systems; the clerk passes the item's bar code over the reader and the computer automatically looks up the price of the item in the memory. As an added bonus, the computer can keep track of all of the items that the store sells, and the customer receipt lists the names of the items purchased as well as the prices.

Most of us have taken machine-scored multiple-choice tests.

An optical reader can sense the presence or absence of a pencil mark at a particular location and calculate the score. This type of system is too inconvenient for everyday use; as you might recall, you must use a number 2 pencil, completely fill in the squares you want to mark, and avoid making any stray marks on the paper.

■ scanners. Machine readability will improve significantly when you can transfer data from an ordinary piece of paper into the computer. Scanners with some ability to do this are now available. Suppose you have a picture that you want to incorporate into a document you are developing with a desktop publishing program. A scanner converts the picture into a pattern of symbols that can be stored in the computer's memory. It's much more difficult for the scanner to read a table of text, because the computer needs to convert the visual image of a character into the computer's own representation of the character. For example, the computer does not store the letter "A" as a pattern of dots in the shape of the letter, which is the way that it would store a picture of the letter A. Text reading scanners generally work only with certain styles of type.

OUTPUT

Next, you need to look at how the computer will present output to you. (Note that the terms input and output are always used from the computer's point of view—input is information that gets into the computer, and output is information that comes out.) Possibilities include:

■ monitor. The computer will display its immediate results for you on its monitor, which is like a television screen. There are several possible choices, depending on what purpose you will be using the computer for. The basic choice is whether to get a color or monochrome monitor. Color is essential for many games (after all, you should also be able to have some fun with the computer), and it is very helpful for graphics programs and mapping programs. Also, many business programs such as spreadsheets now use color to highlight important information.

However, there are some drawbacks to color. In many cases, you will want to save your output on paper, and the color effects will be lost unless you have a color printer (which are very expensive now, although the price will probably drop in the future). Also, unless you obtain a high-quality color monitor, the text will be less sharp than with a standard monochrome monitor, a disadvantage if you plan to use the machine predominantly for word processing. Finally, color monitors are more expensive. If you will be purchasing several microcomputers for your business, you will probably want at least one color monitor, but you may decide that monochrome monitors are a good choice for some of the machines.

Monochrome does not necessarily mean black and white; you have a choice as to what color you think is easiest to read. Amber on black and green on black are two popular choices; they are both easy on the eye. Other monitors present the text as black on white, more like the actual appearance of paper. However, you should compare to see which type of monitor is best suited for your eyes. If you have a color monitor, you may be able to change the color of the background and the text into whatever suits you; you can create some truly hideous color combinations if you experiment a bit. It is also important to make sure that you have adequate light in your work area, but not a lot of light placed so that it causes glare on the screen.

Another choice to make is the size of the monitor. Make sure that the physical size of the monitor is acceptable for you at your normal viewing distance. A typical monitor displays 80 columns and 24 rows of text. If you will be doing a lot of desktop publishing, you may find it worthwhile to invest in an oversize monitor that can display an entire page on one screen. (You definitely do not want a 40-column screen; no business computer offers this, although such monitors were common on early microcomputers.)

You should also consider the type of graphics capabilities you need. In the early days of microcomputers, it would have been possible to find text-only machines, but those are quite rare now. The graphics capabilities have improved considerably over time. For IBM/PCs, the progression has been from CGA (color graphics adaptor), the type of graphics capabilities on the original IBM PCs, to EGA (enhanced graphics adaptor), an improved version, to VGA (video gate array), the best now available. CGA systems are economical, but the graphics are quite crude by current standards. The choice of graphics is complicated by the fact that you need to have both the monitor and the "graphics card" integrated circuit in the machine so that they match. Make sure that your computer dealer is competent enough to realize this; you don't want to be sold a monitor that doesn't work with your system.

Most computer monitors are based on cathode-ray-tubes (CRT technology), which means that the pictures on the screen are formed as on a television screen: rays of electrons hit luminescent points on the screen. (Some home computers are even designed to be hooked directly to ordinary television screens, although the resulting picture quality is not suitable for business purposes.) CRTs are fine for desktop computers, although they are rather bulky; other types of monitors are offered for laptop computers. LCD (liquid crystal displays) are a common type of monitor on laptop computers. Visit a computer dealer and ask to see a laptop with an LCD screen to see what they look like. Some laptops also offer gas plasma screens, which have better resolution than LCDs but are more expensive and consume more power. As in all other aspects of this choice, there are trade-offs to consider.

▬ printers. In the future we may achieve the paperless office, but for now paper still plays a crucial role in any information storage system. You will need a printer for your computer. There are several types of printers available for microcomputers, and, again, there has been rapid progress in recent years. The most economical printers are dot-matrix printers, which form characters by firing little needles at the ribbon in contact with the paper, creating a pattern of dots. Some dot-matrix printers can be obtained for as little as a couple of hundred dollars; however, there is considerable variation in quality, so you should compare the results from each printer you are considering before you make your choice. In general, the more pins, the better; a 24-pin printer produces sharper characters than does a 9-pin printer. Some dot-matrix printers provide two speeds—a fast, one-pass speed for rough drafts and a slower, two-pass speed for better-quality type.

Dot-matrix printers are not suitable for high-quality letter-perfect work. Two types of printers became common in the late 1980s: ink-jet printers and laser printers. Ink-jet printers are the most economical choice for many businesses; the prices have fallen considerably since their introduction. The characters are formed by spraying fine jets of ink at the paper. They are sharp, high-quality characters. Laser printers are the best-quality printers available for microcomputers; you definitely should invest in a laser printer if you are doing a lot of desktop publishing work. They are very fast and very quiet, which are also important advantages. However, they are expensive, although again the prices have been falling and newer, better models are being introduced. If you have an office with several microcomputers, you will likely find it worthwhile to obtain at least one laser printer, although it may very well be too expensive to obtain laser printers for each machine. You may find it convenient to network the computers together so that one laser printer supports several machines. It often works well to use dot-matrix printers for rough drafts or for internal documents that don't require a high-quality appearance and a laser printer for the final product and those requiring a polished appearance.

The system for sending text from a computer to a printer is fairly well standardized, but the codes that govern graphics and other specialized features vary quite a bit from printer to printer. Therefore, when you obtain a new piece of software, you usually need to install it before you run it. During the installation procedure you indicate what type of printer you have, what type of monitor you have, and other features of your system. Most software programs come with several units, called *drivers,* that tell it how to send codes for different printers. After you install your software, it will look for the appropriate driver for your printer and make sure that it uses the driver every future time you use the program (until you obtain a new printer, in which case you will have to re-install the program so that it will use the driver appropriate for the new printer).

— speech synthesizers. Computers can talk to you by adding a device that converts text into speech. You have probably heard the results, which definitely sound like they come from a machine. There are likely to be considerable improvements in the quality and affordability of speech synthesizers in the coming years.

STORAGE

Computer memory has one major disadvantage: it goes blank when the power to the computer is turned off. (There are a few exceptions: Many pocket computers are equipped with a type of memory that does not vanish when the power is off.) A computer needs other devices to store your data when the power is off. The most commonly used storage devices use a magnetic medium to encode the information. The principle is similar to that used in audiotape recorders; some early microcomputers even used ordinary audiotape as a storage device. However, tape has one major disadvantage: in order to reach a point halfway into the tape, it is necessary to read through all points on the tape prior to that point. Therefore, it is much more convenient to use a disk storage device, on which the magnetic medium is arranged on a disk that is then inserted into a device called a "disk drive." The drive can rotate the disk so that it can quickly find any point on the disk.

Microcomputer disks come in two basic types: "floppy disks," which are small flat disks that must be inserted into the computer each time they are to be used, and "hard disks," which are installed permanently in the machine. Floppy disks, which aren't really floppy, come in two common sizes: 5¼ inches and 3½ inches. The 5¼-inch size was the most common throughout the 1980s, although the 3½-inch size will likely become dominant in the 1990s. The 3½-inch disks are more convenient, and they store more information despite their smaller size. The exact capacity of each type of disk varies; traditional 5¼-inch disks store 360 kilobytes, while high-density 3½-inch disks typically store 1.4 megabytes. (360K corresponds to about 100 pages of text with 70 characters per line and 52 lines per page.)

In the early 1980s, microcomputers often had two floppy disk drives, called "A" and "B." However, as software packages became more complicated, they began to fill several floppy disks, and it became very inconvenient to have to switch disks constantly. A hard disk has a much greater storage capacity and it can be read much more quickly by the computer. It became common for computers to offer 10 MB hard drives in the early 1980s; as more and more uses were found for computers, the software and data began requiring more and more space, and 20 MB, 40 MB, and even larger drives became increasingly common. Any business computer you purchase should have a hard disk with at least 40 MB capacity; it will be more expensive than a machine without a hard disk, but the added convenience and improved access to your data makes the higher cost worthwhile.

Mainframe computers store data on disks arranged in packs stacked on top of each other or on reel-to-reel tape. Tape storage is more economical than disk storage, so it is a good choice for large data sets, particularly if the data items can always be processed in the same order, as with a payroll. Tape is not a good way to store data if you frequently must find one particular item at a random location in the middle of the tape.

COMMUNICATION

Computers can communicate with other computers via two devices—modems and networks. A modem is a device that allows a computer to hook up to a phone line. A computer typically has several connections (called "ports") at the back, one of which is labeled the "communications" port and is designed to be connected to a modem (although it is now becoming more common for computers to have built-in modems). The modem also contains a cable that can be plugged into a telephone jack. In order to use the modem, you must have the appropriate communications software. Modems are rated by their speed of data transmission (1200 Baud, or 1200 bits per second, is common) and by the command structure that they recognize (Hayes-compatible is common). Type the command that starts your communication software, then type the telephone number of the computer that you wish to contact, and you can put yourself in touch with a friend's computer, a mainframe computer, a bulletin board where callers can leave messages, or an on-line information service such as CompuServe.

A group of computers in the same general area can be linked together in a local area network (LAN). Networks are discussed in Chapter 14.

OPERATING SYSTEMS

In order for the computer to do anything, it must have a set of software known as the operating system. The operating system contains the instructions that allow the computer to read information from its disks and to invoke other programs. The common operating system for business computers is known as MS-DOS (Microsoft Disk Operating System). MS-DOS was sold with the original IBM PC in 1981 and has since become widely used on many different types of computers. As with all other aspects of computer hardware and software, new and improved versions are regularly being introduced.

Microsoft introduced OS/2, a major new operating system, in the late 1980s. OS/2 contains innovations such as the ability to perform multitasking (that is, have more than one task running on the computer at the same time). OS/2 will probably be common in the future; however, its acceptance has been slowed because of its high cost and because it requires computers with large hard disks and memories (at least 4 MB for best results). It is probably a safe choice for your business to start with the traditional MC-DOS, leaving open the possibility of upgrading to OS/2 later on if it becomes necessary. However, you should not purchase any computer product just "because it's there"; you should purchase OS/2 when you must perform a business task that cannot be done as well without OS/2.

The traditional MS-DOS uses a command-line user interface. The Apple Macintosh, the program Microsoft Windows, and the OS/2 Presentation Manager use a newer graphics user interface. The appendix contains a brief description of each of these. However, you will spend most of your time working with your applications software, rather than the operating system, so it is more important to be concerned about the user interface of those programs rather than the user interface of the operating system.

CHAPTER PERSPECTIVE

First determine the goals of your organization; then determine what information processing tasks will be needed to achieve these goals. On this basis you can select the software that will perform those tasks and the hardware that will run the software.

Brief History of Information Processing

CHAPTER 2

SUMMARY AND MAIN POINTS
We can learn the key concepts of information processing by tracing the history of key inventions. We take many of these for granted now, but we should remember how crucial each of these advances was.

After studying the material in this chapter:

— You will understand the importance of the symbolic representation of information, and how this concept has developed.
— You will be familiar with the history of computational aids and early computers.
— You will understand the revolution in computer software and hardware that occurred with the introduction of microcomputers.

SYMBOLS AND THEIR PHYSICAL REPRESENTATION
The history of written communication goes back to ancient times and is marked by the invention of basic elements that underlie communications today. With all our fancy gadgetry, these fundamental tools and concepts are as necessary to us today as they were 2,000 years ago.

Writing
One day, sometime before 3,000 B.C., a scribe in southern Mesopotamia needed to keep track of ten goats. There happened to be some soft clay and a sharp reed nearby, so he used the reed to sketch a picture of a goat on a chunk of clay and then sketched a circle that he decided would remind him of the number 10. This proved to be such a convenient system that soon scribes all over Mesopotamia were recording symbols on clay tablets. Instead of drawing pictures of objects each time, they developed standardized symbols to represent words, thus inventing writing. Writing was the invention that made civilization

possible. Using symbols to represent concepts underlies all subsequent information processing.

The clay tablet texts became known as cuneiform (which means wedge-shaped writing). A large majority of the cuneiform texts uncovered by archaeologists deal with economic records: how many items of food, livestock, and other goods entered or left a city. They thus provide one of the earliest examples of an information-processing system. The scribes must have developed an orderly filing system for the tablets, ways to retrieve tablets that met certain characteristics, and ways to consolidate the data on individual tablets to prepare summary reports (although this last task clearly would have been much more difficult without computational aids).

Paper

Clay tablets are a convenient way of storing data if you want it to survive for thousands of years. (Modern archaeologists certainly appreciate this.) However, they are bulky if you need to store a large quantity of information. One day an ancient Egyptian took some stems from the papyrus plant that grew in the river, pressed them together, and dried them to form a smooth writing surface. Paper as we know it now, which is a substance made from processed wood fibers, seems to have been developed in China about 100 A.D.; it was several centuries later before it became common in Europe. As long as paper was an expensive commodity, information processing was severely hindered; now we are used to the widespread availability of cheap paper.

The Alphabet

Sometime between 1700 B.C. and 1500 B.C., some people along the eastern shores of the Mediterranean (possibly Hebrews or Phoenicians) developed a system of writing in which symbols stood for individual sounds (instead of words or syllables). Words were formed by combining these symbols. Thus was created the concept of the alphabet, which provided a huge advantage: a very small number of symbols could be used to represent a very large number of words, since the symbols could be combined in many different ways. The 26-letter Latin alphabet that we now use seems to have been adapted from earlier alphabets in the 7th century B.C.

All of our modern data storage systems are based on the fact that it is necessary for the memory system to be able to recognize only a small set of symbols. In fact, computers carry this principle to the ultimate extreme by storing only two symbols: 1 and 0. If you provide a long enough series of 1s and 0s, and you have agreed on the meaning of each pattern, then you can represent any data item this way. However, the binary 1 and 0 system is very awkward for people, so it is customary for computers to use an "alphabet" of 256 characters, called the ASCII code. These codes provide the symbols for all of the letters (both upper and lower case), plus the numerical digits, punctuation symbols, and other, more specialized symbols. The computer itself stores each of these characters as a pattern of 8 binary digits (bits) (since 2^8 equals 256, there are 256 different combinations), but human computer users never need to know that the computer is really working with binary numbers.

Positional Number System

Complicated calculations with Roman numerals (I, II, III, IV, V, VI, VII, VIII, IX, X, etc.) are very cumbersome, so it was a big improvement when a positional number system was developed. We tell the difference in value between the digit "1" in the numbers "10" and "1,000" by the position of the digit within the number. Although zero represents "nothing," the development of the number zero was a major conceptual advance when it was developed by the Hindus some time before the 9th century. The digit symbols we use (0,1,2,3,4,5,6,7,8,9) were also developed by Hindu mathematicians and introduced to the western world by the Arab mathematician al-Khwarizmi during the 9th century. (Al-Khwarizmi's name is remembered as the source of the world algorithm.)

Double-entry Bookkeeping

Structured financial recordkeeping became possible after the development of double-entry bookkeeping during the 15th century in Italy. Each transaction must have two effects on the organization (for example, money spent means that there will be a decline in cash and an increase in spending). The rules of accounting have developed to make sure that each transaction is properly recorded. Computers have become very valuable tools for performing the computations involved in accounting, although they cannot help in cases where a judgment call must be made to determine how a particular transaction is to be recorded.

The Printing Press
About 1455, Johannes Gutenberg completed the development of a printing press that used movable-type elements. This quickly led to a vast increase in the ability to reproduce information for a wide audience. The use of movable-type elements was a big improvement over earlier methods such as woodblock printing, but it still required a lot of work to set the type and therefore was not a solution for day-to-day office communication needs. (Desiderius Erasmus, a widely published scholar of the early 1500s, was able to develop a type of word processing capability by staying with his publisher while his books were typeset, examining each page after it was set and making changes right at that time. This process was too time-consuming to be available for most authors.)

The Jacquard Loom
Joseph-Marie Jacquard, who developed a new type of loom that could weave cloth into intricate patterns, needed a coding system for describing the patterns, as well as a way to transmit those codes to the loom. In 1805, he developed a system of cards with holes punched in them. The presence or the absence of a hole at a particular place on the card determined an element of the loom's pattern. He thus created a type of binary code system with two symbols: hole or no hole; it took a large number of cards, each containing many symbol locations, to determine a pattern. The key advance that was achieved was machine readability; once the holes had been punched into the deck of cards, the machine could read those cards any time that particular pattern was desired. There was no need for a person to reenter all of the instructions.

The Telegraph
Imagine you needed to contact a branch office at the other end of the country (or across the ocean) in 1830. Information could travel no faster than people could, which was very slow. In the late 1830s Samuel Morse developed a system that could transmit information practically instantaneously. The first telegraph line, between Baltimore and Washington, allowed information to be transmitted as electronic impulses. Morse developed a code that used two "symbols," long dashes and short dots, for use in transmitting messages.

The Typewriter

In 1868 Christopher Sholes received a patent for his invention of the typewriter. This machine meant that it was finally possible to prepare documents easily on a day-to-day basis. Even more important, the concept of the typewriter keyboard provided a relatively easy way for people to transmit information to machines. Each alphabet symbol is represented by a button; with practice, people can hit the intended buttons at a high rate of speed. Unfortunately, the keyboard layout in common use now dates from the early days when people could type faster than the machine could work, so the key layout was designed to slow the typist down. Other keyboard layouts have been developed that make typing faster, but the cost of changing would be great because typists are so used to the current layout. Until such time as voice recognition systems become common, keyboards will continue to be the dominant way for people to enter information into computers.

Punched Cards

Imagine that you had the job of processing data from the 1880 U.S. census. The data for each person are entered on a sheet of paper, and you have the job of tabulating the sheets to find the total number of people of each age, the number of people in each city, and so on. What a nightmare! By 1880, the population was large enough that it took several years to complete the tabulation. It was clear to Herman Hollerith that it would take longer than ten years to process the 1890 census unless a better method could be found.

What he needed was some form of system to make the data on the census forms machine-readable. Hollerith developed the same concept that had run the Jacquard loom: punched cards. The census data for 1890 were transferred to punched cards by clerks who read the original census forms and then pressed buttons on a machine that punched holes into the correct locations. (This was a big job in itself, but it was easier than tabulating the data by hand.) Hollerith developed machines that could sort and tabulate the cards. For example, suppose you wanted to separate the population by education. The cards were loaded into the sorting machine and passed one at a time through sensors that determined the presence or absence of a hole at a preset location and dumped the card into one of several bins accordingly. For example, the sensor determined if there was a hole in the location that indicates high school education. If there was, then the card was dropped into the bin for high school graduates; if not, the card passed over that bin and on to next sensor location, which determined if it should fall into the next bin. Once all the cards had been passed through the machine, a machine counted the number of cards in each bin giving you a tabulation of the education distribution of the population.

Hollerith's punched-card system preceded the development of computers by about 50 years, and punched-card data processing systems were in widespread use in businesses before computers became available. Many refinements were quickly added; for example, codes were developed so that numbers could be stored on the cards and then machines could add all the numbers on a deck of cards.

Punched cards were once the dominant way to feed information into computers. A standard punched card consisted of 80 columns, each representing one character. Each column consisted of 12 possible locations where holes could be punched, and a standardized coding system determined the pattern of holes for each character. The cards were punched by people using machines called keypunches, which used typewriter-like keyboards. Electronic card readers read the cards at a fast rate and then translated the information into electrical signals to be sent to the computer. This information could be either a set of instructions for the computer to follow (a program) or the data the computer were to manipulate. Punched cards had some disadvantages: they could not be read by the machine if they were folded, spindled, mutilated, or wet, and a large deck of cards was awkward to carry around. (If you dropped the cards and their order became scrambled, you were in real trouble.) Punched-card systems were still widely used throughout the 1970s, but by the 1980s they had generally been replaced with terminal systems in which users typed on terminals (keyboards and CRT screens) that were directly wired to the computer. However, Hollerith's concept of data operations still applies today. Data elements still need to be categorized according to some criteria and then tabulated. But, now the data are stored on an electronic medium instead of on cards and the tabulation process is done under the direction of a computer program instead of mechanically by a card-sorting machine.

The Copy Machine
The copy machine was invented by a lone inventor who tinkered in his kitchen. In 1940 Chester Carlson obtained his first patent

for an electrostatic copier, but many companies turned down the chance to develop and market the idea. It was several years later that a small company that eventually became the Xerox Corporation began working with him. It took until the late 1950s to develop an improved copy machine that became widely used in offices. We are so used to copy machines now that it is hard to conceive of offices without them. Ebenezer Scrooge made his clerk Bob Cratchit copy documents by hand; Thomas Jefferson used a device with two pens connected together so that when he wrote a letter with one pen, the other pen automatically followed his movements to make a copy of the letter. Previous methods of office reproduction (such as carbon paper or mimeographs) required special preparation at the time the document was created.

The ability to reproduce information easily was a huge improvement, although it can lead to another danger: information overload. Just because something can be copied doesn't mean it should be copied. One of the challenges of modern offices is to make sure that the information system does not spew out more information than the people can digest.

Copy machines have one important advantage: The information they reproduce can include diagrams as well as text. (A typewriter keyboard, by contrast, deals only with text.) A photocopy is not machine readable, however. Although the machine can copy the data it has no way of processing it. The same advantages and disadvantages apply to facsimile (fax) machines, essentially two copy machines connected by a telephone line so that the copy does not have to be made at the same location as the original. Fax machines became common office fixtures in the late 1980s.

COMPUTATIONAL AIDS

Like the history of writing, the history of computational aids is long and goes back thousands of years.

Abacus

The abacus (see Figure 2-1) was developed in ancient times. Any calculating machine needs a physical system for representing data; unlike writing, it is necessary that data items be easily changed. On the abacus, numbers are represented by the positions of beads along a rod. The operator moves the beads by hand; 1 + 2 is easily calculated by moving two beads on top of one bead. An adding machine must also have a way of handling carries; that is, the result of addition that moves to the next column. On the abacus the operator performs carries by hand.

Pascal's Calculator

Blaise Pascal developed a calculating machine in 1642 that used rotating wheels to represent digits and a system of gears so that carries could be handled automatically. Over the next three hundred years many refinements to this basic design were developed. By the early 1900s mechanical desktop calculators were common, some driven by hand cranks and others by electronic motors that turned the wheels.

Slide Rules

Slide rules work on a totally different approach. Suppose you take two rulers that slide along each other. To add 2 + 5, all you need to do is put the base of the second ruler opposite the 2 on the first ruler and then read the result by seeing the number from the first ruler that is next to the 5 on the second ruler (see Figure 2-2a.) You can also add fractions, provided that you are very careful about reading the scales. In this type of device, called an *analog* device, numbers are represented by a physical system that can vary continuously, as can the position of the ruler. If you could measure the positions of the ruler perfectly, then you could obtain perfect accuracy; however, in reality the accuracy of analog devices is severely limited.

A slide rule is an analog device for performing multiplications by taking advantage of logarithms, which were developed by John Napier in 1614. Because $\log(ab) = \log a + \log b$, a multiplication problem can be converted into an addition problem in which the two logarithms are added. Slide rules were the common tools for engineering calculations until the 1970s, when pocket electronic calculators became widespread. By contrast, the abacus and the wheeled adding machines described above are called *digital* devices. On an abacus, a bead is either up or down; there is no meaning for putting the bead one third of the way up. On a digital device the data are represented by a device that has only a small number of discrete positions, instead of an

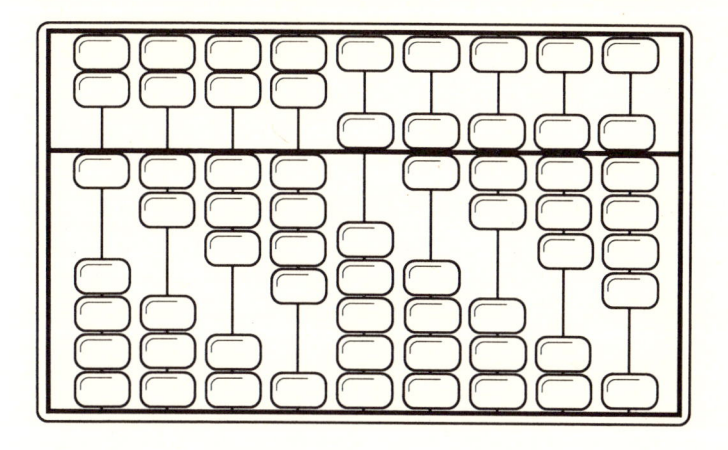

Fig. 2-1. The number 123,456,789 represented on an abacus.

infinite number of continuously varying positions. All modern general-purpose computers are digital; as we have seen, they are based on storage devices that have only two positions—1 and 0.

Babbage's Analytic Engine

Charles Babbage worked on the design of a mechanical computing device in the 1830s. He used gears to represent data items, which could be transferred from one location to another. He developed the concept of memory (which he called the store) and the central processing unit (the mill), which are key parts of all modern computers. He conceived of the analytic engine as a football-sized machine powered by steam engines. Babbage's design illustrates that, theoretically, the physical representation of symbolic data can take forms different from the electronic forms to which we are accustomed today. Unfortunately, in practice the physical structure of Babbage's machine didn't work. Building the complete machine would have required engineering technology beyond that which was available in his day; consequently, only parts of it were ever built. Sadly, the

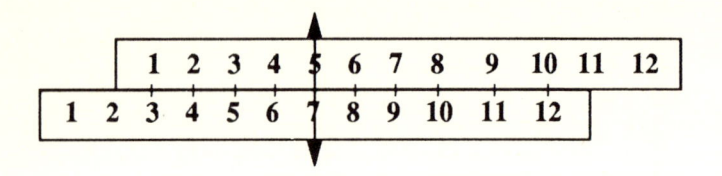

Fig. 2-2a. Slide rule for addition: 2 + 5 = 7.

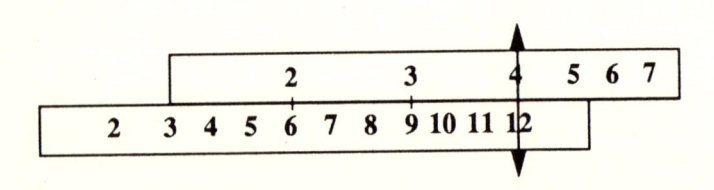

Fig. 2-2b. Logarithmic scale slide rule for multiplication: 3 × 4 = 12.

developer of such key concepts of computers was simply too far ahead of his time.

EARLY COMPUTERS

Throughout the years prior to World War II, many improved versions of calculating machines (partly electrical and partly mechanical) were developed. Howard Aiken and John Atanasoff were two of the most noteworthy contributors to the growing technology. However, in order for a machine to be both reliable and fast, it was necessary for it to be made with completely electronic components; what was needed was the electronic equivalent of switches that could be turned on or off by sending the appropriate signals. Mechanical relays were used in some computer forerunners; the only suitable purely electronic device available at the time was the vacuum tube, which had been developed by Lee De Forest in 1907 and which had been used as amplifiers in radios.

The Electronic Numeric Integrator and Calculator (ENIAC), developed by a team led by John Mauchly and Presper Eckert in 1946, can be said to be the first operational fully electronic digital computer. The ENIAC was a huge machine consisting of 18,000 vacuum tubes. The tubes generated a lot of heat, and they frequently needed to be replaced, but the ENIAC nevertheless provided reliable service for about ten years. The early computers made with vacuum tubes have become known as *first-generation* computers.

Support for the development of the ENIAC came from the U.S. Army, which wanted a way to reduce the enormous effort that went into the calculation of ballistics tables used for aiming weapons properly. The British also worked on developing early computers to simplify the effort to crack German codes. Massive scientific calculation, rather than commercial data processing, provided the incentive for the development of the early computers.

Stored Program Concept

Once computer hardware became available, it was necessary to figure out the best way to give instructions to the computer. As we have seen, computers operate by storing their data as binary code; the striking realization was that the computer's instructions could also be stored as a binary code and that the instructions could be stored in the memory along with the data. (Of course, the computer would need to keep track of the locations of instructions and data, so it wouldn't mistakenly try to process a data item as if it were an instruction, or vice versa.) Credit for this insight is often given to the mathematician John von Neumann, who worked with the developers of the ENIAC on the development of a new machine using the stored program concept.

A "computer" is now distinguished from a "calculator" because the computer is able to store its own instructions. For example, adding all the numbers from one to one million on a calculator would take a long time. If you had a computer, you would just need to write a short program and then the computer would take it from there. (Prior to the development of what we now call computers, the word "computer" was used to refer to a person who performed computations.)

Transistors

In order to improve computers, it was necessary to develop electronic switches that would be more convenient to use than vacuum tubes. The answer was provided in 1947 by scientists at Bell Laboratories—the transistor, a semiconductor device made largely of silicon that could perform the same functions as a vacuum tube but was much smaller, cost much less, used less power, and generated much less heat (see Figure 2-3). It took several years of research during the 1950s to perfect the use of transistors in computers. In 1957 IBM introduced the 608 calculator, the first commercial product with all transistors and no tubes. In the same year IBM announced that it would make no new products with tubes; transistors would be the wave of the future. Computers with transistors are known as *second generation*.

Integrated Circuits

Researchers knew that further improvements in computer hardware would be possible if the components could be made even smaller. The trick was to put many components on a single silicon chip instead of using discrete transistors wired together. Semiconductor integrated circuits were developed in the late 1950s; many recent improvements in computer technology have resulted from improvements in such circuits, making it possible to include an ever larger number of components on a single chip. Computers with integrated circuits became known as *third generation*.

Vacuum Tube

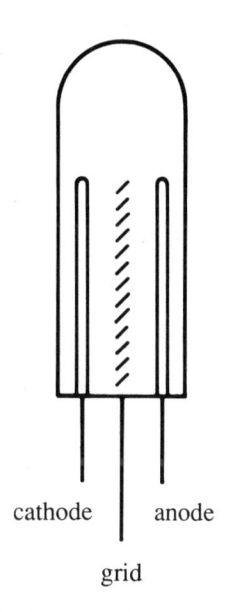

cathode | anode

grid

cathode to anode current
is controlled by voltage at grid

Transistor

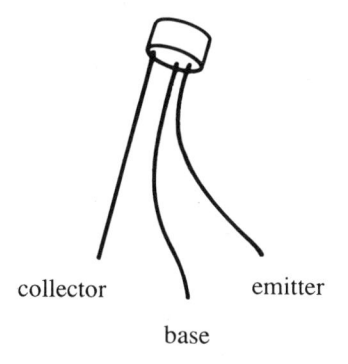

collector   emitter

base

collector to emitter current
is controlled by voltage at base

Fig. 2-3. **The transistor.**

Commercial Data Processing Computers
In the late 1940s some people believed that computers would be used only for extremely complicated numerical calculations, so the world would need only a handful of computers. However, businesses soon realized that electronic computers could offer many advantages over existing punched-card systems for data processing operations. The promise could be realized only when the hardware advances had progressed to the point that business computers could be made economically. One of the earliest computers used for data processing was the UNIVAC, built by Eckert and Mauchly in 1951 for the U.S. Census Bureau.

International Business Machines (IBM), the company that became the biggest name in data processing, was descended from a company started by Herman Hollerith, the inventor of the punched-card data processing system. IBM was a big producer of office equipment, such as typewriters and time clocks, in the first half of the century; its success came largely from its ability to provide a trustworthy network of service for its business customers. IBM introduced the 701 series of computers in 1952, only a handful of which were produced and rented to businesses for several thousand dollars per month. Improved first-generation machines were developed throughout the 1950s, when the introduction of solid-state semiconductor technology (transistors and integrated circuits) led to rapid improvements. One landmark product in data processing history was the IBM 360 computer; introduced in 1964, this machine and its successors set the standard for data processing machines for more than a decade.

Programming Languages
Suppose you wanted an early computer to add two numbers. You would have to write a set of binary coded instructions telling the computer the details of how to perform the task, including how to find the numbers in the memory and then transfer them to the registers where the computation could take place. Suppose the next day several coworkers also needed to add two numbers together. It would seem silly for them to have to start from scratch and write the same set of instructions again. This illustrates an important principle in the practical use of computers: Try to avoid the "reinventing the wheel" syndrome. It is not efficient to spend your time writing the same set of instructions over and over again.

Computer operators realized that it would make computers easier to use if it were possible for the user to write a simple instruction for adding two numbers, such as 2 + 3, and then have the computer automatically look in its memory to find the detailed binary code for performing this task. The same principle should be applied to all of the common operations: multiplication, division, subtraction, input, output, etc.; once a set of standard instruction codes is available, then people (*programmers*) can write their instructions (*programs*) in this code (called a *programming language*.) The earliest computer programs were written in languages that we would now call *assembly languages*. These languages require the programmer to specify in detail exactly how the data will be moved between the various register locations in the computer, and the available command set corresponds directly to the commands that are built in to the machine. These languages are oriented toward the needs of the machine, but they are not convenient for people. Assembly language programs can become very cumbersome, and they require the programmer to spend time thinking about the detailed machine architecture instead of about how to solve the problem.

In 1957 IBM began shipping a computer program (called a *compiler*) that could read a set of mathematical instructions and convert them into machine language. This allowed people to write computer instructions in a programming language known as FORTRAN (short for Formula Translation). FORTRAN statements were similar to ordinary algebraic notation (for example, $A*X + B*Y + 2$), so it was much easier for programmers to prepare computer instructions. FORTRAN quickly became a common language for scientific calculation purposes. Later programming languages reflected improvements as scientists began to learn more about the nature of computer programming.

The computer language COBOL (an acronym for Common Business Oriented Language) was developed by several computer manufacturers and the U.S. Department of Defense in the early 1960s to provide a standard language for expressing business data processing problems. COBOL is best suited for operations on large sets of data, such as processing a payroll. COBOL is still an important language for many business mainframe computer systems; if your business is large enough to require a mainframe computer, you will probably need to hire professional COBOL programmers.

Some other well-known programming languages are:
- BASIC: good language for beginners to learn; it often is sold along with microcomputers
- Pascal: developed in the early 1970s as a language to help programmers write well-structured programs
- C: developed by Bell labs; has some of the advantages (but not the disadvantages) of assembly languages
- Prolog: short for Programming in Logic; a language used for tasks involving the logical relations between concepts; used for developing expert systems
- LISP: a language often used in artificial intelligence work for highly complex problems
- PL/I: developed by IBM in the early 1960s to accompany the 360 computer; it is suitable for a wide variety of tasks but is not found on microcomputers
- APL: best suited for complex operations on arrays

Most of these languages have several different versions, and programs written in one version might not work in another version of the same language.

MICROPROCESSORS AND MICROCOMPUTERS

The microcomputer became possible in the mid 1970s with the development of microprocessor chips that contained the entire central processing unit of the computer on a single integrated circuit. The memory capacity of computers also dramatically increased as memory integrated circuits improved. Some notable early microcomputers include the Commodore 64, the TRS-80 (sold by Tandy Corporation's Radio Shack stores), and the Apple II (developed by Steve Wozniak and Steve Jobs, who began work in a garage but whose company grew into one of the major microcomputer innovators).

The advent of microcomputers led to a stunning change in the way computers were viewed—computers could now be available to anyone, not just specialists. However, the mere availability of the hardware didn't lead to a dramatic increase in computer use. At first, home microcomputers were largely purchased by hobbyists. In order for the machines to become really widely used, new software was needed. In response, a number of user-friendly programs were developed, including spreadsheets and word processing software.

Spreadsheets

Businesspeople had used paper spreadsheets to arrange calculations for a long time (although they didn't call them "paper" spreadsheets at the time—obviously spreadsheets were on paper, since there were no other kinds). Paper spreadsheets have one major disadvantage: If one of the numbers changes, you must redo the calculations and change all of the other numbers that depend on it, a very difficult job. In the late 1970s, some business school students became frustrated with this problem. Since microcomputers had just become available, they came up with the idea to develop an electronic spreadsheet that would allow you to type the numbers and formulas into the computer, and with all recalculations made automatically if one of the numbers changed. They wrote a computer program, which became known as VisiCalc, to perform this task. Although VisiCalc seems primitive compared to today's spreadsheets (partly because of the memory limitations on the computers it was used with), it was a landmark development. VisiCalc was widely used on early Apple II computers and contributed to their sales.

This illustrates an important point: Electronic hobbyists buy the microcomputer hardware and then figure out what to do with it; businesspeople discover software that will help with a task (in this case, VisiCalc) and then obtain the necessary hardware (in this case, the Apple II).

The next generation of electronic spreadsheet programs was introduced with the product Lotus 1-2-3, developed by Lotus Development Corp. in 1983. Lotus 1-2-3 was considerably more flexible than previous spreadsheets, and graphics capability was integrated into the program. The Lotus 1-2-3 program was one of the main reasons that business computer users turned to microcomputers for financial calculations. This meant that they had to buy IBM PCs in order to run the software, which contributed to the rapid expansion of the IBM PC into the business world. (Lotus 1-2-3 would not fit on computers with 64K of memory, which had previously been a common size.) Another, newer spreadsheet program is Microsoft's Excel, first introduced in 1985 for the Macintosh.

Word Processing

Word processing systems were set up by newspapers in the 1970s to make it easier for reporters to type and edit stories. Early word processing systems were based on time-sharing systems on mainframe computers. When microcomputers became available, word processing programs became available for them. Wordstar was one of the earliest popular programs; some newer programs that have become widely used are Microsoft Word and WordPerfect. Newer programs usually contain improvements, partly because the hardware itself is constantly being improved.

Computers of the 80s—the IBM PC Standard and the Macintosh

IBM entered the microcomputer market with the first IBM PC, introduced in 1981. In the early 1980s a wide variety of different microcomputers were competing with each other, providing choices for the consumer but also creating one problem: Most of these different computers were not compatible with each other, and the programs that would run on one computer could not run on others—in most cases the disks could not even be read by other machines. There is a difficult trade-off here between innovation and standardization: It is good if companies are able to come up with new ideas that make their products better than the competitors, but it is also good if there is considerable interchangeability. If your company has just set up a system with several Brand X computers, you will be reluctant to change suddenly to a system based on Brand Y computers if they are incompatible with the ones you already have, even if the Brand Y computers are better.

Fortunately, by the late 1980s customers were able to get many of the benefits of both competition and standardization. The IBM PC had become established as a standard; its format for storing data on disks and for controlling video displays was used on many different machines. Other companies began making computers that conformed to the IBM PC standard but that had some innovations of their own. When whole new classes of machines, such as the PC AT and the PS/2, were introduced, they were designed so that the programs from earlier machines would still work. (Of course, a program written for the newer machines would likely use special features of that machine and so would not run on the older machines.)

An important part of the IBM PC standard was the operating system MS-DOS, developed by the Microsoft Company, which was then quite small. Microsoft grew rapidly in the 1980s with updated versions of MS-DOS being one of its main products;

after all, one copy of DOS was sold with every machine that fit the IBM PC standard.

IBM's main competition was the Macintosh, introduced in 1984 by Apple and totally unlike its earlier Apple II line. Macintosh commands are given with a menu system, with pictures representing the commands (called *icons*) appearing on the screen. Choices often appear in small windows on the screen (called pulldown menus or dialog boxes) that appear on top of other parts of the screen, but then disappear (revealing the screen segment underneath) when the user is finished with it. The user points to the icons by using a mouse. These concepts had been developed earlier, but the Macintosh was the first machine to make them widely used. The mouse allowed much greater flexibility in computer drawing programs; because the screen was always in graphics modes, word processing programs on the Macintosh are able to change font styles and type size, showing the results immediately on the screen. The early Macintosh with its small, monochrome screen and lack of a hard disk looks rather primitive now, but improved versions were quickly developed.

When a revolutionary new computer is introduced, naturally other computer makers try to adopt the good features for their machines. The program Microsoft Windows makes is possible to take advantage of many of the Macintosh concepts on IBM PCs. This has led to a controversy and another trade-off. On the one hand, the innovators should be able to profit from the success of their innovation before others imitate it; on the other hand, when a new, improved user interface is developed, it is to everyone's advantage if this becomes a standard, making it much easier for people to learn to use the computer. If each program has a totally different interface, it is harder for people to learn different application programs. This controversy is still under litigation (as of 1990); Apple is claiming that Microsoft appropriated concepts that belonged to Apple when developing the program Microsoft Windows (actually, Microsoft helped write the software for the Macintosh; Apple claims that it bought the concepts from Microsoft and now owns them).

Other lawsuits have been filed over the issue of the "look and feel" of a program. Nobody claims to have a copyright on the concept of a menu in a computer program (how would other software developers write programs if they could not use menus?). The controversy is whether the developer of a specific menu owns the rights to that menu, and whether other companies can use the same menu in the interests of standardization. This issue is unsettled; the field of copyright law for computer software is still very new. Both sides have a valid point; so some form of compromise perhaps can be reached.

Desktop Publishing

Consider a newspaper; it needs to arrange the stories on the page, place headlines of different sizes, and include pictures. In order to computerize newspaper production, it is necessary to have a computer that operates in graphics mode and has a pointing device, such as a mouse, so you can move stories to different locations around the page. The program must be able to take the text of the story from a word processing program and arrange it in columns or whatever shape is needed to fit the space, allowing for some of the story to run to another page if necessary. In 1985 Aldus Corp. (which also started out very small) introduced PageMaker, a program for the Macintosh that made it possible to design page layouts. Other desktop publishing programs were soon introduced, providing a major reason for businesses to buy Macintoshes (as the Lotus 1-2-3 program had earlier provided a major reason for businesses to buy IBM PCs). As would be expected, desktop publishing programs for the IBM PC world were introduced soon, as well.

There is one important lesson in this history: Nobody has a monopoly on good ideas. One reason the IBM PC prospered is that the company encouraged other companies to write software for the machine; creative people at companies other than IBM wrote much of the software responsible for making the IBM hardware such a big success. Computer companies that tried to force customers to buy all their computer products from one source were not as successful.

This brings us up to date as of the writing of this book. However, probably at this very moment somebody is thinking of an idea that will turn into the next revolutionary software product, and a new wave of computer applications will begin.

CHAPTER PERSPECTIVE

The history of information processing has centered on improvements in the physical representation of symbolic data. The modern digital general-purpose computer developed from many of these earlier ideas. The flexibility of computers holds the promise that there will be continued rapid improvement in the way that information can be processed as new software and hardware are developed.

REFERENCES
Bashe, Johnson, Palmer, and Pugh, *IBM's Early Computers* (Cambridge, MA: MIT Press), 1986.
Encyclopedia Britannica.
Ritchie, David, *The Computer Pioneers* (New York: Simon and Schuster), 1986.
Walker, C.B.F. *Reading the past: Cuneiform* (London: British Museum Publications), 1987.

Spreadsheets: Making Optimal Decisions

CHAPTER 3

INTRODUCTION AND MAIN POINTS

Running a business calls for many judgment decisions; computer data can never substitute for a well-thought-out decision. However, the computer can help perform calculations and leave you more time to think about the serious judgment calls. For example, one key decision you must make is determining what price to charge. In order to make this decision, you need to take into account both factors that relate to the cost of production and factors that relate to the demand for the product. There are many variables to consider, a change in any one of which can lead to significant changes in the result. This is where computer spreadsheets come in: They can quickly perform calculations of the type "If variable X changes, what happens to all of these other variables?"

After studying the material in this chapter:
■ You will know the basic command structure of Lotus 1-2-3.
■ You will know how to determine the profit-maximizing price when you are given information on the demand for the product and the cost of production.

LOTUS 1-2-3 WORKSHEETS

Several computer spreadsheet programs are available for microcomputers. We will talk about the program Lotus 1-2-3, which, since its introduction in 1983, has become the most widely-used business spreadsheet. Another popular choice is Excel from Microsoft, originally sold for the Apple Macintosh and now also available for IBM PC compatibles. The general principles are similar, so you should be able to convert the spreadsheet discussed in this chapter to another program without too much difficulty.

Specifically, we will focus on Lotus 1-2-3 Release 2, which contains several improvements over the original Release 1. Release 2 works fine for many business decision-making purposes;

SPREADSHEETS: MAKING OPTIMAL DECISIONS

if you need to develop very large spreadsheets—for example, if you are putting together a budget with many subsections—you should obtain Release 3, which contains some fundamental enhancements that make it much easier to work with large spreadsheets (these will be discussed in Chapter 12).

The focus in this chapter is on the business principles behind the spreadsheet, rather than the details of how to make Lotus 1-2-3 work. However, we cover enough of the specifics that you will be able to follow the material even if you have never used a spreadsheet before. You should follow along on your own computer; the only way to learn one of these spreadsheets is to put your own fingers on the keys. A spreadsheet program such as 1-2-3, which is complicated because of its many capabilities, can be intimidating when you are starting out. However, don't despair. You don't need to learn all of the capabilities before you begin using the program; the best way to learn it is to start working with it to solve the problems you need to solve and then learn about the various additional capabilities as you need them. This book focuses on the business tasks themselves, rather than the computer, and does not cover all of the capabilities of the program. We introduce only the features that we need to solve our problems; your reference manual gives you complete information on all of the other features.

When you first enter the Lotus 1-2-3 program, your screen will look like the illustration on page 44.

The top three lines give information about the status of your work; the rest of the screen consists of the worksheet where you actually put your data. When the word READY appears at the upper right-hand corner, the program is ready for you to enter data into the worksheet. The worksheet consists of a grid of cells. Each cell is a location where you may put a number, a formula, or a label. The cells are arranged in rows and columns, which are labeled on the screen. Note that columns are labeled with letters; rows are labeled with numbers. Somewhere on the worksheet is a highlighted cell. The highlighted area is called the cell pointer; it indicates where you may enter data. At the start, the cell pointer is at the upper left-hand corner. This cell is called cell A1; cells are identified by the letter of their column and the number of their row.

The keyboard contains four arrow keys; pressing these moves the cell pointer up, down, left, or right. Experiment with this a bit now. (If you have an old-fashioned IBM PC keyboard with the numeric keypad and the arrows on the same keys, the

BARRON'S BUSINESS LIBRARY

```
A1:                                              READY
```

	A	B	C	D	E	F	G	H
1								
2								
3								
4								
5								
6								
7								
8								
9								
10								
11								
12								
13								
14								
15								
16								
17								
18								
19								
20								

arrows work only when NUMLCK is off.) Note that the upper left-hand corner of the screen gives the coordinates of the current active cell.

EXAMPLE: ICE CREAM SHOP
Now you're ready to go to work. Suppose you are considering the purchase of an ice cream shop and are trying to decide what price to charge for an ice cream cone. This ice cream shop sells

SPREADSHEETS: MAKING OPTIMAL DECISIONS

only one kind of ice cream cone. (In reality you would need to develop a more comprehensive plan, taking into account the sales for each type of product.)

You know that raising the price will cut down on the number of cones that you sell, also affecting your costs. So you want to develop a worksheet that shows how your revenues and costs will be affected if you change the price.

First, you make a column for the price. It would be very confusing if you made a table consisting of nothing but numbers; imagine trying to figure out what anything meant. So, you need to include a label at the top of the column. This is very easy to do; simply type "Price when the pointer is pointing to cell A1. Press the down arrow key when you are done, and the label "Price" will appear in cell A1. Here are some things to note when you are typing information into cells:

— Use the backspace key if you need to go back and fix a mistake.

— When you are finished typing in a cell, you may press either the RETURN key or one of the four arrow keys. If you press the RETURN key, the pointer will stay in the current cell. If you press one of the arrow keys, the pointer will move to the next cell in that direction shown on the key. If you know which cell you want to move to next, the best thing to do is press the arrow key that points in that direction.

— The double-quote mark in front of "Price" causes the label to be lined up with the right edge of the cell, which is best because that way the label will line up with the numbers in that column. (If you leave out the double quote mark, the label will be lined up with the left edge of the cell.)

Now, suppose you want to consider possible prices from $0.8 up to $2. Type these numbers into the cells as shown below. After you have typed each number, then press the down arrow key to move down to the next cell (see figure 3-1 on page 46).

THE COMMAND MENU

Next, move to cell B1 and type "Quantity to enter the label into that cell. You know that the quantity of ice cream cones you sell per month depends on the price you charge, but it can be very difficult to figure out the exact relation (see a book on statistics). For now, suppose you have estimated that the quantity sold can be written as the following straight-line function of the price:

```
A14: 2                                        READY
```

	A	B	C	D	E	F	G	H
1	Price							
2	0.8							
3	0.9							
4	1							
5	1.1							
6	1.2							
7	1.3							
8	1.4							
9	1.5							
10	1.6							
11	1.7							
12	1.8							
13	1.9							
14	2							

Fig. 3-1.

$$q = 16000 - 6200p$$

The number -6200 is said to represent the *slope* of the line, and 16000 is the *intercept*.

You might be tempted to move to cell B2 and type this formula: 16000−6200P. However, there is a problem. First, the computer will not recognize the label *p* unless you tell it what it means. To accomplish that, Lotus 1-2-3 provides the Name command, which allows you to attach a name to a cell or range of cells. You can refer to cells by their coordinates if you wish, but that can quickly get confusing because the coordinates don't tell you anything about what a cell means. For example, if you look at the formula next week, you're not likely to remember that cell A2 means price. It's good practice to create cell names that give some indication of the cells' meaning.

First, move the pointer to the cell you want to name (in this case, cell A2). If you're using Lotus 1-2-3, you tell the program that you want to use the Name command by hitting the slash key, /, at the start of a command. As soon as you hit the slash key, the appearance of the top of the screen changes:

```
A2: 0.8                                              MENU

 Worksheet  Range Copy Move File Print Graph Data System Quit
 Global, Insert, Delete, Column, Erase, Titles, Window, Status, Page
```

	A	B	C	D	E
1	Price	Quantity			
2	0.8				
3	0.9				

First, the word READY has disappeared from the upper right-hand corner and has been replaced by the word MENU. A menu is a list of choices. All of the Lotus 1-2-3 commands are arranged in menus, which makes it easier for you because you do not have to remember them all. You can look at the menu to see the choices. The second line of the screen now gives the main menu choices.

Lotus 1-2-3 gives you a choice about how to give commands, depending on whether you are a person who likes to type or a person who likes to point. If you press the first letter of a command name, that command will be called. For example, pressing w calls the Worksheet command. You can also call the command by moving the menu pointer to the command you want and pressing RETURN. Notice that after you press the / key and the menu first appears, the word WORKSHEET is highlighted, meaning that the menu pointer is pointed at the Worksheet command. This means that the program is guessing that you wish to use the Worksheet command. Often the program will try to guess your intention and highlight that choice; if it guesses correctly, it will save you work. In this case, it has not guessed correctly, because you don't want the worksheet command.

What does the Worksheet command do? you are probably asking. Look at the third line of the screen, which gives the submenu for the Worksheet command. Many of the Lotus 1-2-3 commands have submenus that give you more detailed choices about that command. This is actually a very logical way to organize commands; the menu structure is one of the reasons that Lotus 1-2-3 became so popular. To understand the concept of a submenu, suppose you go to a restaurant and select a salad from the menu, and the waiter presents you with three choices for salad dressing. Think of the three dressings as three choices in the submenu for the Salad command from the main menu. You can think of the command menu as a large house (or perhaps a maze); each menu is like a hallway with several doors. After you enter one room you might have a choice of additional rooms that branch off the room you are in.

The submenu for the Worksheet command appears in figure 3-2 on page 49.

Some of the Worksheet command items, such as insert, delete, erase, have obvious meanings; others are more complicated. Consult your reference manual.

THE NAME COMMAND

At this point you do not want the Worksheet command, so use the right arrow key to move the pointer so that the Range command is highlighted. The third line of the screen will now show the submenu for the Range command:

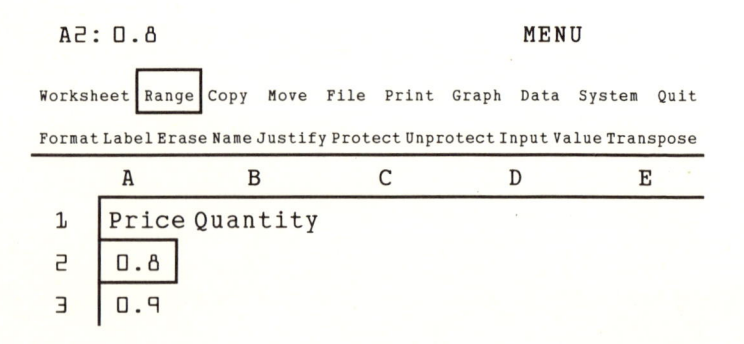

```
A2: 0.8                                    MENU
```

| Worksheet | Range | Copy | Move | File | Print | Graph | Data | System | Quit |

Format Label Erase Name Justify Protect Unprotect Input Value Transpose

	A	B	C	D	E
1	Price	Quantity			
2	0.8				
3	0.9				

Note that the Name command is the fourth choice on this submenu. In order to call up the Range submenu, type RETURN (since the Range command is the one that is currently highlighted) or type R. The screen now looks like:

Entry to Main Menu

| Worksheet | Range | Copy | Move | File | Print | Graph | Data | System | Quit |

File: | Retrieve | Save | Combine | Xtract | Erase | List | Import | Directory |

Range: | Format | Label | Erase | Name | Justify | Protect | Unprotect | Input | Value | Transpose |

Name: | Create | Delete | Labels | Reset | Table |

Format: | Fixed | Scientific | Currency | , | General | +/- | Percent | Date | Text | Hidden | Reset |

Worksheet: | Global | Insert | Delete | Column | Erase | Titles | Window | Status | Page |

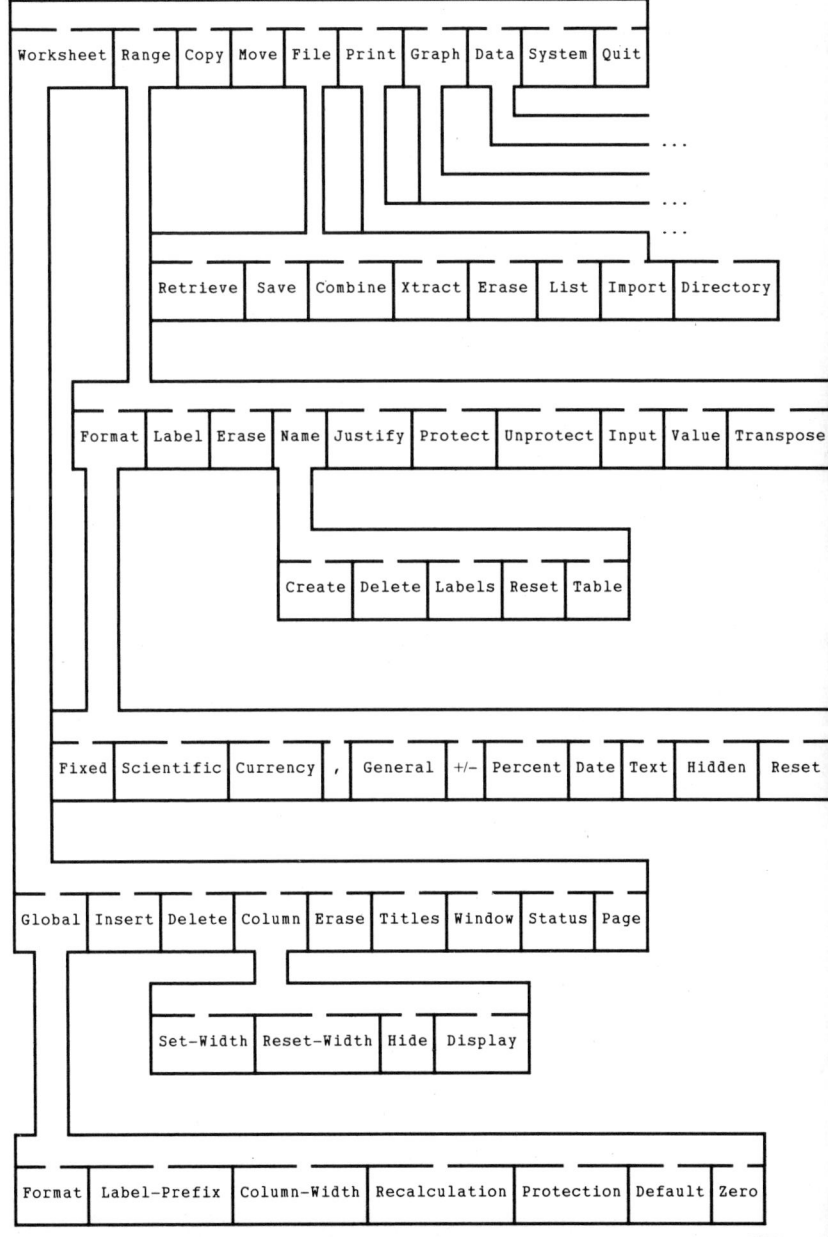

Column: | Set-Width | Reset-Width | Hide | Display |

Global: | Format | Label-Prefix | Column-Width | Recalculation | Protection | Default | Zero |

Fig. 3-2. **Part of Lotus 1-2-3 command menu.**

```
A2: 0.8                                              MENU
```
| Format | Label Erase Name Justify Protect Unprotect Input Value Transpose |

Format a cell or range of cells

	A	B	C	D	E
1	Price	Quantity			
2	0.8				
3	0.9				

Note that the Range submenu has now jumped up to the second line. The Format command is highlighted, and the third line of the screen now contains a description of the Format command. (We will come back to this command very shortly.)

In order to invoke the Name command, you have two choices: either type N or move the menu pointer so that it highlights NAME. When you move the pointer, you see:

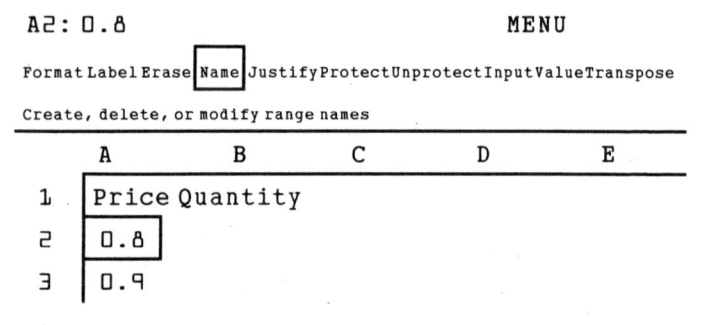

```
A2: 0.8                                              MENU
```
Format Label Erase |Name| Justify Protect Unprotect Input Value Transpose

Create, delete, or modify range names

	A	B	C	D	E
1	Price	Quantity			
2	0.8				
3	0.9				

Line 3 now contains a description of the Name command. Press the RETURN key, and the submenu for the Name command jumps to line 2.

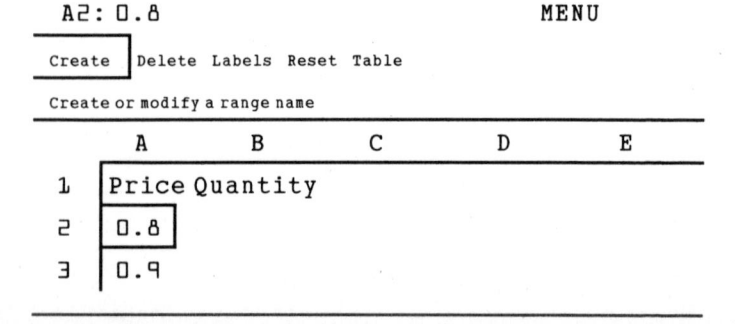

```
A2: 0.8                                              MENU
```
| Create | Delete Labels Reset Table |

Create or modify a range name

	A	B	C	D	E
1	Price	Quantity			
2	0.8				
3	0.9				

SPREADSHEETS: MAKING OPTIMAL DECISIONS

The Create command is used to create a name; invoke this command by pressing either C or RETURN. (Remember, pressing RETURN always selects the command that is highlighted.) The program now needs two pieces of information: the name you wish to give and the cell or cells to be named. The prompt ENTER NAME: appears on the screen:

```
A2: 0.8                                    EDIT
Enter name:
```

	A	B	C	D	E
1	Price	Quantity			
2	0.8				
3	0.9				

Since you want to give the name P, press the key for P and then RETURN. Next, the program will ask for the range of cells to be named:

```
A2: 0.8                                    POINT
Enter name: P                   Enter range: A2..A2
```

	A	B	C	D	E
1	Price	Quantity			
2	0.8				
3	0.9				

Note that the program guesses the range you want: in this case, it guesses that you want to give the name to cell A2. Why did it guess this cell? Because the cell pointer was pointing to cell A2 when you began entering the command menu. It is a good idea to move the cell pointer to the cell you wish to name before entering the name command so you can take advantage of this guessing feature. (Note that the program did not even dare to guess what name you wanted to use, since it had no way of knowing what you were thinking of.) If the cell pointer is not pointing to the cell you want to name, then you can type in the range this way: A2..A2. You can also give a name to a group of cells by typing the coordinates of the upper left-hand corner and the lower right-hand corner, separated by two periods. After you have typed RETURN to enter the range to be named, the menu lines vanish, the word MENU changes back to the word READY, and you are able to enter data again.

The fast way to use the Name command is to simply type these keys: /RNC (Range Name Create). Then you would not have had to look at the menus at all. When you are new to the program, the menus are a valuable aid. However, just as if you know a restaurant well, you can skip the menu and simply tell the waiter what you want, so too with Lotus 1-2-3; once you get to know the program, you can enter the commands more quickly by typing their first letters without bothering to look at the menus.

THE FORMAT COMMAND

There is one more problem with your spreadsheet that should be fixed before you proceed. Note that the numbers in the price column (0.8, 0.9, 1) do not line up, since the 1 does not have any numerals after the decimal point. A column of numbers always looks better if all of the numbers in the column are displayed with the same number of decimal places (in this case, one decimal place); for instance, "1" should be displayed as "1.0." In order to tell the program to do that, use the Range Format command. Enter this command sequence: /RF (Range Format), or look at the menus at the top of the screen and use the arrows, as described above. The program will display a line giving several format choices:

FIXED SCIENTIFIC CURRENCY, GENERAL +/− PERCENT DATA TIME TEXT
HIDDEN RESET

Choose the first option—FIXED. Then the computer will ask you for the number of decimal places that should be displayed with each number. For now, type 1. Then the computer will ask you for the range to format. Type A2..A14 to indicate that you want this particular format to apply to all cells from A2 to A14. Then the screen will look like figure 3-3 on page 53.

The (F1) in the top line indicates that cell A2 has been formatted to fixed format with one decimal place.

Use the Format command for each of the remaining columns that you enter in this worksheet. You will see some examples of the other format options later in the book. For business purposes the most useful ones are the currency format (which includes dollar signs, commas to separate thousands, and negative

```
A2: (F1) 0.8                                    READY
        A       B       C       D       E       F       G       H
   1  | Price
   2  |  0.8
   3  |  0.9
   4  |  1.0
   5  |  1.1
   6  |  1.2
   7  |  1.3
   8  |  1.4
   9  |  1.5
  10  |  1.6
  11  |  1.7
  12  |  1.8
  13  |  1.9
  14  |  2.0
```

Fig. 3-3

numbers enclosed in parentheses as is done in accounting reports) and the comma format, which is like the fixed format except that commas are automatically included. The comma format is the best format for large nonmonetary values.

ENTERING FORMULAS

Now return to your ice cream business. You need to enter the formula for the quantity–price relationship. Move the cell pointer to cell B2 and enter this formula:

$$16000 - 6200*P$$

The formula setup is similar to the way it looks in ordinary mathematical notation, except that an asterisk, *, is used as the symbol for multiplication because the multiplication symbol, ×, looks too much like the letter X and isn't included on the keyboard.

Press the RETURN key, and you will see on the screen:

B2: 16000-6200*P   READY

	A	B	C	D	E
1	Price	Quantity			
2	0.8	11040			
3	0.9				

The program calculated the result and put the answer in cell B2, allowing you to see that if you charge a price of .8, your total sales will be 11040. Note that the formula you typed in appears on the top line of the screen (next to "B2"—the coordinates of the cell to which the cell pointer is currently pointing). When you look at the worksheet itself, you cannot tell the difference between a number that was typed in directly (such as the 0.8 in cell A2) and a number that was calculated as the result of a formula (such as the 11040 in cell B2). However, if you move the cell pointer to a particular cell, the top line of the screen will show you the formula that was typed into that cell.

There is a problem with writing the formula in this manner. What happens if either the slope or the intercept changes? Since you will want to ask "what if" type questions, you need to be able to change these values easily. You can go back and change the formula in a cell by moving the pointer to that cell and then pressing the F2 key to enter the Edit mode, but it is awkward to do that. Also, since you will be copying the formula to all of the locations in that column, you would have to change the formula in all those cells. That would be far too much work.

To avoid that problem, enter the values of the slope and the intercept as data in the worksheet. First, find an open area of the worksheet. In this example, use the space below your table; move to cell A18. Type the label SLOPE here; then move to cell B18 and type the value -6200. (Remember, you should never type a number into a spreadsheet cell without also including a label for it.) Then go down to cell A19, type the label INTCP:, and put the number 16000 into cell B19 (figure 3-4 on page 55).

Now you could enter this formula for the quantity into cell B2: +$B$19+$B$18*P. However, again the formula will be much more meaningful if you have given names to the cells. So, move the pointer to cell B18 for the slope and enter the Name command /RNC (Range Name Create). Enter the name SLOPE, and

B19: 16000				READY
A	B	C	D	E

	A	B	C	D	E
1	Price	Quantity			
2	0.8				
3	0.9				
4	1.0				
5	1.1				
6	1.2				
7	1.3				
8	1.4				
9	1.5				
10	1.6				
11	1.7				
12	1.8				
13	1.9				
14	2.0				
15					
16					
17					
18	Slope:	−6200			
19	Intcp:	16000			
20					

Fig. 3-4

then press RETURN when the computer guesses that you want to give this name to the range B18..B18. Move the pointer to cell B19, type /RNC, enter the name INTCP, and press RETURN to give this name to the range B19..B19.

Now move back to cell B2 and enter this formula: +$INTCP+$SLOPE*P. If you press RETURN, the number 11040 will again appear in cell B2 as the quantity of ice cream cones you would sell at a price of .8. Keep in mind this general rule: In most cases, avoid using numbers in your spreadsheet formulas. Instead, put each number in its own cell, give it a name, and then refer to that name in any formula. This has two major advantages: the name will help you remember what the number means, and it will be easy to make changes, since changing the value of the number in the cell will automatically change the values in all other cells that depend on that number.

You may be wondering why the dollar signs are included in front of INTCP and SLOPE but not in front of P in the formula. The use of the dollar signs in Lotus 1-2-3 is actually very logical, although it can be confusing at first. Before answering this question, we will discuss the next step in the worksheet: copying the quantity formula to the other cells in that column.

THE COPY COMMAND

The program has calculated the quantity of ice cream cones that would be sold at a price of .8; now you need to find out what the quantity would be for each of the other prices. You don't want to type the formula into every cell in the Quantity column. Instead, use one of the most work-saving of the 1-2-3 commands: the Copy command. This will copy the formula from cell B2 into all of the other cells in that column.

Move the pointer to cell B2, then enter the command menu. (Remember, you do that by pressing the / key.) The Copy command is the third choice on the main menu, so you enter that either by typing C or by moving the menu pointer so that it highlights Copy and then pressing RETURN. The copy command needs two pieces of information: where you are copying FROM, and where you are copying TO. In this case, you are copying from cell B2. Since you moved the cell pointer to this cell before you entered the command menu, the program will correctly guess that this is what you are trying to copy from.

```
B2: +$INTCP+$SLOPE*P                              POINT
Enter range to copy FROM: B2..B2
```

	A	B	C	D	E
1	Price	Quantity			
2	0.8	11040			
3	0.9				

SPREADSHEETS: MAKING OPTIMAL DECISIONS

After you press RETURN, the computer will ask where you want to copy TO.

```
B2: +$INTCP+$SLOPE*P                               POINT
Enter range to copy TO: B2
```

	A	B	C	D	E
1	Price	Quantity			
2	0.8	11040			
3	0.9				

Fig. 3-5

It is guessing that you want to copy to the range B2..B2; of course, it has guessed wrong, since it would do no good to copy the formula to the one cell where it is already located. You have two choices for entering the range. Again, some people like to type, and some people like to point. To type the range in, simply type B2..B14. The two dots indicate that all of the cells between the two given cells should be included in the range.

The pointing method takes a little longer, but you are less likely to make a mistake because it is very clear what range you are selecting. First, press the period key. Then start pressing the down arrow, watching the screen closely. The cell pointer, which previously had marked only one cell, now becomes bigger. Keep pressing the down arrow until you reach the bottom of the table (row 14). The screen will look like figure 3-6 on page 58.

Note that the word at the upper right-hand corner has changed to POINT because you are using the Point mode. The RANGE TO COPY TO on line 2 automatically adjusted to B2..B14 as you pressed the down arrow. This entire range is now highlighted on the screen. (You needed to press the period key to "anchor" the range; if you had not pressed the period key, the cell pointer would have moved, instead of becoming bigger, when you pressed the down arrow key.)

Now you come to the magic part. After you have selected the range to copy to, press the RETURN key to execute the copy command. The formula for the quantity will be copied to all of the cells in that column, and their numeric results will be displayed. Press RETURN, and don't blink. The screen will suddenly change to appear as figure 3-7 on pages 58–59.

BARRON'S BUSINESS LIBRARY

```
B14:                                              POINT
Enter range to copy TO: B2..B14
```

	A	B	C	D	E
1	Price	Quantity			
2	0.8	11040			
3	0.9				
4	1.0				
5	1.1				
6	1.2				
7	1.3				
8	1.4				
9	1.5				
10	1.6				
11	1.7				
12	1.8				
13	1.9				
14	2.0				

Fig. 3-6

```
B2: +$INTCP+$SLOPE*P                              READY
```

	A	B	C	D	E
1	Price	Quantity			
2	0.8	11040			
3	0.9	10420			
4	1.0	9800			
5	1.1	9180			
6	1.2	8560			
7	1.3	7940			

8	1.4	7320
9	1.5	6700
10	1.6	6080
11	1.7	5460
12	1.8	4840
13	1.9	4220
14	2.0	3600
15		
16		
17		
18	Slope:	−6200
19	Intcp:	16000
20		

Fig. 3-7

Here you can see the fundamental reason why computers are useful: they can perform calculations very fast.

Now back to the mystery of the dollar signs. A dollar sign in front of a cell address or name means "absolute address." The lack of a dollar sign means "relative address." What does this mean? If you type a formula into a cell and never copy that formula into any other cell, it won't make any difference at all whether you include dollar signs. However, if you do need to copy the formula to another cell, as you have just done, then it makes a big difference whether the dollar signs are included.

Including the dollar signs tells the computer that the address is an absolute address and instructs it never to change this address, no matter where in the worksheet you copy it to. The dollar sign in front of SLOPE in the formula means: this will always refer to cell B18 (the cell to which you assigned the name SLOPE). Use the dollar signs when you have entered a specific number that you want to use in several formulas in different cells.

Suppose you had put a dollar sign in front of the P in the

formula in cell B2. When you copied that formula down to cell B3, the formula would have stayed the same: +$INTCP+$SLOPE*$P, and the result would have been 11040, the same as it was when the price was .8. This is not at all what you want; you do not want to keep the same value for price when you copy the formula down. In cell B2, the P in the formula doesn't mean "Always use cell A2"; it means "Always use the cell that is one cell to the left." That is what the relative means in the term "relative address." Enter the correct formula into cell B2:

$$+\$INTCP+\$SLOPE*P$$

Now copy the formula down the column, and then move the pointer to cell B3. The top of the screen will display the formula there:

$$\$INTCP+\$SLOPE*A3$$

Note that the INTCP and SLOPE have not changed, because of the dollar signs, but that the P has changed to A3. The P in cell B2 meant "the cell that is directly to the left of the current cell"; sure enough, cell A3 is the cell that is directly to the left of the cell B3. Try it yourself by entering these formulas into cell B2 and then copying the result down:

```
$INTCP+$SLOPE*$P
INTCP+SLOPE*$P
INTCP+SLOPE*P
```

In each case try to guess how the computer will go wrong before you enter the formula, and then see if you were right.

Next, you need to calculate your total sales revenue for each possible price. Move to cell B2 and use the Name command to give this cell the name Q, for quantity. Then you should be able to figure out how to enter the formula for revenue. First, move to cell C1 and enter REVENUE as the column heading. Then, move to cell C2 and enter this formula:

$$+P*Q$$

Note there are no dollar signs (you should be able to figure out why; if not, try the formula with dollar signs to see why it goes wrong) and that you must have assigned the names P and Q before using the formula.

There a plus sign at the front of the formula to tell 1-2-3 that this is a formula, not a label. One way to learn the right way to do something is to try it the wrong way first and see what happens. (It is safe to do this on spreadsheets.) Enter this formula into cell C2: P*Q, and you will see this appear:

```
C2: 'p*q                                              READY
```

	A	B	C	D	E
1	Price	Quantity	Revenue		
2	0.8	11040	p*q		
3	0.9	10420			

The program simply displayed the formula, instead of displaying the result of the formula. The program needs a way to know when you want the characters displayed exactly as you typed them and when you want a formula evaluated. You tell it in this way: If the entry starts with a number, or one of these characters:

$$. + - (@ \# \$$$

the program automatically assumes that it is a formula; for example, 2 + 2 will be treated as a formula, and the result 4 will be displayed. If the formula starts with a letter or any other character that is not listed above, the program treats it as a label. By putting a plus sign at the front of the formula, you tell the program that it is not a label. (If you need to enter a label that begins with a number or one of the other formula symbols, putting a single quote mark, ', at the start tells the program that it is a label.)

After you have entered the formula in cell C2, use the copy command to copy the formula to the rest of the cells in that column. The result is:

BARRON'S BUSINESS LIBRARY

C2: +P*Q   READY

	A	B	C	D	E
1	Price	Quantity	Revenue		
2	0.8	11040	8832		
3	0.9	10420	9378		
4	1.0	9800	9800		
5	1.1	9180	10098		
6	1.2	8560	10272		
7	1.3	7940	10322		
8	1.4	7320	10248		
9	1.5	6700	10050		
10	1.6	6080	9728		
11	1.7	5460	9282		
12	1.8	4840	8712		
13	1.9	4220	8018		
14	2.0	3600	7200		
15					
16					
17					
18	Slope:	-6200			
19	Intcp:	16000			
20					

If you raise the price too high we drive away so many customers that the total revenue actually goes down.

COST ESTIMATION

Now you need to consider the cost structure of the ice cream business. This simple business has only three type of costs: variable costs per cone, labor costs, and fixed costs. In a more realistic case there would be more categories here, and the power of the spreadsheet would become even more apparent. Suppose you have entered the information about the cost into the spreadsheet (see page 66).

The variable cost per cone consists of three items: 50 cents for the ice cream itself, ten cents for the cone, and one cent for the napkin. The vertical line, |, is included at the front of each label to separate it from the items to its left.(When you type the vertical line, precede it with a single quote, ', so that 1-2-3 knows it is a label.) To calculate the average variable cost (AVC), move the pointer to cell C20 and enter the label AVC. Then move to cell D20. There are two ways to add up these three items. One way is to enter the formula +D17+D18+D19. That would not be too hard in this case, but there will be times when you will need to add up all the entries in a long column, so you need a quicker way. Lotus 1-2-3 provides a built-in sum function. Type this formula into cell D20: @SUM(D17..D19)

The @ sign is put at the front of all the functions that are built in to Lotus 1-2-3; you will see some more examples of these later. D17..D19 tells the computer to take all of the cells from D17 to D19. If you do this, the program will calculate the value .61 for AVC and display it in cell D20.

To calculate the labor cost, assume that you need to pay an hourly wage of $5.90, that you will need two workers for every hour the store is open, and that the store will be open for 360 hours a month. Multiply these together to get the total labor cost. Therefore, the formula in cell F20 is +F17*F18*F19.

Assume your fixed costs per month are $200 for electricity, $50 for phone, and $75 for insurance. Again, use the @SUM function to add these up. The formula in cell H20 is @SUM(H17..H19).

Use the name command to assign these names: AVC to cell D20, LC to cell F20, and FC to cell H20.

Column D will contain the cost, so label cell D1. In order to calculate the cost, add the fixed cost plus the labor cost, and multiply the cost of each cone by the number of cones. Here is the formula to be entered into cell D2: +$FC+$LC+$AVC*Q

Note there are dollar signs before FC, LC, and AVC, but not before Q. Copy this formula down to the remainder of the cells in column D; as shown on page 66.

To calculate the profit, assign the names TR (for total revenue) to cell C2 and TC (for total cost) to cell D2. Then enter the formula +TR-TC to cell E2 (and quickly think to yourself why there are no dollar signs in the formula). Then copy the formula to the other cells in the column (see page 66).

You can see that the largest possible profit, 1446.2, occurs when you charge a price of 1.6 and sell a quantity of 6080 cones. You can have the program automatically determine the largest profit by using the @MAX function. Find an open space in the worksheet to the right of the table. Enter the formula: @MAX (E2..E14) and include a label above the formula. Then the computer will automatically display the maximum value in the range of cells in the profit column.

GENERAL INFORMATION ABOUT LOTUS 1-2-3
There are some important keys and some important features you should remember about Lotus 1-2-3.

The ESCAPE Key
Suppose you have become trapped in a part of the program where you don't want to be (for example, you might have hit a wrong command key). In general, the ESCAPE key gets you back to where you were before you got to wherever you are now. If you are somewhere in the menu structure, the ESCAPE key gets you back to the previous position in the menu structure. If you hit the ESCAPE key several times in a row, you will eventually leave the menu entirely and return to the ready mode.

The help key (F1)
If you want quick information about how Lotus 1-2-3 works, press the F1 key. You will see choices on the screen; choose one to see information about that topic. Press ESCAPE when you are done with the help screen and are ready to return to your previous work. The F stands for function; the keyboard has ten different F keys. Each F key can be programmed for a specific task, depending on which program you are in. The meaning of each of these keys varies depending on what program you are using.

The edit key (F2)
Suppose you need to change a formula that is typed into a cell. One option is to move the pointer there and type in a new

formula; however, if you need to make one minor change in a long, complicated formula, you don't want to type the whole thing again. Instead, pressing the F2 key allows you to make changes in the cell. Entering Edit mode changes the meaning of the left and right arrow keys; instead of moving the pointer one cell to the left or right, they now move the edit cursor one space to the left or right. The old version of the formula appears at the top of the screen; move the edit cursor to the point where you want to make changes. Use the DELETE key to delete a character. Use the INSERT key to switch back and forth between Insert and Overwrite mode. In Insert mode, any character you type will push aside the characters that are already there, so no characters get lost. In Overwrite mode, a new character will obliterate the old character in the same position and then take its place. Press the RETURN key when you are done editing the formula.

Saving

One important rule when you are performing any task on a computer: Save your work regularly. Work on a spreadsheet is stored in the computer's memory, which goes blank when the power is turned off (or cut off). In order to ensure that your work is not lost, save it on your disk (preferably a hard disk; if not, a floppy disk). To save work under Lotus 1-2-3, enter this command sequence: /FS (File Save). The computer will ask you the name by which you wish to store the file and then save it on the disk. The name that you type must be eight characters or less; it should start with a letter and then may include letters or numbers. The file extension will be added automatically (WKS or WKE or WK1, depending on what version you are using).

Suppose you save the worksheet under the file name SPREAD and at a later time continue working and wish to save the updated spreadsheet under the same name. The old version will get lost when you save the new version, so the program pauses to check with you to make sure that you really want to do this. It gives you two choices: Cancel and Replace. If you choose Cancel, the old version of the file will remain untouched, but your new work will not be saved. Be very careful of this danger; if you choose Cancel and then leave the program, you will later find that the latest version of your work has not been saved. On the other

	A	B	C	D	E	F	G	H
1	Price	Quantity	Revenue	Cost	Profit			
2	0.8	11040	8832	11307.4	-2475.4			
3	0.9	10420	9378	10929.2	-1551.2			
4	1.0	9800	9800	10551.0	-751.0			
5	1.1	9180	10098	10172.8	-74.8			
6	1.2	8560	10272	9794.6	477.4			
7	1.3	7940	10322	9416.4	905.6			
8	1.4	7320	10248	9038.2	1209.8			Max Profit:
9	1.5	6700	10050	8660.0	1390.0			1446.2
10	1.6	6080	9728	8281.8	1446.2			
11	1.7	5460	9282	7903.6	1378.4			
12	1.8	4840	8712	7525.4	1186.6			
13	1.9	4220	8018	7147.2	870.8			
14	2.0	3600	7200	6769.0	431.0			
15								
16			Variable Cost		Labor Cost		Fixed Cost	
17	Slope:	-6200	ice cream	0.5	wage	5.9	elect	200
18	Intcp:	16000	cone	0.1	workers	2	phone	50
19			napkin	0.01	hours	360	insur.	75
20			AVC	0.61	LC	4248	FC	325

hand, if you choose Replace, the old version of the file will be lost forever, but your new work will be safely saved. Normally this is what you want. However, there can be a danger here, too. If you saved yesterday's work under the name SPREAD and then save today's work on a totally different problem under the name SPREAD as well, yesterday's work will be totally lost. That is why a generic name such as SPREAD is actually a very poor choice for a spreadsheet name. Instead, the name should relate very specifically to the work contained in that file; choosing a descriptive name makes it clear to you in the future what is contained in the file, and reduces the likelihood that you will accidentally give another file the same name.

Retrieving Files
When you wish to work on a file that you have previously saved, use the /FR (File Retrieve) command sequence. The computer will ask you for the name of the file you wish to retrieve (and it will even display a list of available files for you). After you provide the file name, work in that file will appear on the screen.

Printing
At some point you will probably want your work on paper. Enter the /PP (Print Printer) command sequence. You may not want your entire spreadsheet to be printed, so you must enter the range that you do want printed. As in every case where you need to specify a range, you have a choice between typing in the coordinates of the two corner points of the range (such as A1..G30) or using the point feature by pressing the period key and then using the arrows. Then press G (for Go) to commence the printing. The Print command has several other options; for example, you can advance to the top of the next page or adjust the margin settings on the paper.

Another variant of the print command is the /PF (Print File) command sequence. Suppose that you want to incorporate your spreadsheet into a document that you are typing with a word processing program. In that case an image of the printer output must be stored in a disk file, instead of being sent to the printer. When you enter the /PF sequence, you enter the name of the file where the printer output will be sent, then select the range and press G, just as you would if you were sending the file directly to the printer. You will not be able to see anything happen, but an image of the file will be written to the disk file that you specified. Later, when you have exited 1-2-3 and returned to MS-DOS, use the Type command to see the file displayed on the screen. For example, if you sent the output to the file BUDG95.PRN, then the command TYPE BUDG95.PRN will display it on the screen. (Do not use the Type command with one of the worksheet files with extensions beginning with WK; these files contain special characters that are not intended to be displayed.) Your word processing program will have a command that allows it to read in text (called an ASCII file) from the disk, so you can read the file BUDG95.PRN into the document.

Column Width

What happens if the information you wish to display in a column is too wide to fit in that column? If you are typing a label and the cell to the right is empty, there is no problem; the display will simply spill over into the adjacent column. However, there will be a problem if you later need to put some data into the adjacent column, because you will not be able to see all of the original cell. A number will not spill over into the adjacent column. If you try to enter a number that is too wide for the cell, you will see a row of asterisks: *******. Don't panic; your number isn't lost. In order to see the number, you need to increase the width of that column. Enter this command sequence: /WCS (Worksheet Column Set-Width). Then the computer will ask you to type in the number of characters you would like the column to accept. As you work on a worksheet you can adjust the widths of the various columns to improve the appearance of the worksheet.

Other Capabilities

There are many more @ functions included with 1-2-3; you will use some of them later in this book. See your reference manual for the complete list. Other important parts of the program are its graphic capabilities and its data base management capabilities, some of which will be discussed later in the book.

Templates

Performing spreadsheet calculations on a computer spreadsheet is easier than doing them on paper, but it still takes work to set up the computer spreadsheet. In order to avoid the reinventing-the-wheel syndrome, you can use preformed spreadsheets known as templates. Business software stores usually have templates that can be used with common spreadsheet programs available for common business applications. The templates come with the labels and formulas built in; you need only enter the specific data for your situation.

Macros

One day, as you are repeatedly typing a set of 1-2-3 keystrokes, you might remember the definition of a computer—a machine that can store its own instructions—and wonder if those instructions can also include a set of keystrokes. It would save you a lot of work if you didn't have to keep repeating the same keys. In Lotus 1-2-3, a set of stored keystrokes is called a *macro*. You need to know two things: how to store the keystrokes and how to execute them when you need them. We will discuss several macros later in the book.

Quitting 1-2-3

When you are done using 1-2-3, enter the /Q command. The computer will check with you to make sure that you really want to leave the program. (The program expects you to have so much fun that it is hard to believe that you want to leave it.) Actually, the point of checking is to give you one last chance to make sure that you have remembered to save your work before you leave. Once you indicate yes that you are done, the computer will return you to the operating system. In any computer system, when the user is about to enter the command that will lose data, such as erasing an entire spreadsheet or leaving the spreadsheet program, there should be a confirmation check to lessen the chance that an erasure will happen accidentally. Here is another example of that same principle. You may have learned that the way to completely reset an IBM PC is to press three keys simultaneously: CONTROL, ALT, AND DELETE. At first you may think that this is needlessly complicated, but you quickly should realize the value in making it difficult to reset the computer. A single key that can reset the computer is likely to be hit accidentally fairly often, causing a lot of grief to users. Requiring three keys to be hit at the same time significantly reduces the chance of catastrophe.

CHAPTER PERSPECTIVE
Computer spreadsheet programs are very valuable tools for business decision making. In particular, they are very helpful when you need to ask "what if" questions, since the results can be automatically recalculated if you change one of the assumptions.

Spreadsheets: Budget Development

CHAPTER 4

INTRODUCTION AND MAIN POINTS

A budget is a plan that helps you achieve your organization's goals. You will need resources to fulfill those goals; your budget is the specific part of the plan that determines how you will obtain and allocate resources. A corny old joke says: "It's tough to make predictions—particularly about the future." Because the future is so uncertain, any budget is only an estimate, and you cannot expect to follow it perfectly. The budget process involves both budget development and budget monitoring; you will need to compare actual results with budgeted results and perhaps make changes in your future plans.

Unless your organization is very small, it should be divided into different budget units. You should develop a plan for each unit that includes estimated revenue and expenses by category. The process of developing a budget is very complicated, requiring a lot of judgment and teamwork, neither of which can be provided by computers. It also requires tedious calculations—the perfect job for the computer.

After studying the material in this chapter:

— You will know how to set up a budget development spreadsheet.

— You will be familiar with features of Lotus 1-2-3, including protection for cells and the printing of the worksheet formulas.

SMALL BUSINESS BUDGETING: EASY VAN COMMUTING SERVICE

A budget system is an information system. You need to determine what information you want the system to provide, to whom, and when. Once you have determined your information needs you need to figure out how the computer can provide for them.

A budget is typically developed to cover one year. The budget year, called the *fiscal year,* does not have to coincide with a calendar year. The federal government uses a fiscal year that runs from October 1 to September 30; department stores typically use fiscal years that run from February 1 to January 31. You need to determine which is the most convenient fiscal year for your organization. Ideally, the fiscal year break will occur during a slow period for your organization. For example, a ski resort or a school should not break its fiscal year on December 31, since that is right in the middle of the busy season. At the end of the year, you will prepare summary reports comparing your actual performance to the budget. However, by then it is too late to affect the results, so it is necessary to prepare budget performance reports more often. Typically, budget performance reports are printed every month; it may be necessary to do them more often in your organization. In Chapter 8 we will consider how to generate the performance reports.

What follows is an example of a budget plan for a very small business. Suppose that there is a demand from commuters for transportation between Smalltown and BigCity, 36 miles away. Parking is very expensive in the city and public transportation is nonexistent, so you plan to start a business that will provide rides in vans with door-to-door service. The Easy Van Commuting Service will start with one van. You need to develop a budget to figure out your plans for the next year. Here is the Lotus 1-2-3 spreadsheet reflecting this plan:

	A	B	C	D
1	EASY VAN COMMUTING SERVICE			
2	Budget -- Next Year			
3			Van Purch, Price:	$30,000
4	Max. Passenger Cap.	12	Est, Life (yrs):	8
5	Price per ride:	$6.00	Maintenance	
6	Highway Miles:	36	Miles per tire set	20,000
7	Extra Miles per Pas	1	Cost of tire set	$500.00
8	Fuel Use (MPG):	12	Miles per oil chng	5,000
9	Fuel Cost, per gall	$1.10	Cost of oil chng	$100.00
10	Wage per day	18		
11				

SPREADSHEETS: BUDGET DEVELOPMENT

12	REVENUE	Year	Jan	Feb	Mar	Apr
13	#Days	253	21	19	22	21
14	Capacity	3036	252	228	264	252
15	Occupancy	0.74	0.85	0.85	0.85	0.85
16	Actual	2240	214	194	224	214
17	Total Revenue	$13,440	$1,284	$1,164	$1,344	$1,284
18	COST					
19	Miles	20456.0	1726.0	1562.0	1808.0	1726.0
20	Fuel (gal.)	1704.7	143.8	130.2	150.7	143.8
21	Fuel Cost	$1,875	$158	$143	$166	$158
22	Maint – tires	$511	$43	$39	$45	$43
23	Maint – oil chng	$409	$35	$31	$36	$35
24	Wage	$4,554	$378	$342	$396	$378
25	Depreciation	$3,750				
26	Insurance	$1,400				
27	Office	$400				
28	Other	$400				
29	Total Cost	$13,300				
30						
31	PROFIT	$140				
32						

The first thing to notice about this spreadsheet is that it is too big to fit on the screen. This is very common except in the very simplest situations, such as the one looked at in the last chapter. The computer has the capacity to store a giant spreadsheet. If you use the arrow keys to move the cell pointer off the edge of the screen, you will be able to see more rows or columns in that direction but you will lose some rows or columns at the

	G	H	I	J	K	L	M	N
12	May	Jun	Jly	Aug	Sep	Oct	Nov	Dec
13	22	21	21	23	19	23	21	20
14	264	252	252	276	228	276	252	240
15	0.65	0.60	0.60	0.60	0.60	0.85	0.85	0.70
16	172	151	151	166	137	235	214	168
17	$1,032	$906	$906	$996	$822	$1,410	$1,284	$1,008
18								
19	1756.0	1663.0	1663.0	1822.0	1505.0	1891.0	1726.0	1608.0
20	146.3	138.6	138.6	151.8	125.4	157.6	143.8	134.0
21	$161	$152	$152	$167	$138	$173	$158	$147
22	$44	$42	$42	$46	$38	$47	$43	$40
23	$35	$33	$33	$36	$30	$38	$35	$32
24	$396	$378	$378	$414	$342	$414	$378	$360

other end of the screen. The PAGEUP and PAGEDOWN key allows you to move up or down a whole screen at a time; the HOME key always returns you to cell A1 at the upper left-hand corner of the whole worksheet.

When you print your spreadsheet, you are limited by the size of the paper. That is why the months from May to December in the spreadsheet don't fit on the same page as the rest; they will be printed on the next page. You have several options for joining the two pages so that the adjacent columns are next to each other. One is to tape them together. The other three are to print the spreadsheet sideways, obtain a printer that prints wider-than-normal paper, or use compressed print.

As you examine the spreadsheet's construction, you will think at first glance that the cells seem to contain two types of items: labels and numbers. However, now that you have some spreadsheet experience, you realize that some of the cells that appear to contain numbers really contain formulas. After you have developed a spreadsheet such as this, you will likely need

SPREADSHEETS: BUDGET DEVELOPMENT

to change the basic numerical data to reflect different possibilities; you will not want to change the labels and the formulas nearly as often. One helpful option is the protect option, which allows you to protect the contents of some cells from being changed. This can prevent you accidentally typing over a key formula in your spreadsheet or from an even greater disaster if you don't realize that you have typed over the formula and that the results in distant parts of the spreadsheet are all wrong. Also, if your planning spreadsheet will be used by someone else who will experiment with different numbers, it will be helpful to have the formulas protected.

To start the protection, use this command sequence: /WGPE (Worksheet Global Protect Enable). This command has the effect of protecting all of the cells. Now you need to "unprotect" the cells that will be subject to change. Enter this command sequence: /RU (Range Unprotect). Then the computer will ask you for the range to unprotect; as before, you may enter the range either by typing coordinates (such as B2..B7) or by pressing the period and then using the arrow keys in Point mode. If you have a color monitor, the unprotected cells will show up in a different color than the protected cells.

This is the information that you need to develop the budget:
- the number of passengers that can ride in the van
- the price they will pay per day for one trip to the city and back
- the distance along the highway between the small town and the big city
- the average distance required by each additional passenger to provide door-to-door service. Clearly, door-to-door service is economical only if the passengers live in the same neighborhood.
- the fuel use (in miles per gallon) for the van
- the cost of the fuel (dollars per gallon)
- the wage that will be paid the driver per day (the driver works approximately two hours per day, one in the morning and one in the evening. In practice, the driver will likely be one of the commuters who needs to reach the city for the day.)
- the purchase price of the van
- the estimated useful life of the van
- the number of miles the van can travel before a new set of tires is required, and the cost of that set of tires

■ the number of miles the van can travel before an oil change (and other standard maintenance) is needed, and the cost of such maintenance.
■ insurance expense, office expense, and other expense

Estimated values for all of these quantities have been entered into the spreadsheet; you need to experiment with different values for these quantities to see how your business will be affected if some of these change.

You also need to estimate ridership. The spreadsheet includes calculations for each month of the year. First, enter the number of business days each month (your van does not run on weekends or holidays). Multiplying that total by the capacity of the van (12) gives you the total number of rides per month you can offer if you run at full capacity. Then you need to estimate the percentage of capacity that will actually be used in a given month. These estimates are given in row 15; these are the only numbers in this section of the worksheet that are highlighted. That means these are unprotected—that is, they consist of numbers, not formulas. As with the ice cream example in the previous chapter, these numbers are very difficult to predict accurately. You would expect that the number of people riding your van will depend on the price that you charge; it will also depend on many other factors. One factor that may make a difference is the season; in the summer more people take vacations, so there will be fewer people interested in riding your van. This pattern is reflected in the numbers shown in the table.

All of the other numbers shown are calculated from formulas. We need a way to print out all of the formulas used in the worksheet. You should keep such a printout in your budget development file so you can see how the spreadsheet was constructed. In Lotus 1-2-3, enter the command sequence /PPOOC (Print Printer Options Other Cell-Formulas). This will cause the cell-formulas to be printed, instead of the numerical results. In many cases the formula entered into a cell will be considerably wider than that cell, so you cannot print the spreadsheet in the same form when you want the formulas. Instead, the program prints one cell per line. A part of the formula table (the dots indicate that repetitive formulas have been left out) is shown on pages 77 and 78.

The list of all of the formulas is much longer than the original spreadsheet, but you do not need to read through the whole list. Save it for reference and refer to specific cells when you need

SPREADSHEETS: BUDGET DEVELOPMENT

to remind yourself how they were calculated. Some general points about the formula list:

▬ a w indicates the width of the cell (for example, [W19] indicates the cell has been set to a width of 19 characters)

```
A1: PR [W19] ' EASY VAN COMMUTING SERVICE
A2: PR [W19] ' Budget — Next Year
D3: PR 'Van Purch. Price:
F3: (C0) U [W9] 30000
    ...
A12: PR [W19] '   REVENUE
B12: PR "Year
C12: PR "Jan
    ...
A13: PR [W19] '#Days
B13: PR @SUM(C13..N13)
C13: PR 21
    ...
A14: PR [W19] 'Capacity
B14: PR@SUM(C14..N14)
C14: PR +$MAXP*C13
    ...
A15: PR [W19] 'Occupancy
B15: (F2) PR +B16/B14
C15: (F2) U 0.85
    ...
A16: PR [W19] 'Actual
B16: PR @SUM(C16..N16)
C16: PR @ROUND(C15*C14,0)
    ...
A17: PR [W19] 'Total Revenue
B17: (C0) PR @SUM(C17..N17)
C17: (C0) PR +$PRICE*C16
    ...
A18: PR [W19] ' COST
B19: (F1) PR @SUM(C19..N19)
C19: (F1) PR 2*$HMILES*C13+$MIPERPAS*C16
    ...
```

```
A20: PR [W19] 'Fuel used, gallons
B20: (F1) PR @SUM(C20..N20)
C20: (F1) PR +C19/$MPG
     ...
A21: PR [W19] 'Fuel Cost
B21: (C0) PR @SUM(C21...N21)
C21: (C0) PR +C20*$DPG
     ...
A22: PR [W19] 'Maint - tires
B22: (C0) PR @SUM(C22..N22)
C22: (C0) PR +C19/$MPTIRSET*$CTIRSET
     ...
A23: PR [W19] 'Maint - oil change
B23: (C0) PR @SUM(C23..N23)
C23: (C0) PR +C19/$MPOILCH*$COILCH
     ...
A24: PR [W19] 'Wage
B24: (C0) PR @SUM(C24..N24)
C24: (C0) PR +$WAGE*C13
     ...
A25: PR [W19] 'Depreciation
B25: (C0) PR +$VPURPR/YRSLIFE
     ...
A27: PR [W19] 'Office
B27: (C0) U 400
A28: PR [W19] 'Other
B28: (C0) U 400
A29: PR [W19] 'Total Cost
B29: (C0) PR @SUM(B21..B28)
A31: PR [W19] ' PROFIT
B31: (C0) PR +B17-B29
```

SPREADSHEETS: BUDGET DEVELOPMENT

■ a U indicates that this cell is unprotected; PR indicates that it is protected

■ (CO) indicates currency format with zero decimal places

We also need to print out a list of all of the names we have used. Enter this command: /RNT (Range Name Table). The program will ask you for a range where you want this name table to be displayed. Choose an empty area of the worksheet for this; for this example, the range below the main table (starting in row 33) will work fine. Then, after this name table is created, print it out. Here is the result:

```
33    NAME TABLE
34    DPG                   B9
35    HMILES                B6
36    MAXP                  B4
37    MIPERPAS              B7
38    MPG                   B8
39    PRICE                 B5
40    WAGE                  B10
41    VPURPR                F3
42    YRSLIFE               F4
43    MPTIRSET              F6
44    CTIRSET               F7
45    MPOILCH               F8
46    COILCH                F9
```

Both the formulas list and the name table should be kept in your budget development folder.

To make it easier to see how the formulas work, on page 80 appears a portion of the spreadsheet with the formulas inserted in place of the numbers.

According to this budget plan, you will make a small profit. You clearly cannot expect to make a very big profit running only one van, so you will see about expanding later on. Experiment with changing some of the numbers so you can see how much the budget depends on each assumption. Also, consider the relevant interest rate to determine whether this business really is a good investment.

This example illustrates some principles that you should follow in developing a budget:

■ You should estimate the activity level of your organization. For a business, the activity measure will relate to sales; for a

	B	C
	Year	Jan
12	REVENUE	
13	#Days	@SUM(C13..N13)	21
14	Capacity	@SUM(C14..N14)	+$MAXP*C13
15	Occupancy	+B16/B14	0.85
16	Actual	@SUM(C16..N16)	@ROUND(C15*C14,0)
17	Total Revenue	@SUM(C17..N17)	+$PRICE*C16
18	COST		
19	Miles	@SUM(C19..N19)	2*$HMILES*C13+$MIPERPAS*C16
20	Fuel used, gallons	@SUM(C20..N20)	+C19/$MPG
21	Fuel Cost	@SUM(C21..N21)	+C20*$DPG
22	Maint - tires	@SUM(C22..N22)	+C19/$MPTIRSET*$CTIRSET
23	Maint - oil chng	@SUM(C23..N23)	+C19/$MPOILCH*$COILCH
24	Wage	@SUM(C24..N34)	+$WAGE*C13
25	Depreciation	+$VPURPR/$YRSLIFE	
26	Insurance	$1,400	
27	Office	$400	
28	Other	$400	
29	Total Cost	@SUM(B21..B28)	
30			
31	PROFIT	+B17-B29	

nonprofit organization you will need some type of activity measure that is appropriate in your case.

▬ Cost estimates need to be developed taking estimated activity level into consideration. Some costs are fixed and will be the same no matter what your business does (for example, the lease on a facility is usually a fixed cost). Other costs vary with the activity level. Look at historical data to try to estimate this relation; see books on statistics and managerial accounting for suggestions about how to do this.

EXAMPLE: DEPARTMENTAL PERSONNEL BUDGET

For a very small company, one person can create and monitor the entire budget. However, a growing company quickly becomes too big for one person to watch all of the financial affairs, and the budget development and monitoring process becomes more complicated. Suppose that after several years the Easy Van Commuting Service has grown into a large shipping company with numerous branch offices. A large organization can take one of two approaches to budget development: the *top down* approach and the *bottom up* approach. In the bottom up approach, each division figures out what resources it will need, then sends its needs to the central office where each division's figures are added to form the budget. In the top down approach, the central office determines what resources will be available to the organization and then decides how to divide those resources among the divisions. Neither approach works very well on its own. If each division is able to set its own budget, the total planned spending will probably exceed available resources. On the other hand, if the central office determines everything, it is likely that the needs of each individual division will not be fully understood. The best system is a compromise in which each division develops its budget in cooperation with the central office.

We look now at an example of how the South Hill office of the Easy Express Shipping Service can develop its personnel budget. To start with, the budget manager needs information on the pay rates for the various classes of employees. Suppose that this information is contained in the Lotus 1-2-3 spreadsheet as follows:

	A	B	C	D	E
1	Hourly Wage Table				
2	Class|Exp:	1	2	3	4
3	ACCT	$14.50	$15.37	$16.29	$17.27
4	DISP	$14.80	$15.69	$16.63	$17.63
5	DRV	$12.00	$13.80	$15.87	$18.25
6	MGR	$14.90	$15.79	$16.74	$17.75
7	MRKT	$12.20	$12.93	$13.71	$14.53

Each worker at the office can be classified into one of five categories designated by the abbreviations shown and further classified into one of four experience categories based on length of time with the company. Then the hourly wage rate for each worker can be determined from the two-dimensional grid shown above. This information comes to the South Hill office from the central office. (The central office cannot dictatorially decide the pay rates; it needs to negotiate with the workers so that it pays them enough that they are willing to work for the company.)

Next, you need information on the workers at the South Hill office. You can enter that information into a table as follows:

	G	H	I	J	K
18	Name	SS NUM	Class	Exp	Hrs
19	Tim	123-45-6781	DRV	1	2,083
20	Sue	123-45-6782	DRV	4	2,083
21	Joe	123-45-6783	DRV	2	1,040
22	Joan	123-45-6784	DISP	1	2,080
23	Bill	123-45-6785	ACCT	3	1,040
24	Mary	123-45-6786	MRKT	2	2,080
25	VACANT		DRV	1	2,083
26	VACANT		MGR	1	2,080

SPREADSHEETS: BUDGET DEVELOPMENT

The number of authorized positions must be determined by negotiation between South Hill and central; typically, each division wants more workers to help with the work, and the central office needs to make sure that there are enough workers in each office without the cost exceeding the available resources. Note that South Hill currently has two positions that are vacant.

For each employee, you need the job classification and the number of hours that person is expected to work. For some of the positions, the number of hours will be entered as a number; for the full-time driver positions, however, the number of hours depends on the total business done by the company.

Now you need to determine the total pay for each worker. Given the job class and experience in the personnel table, look up the hourly wage rate in the wage table. The 1-2-3 function that does this is called @VLOOKUP. Here is how it works in general:

@VLOOKUP *(item to find, range to look in, number of columns to move right)*

The @VLOOKUP function takes three arguments. First, give the item that you wish to find in the table. Second, give the range containing the table, with the first column of that table the column where you will look. Once the computer has found a match, it will move to the right the number of columns specified by the third argument. The result of the function will be whatever it finds in that particular cell.

Now we can find Tim's pay. Move to cell L19 and enter this formula:

@VLOOKUP(I19,$A$3..$E$7,J19)*K19

Cell I19 contains Tim's job classification (DRV), the item you must find in the wage table. $A$3..$E$7 is the range specifying the wage table; note that the first column gives the job classification, as it must for the @VLOOKUP function to work. Cell J19 gives Tim's experience class (1), which tells you the number of columns to move to the right. The computer will look down column A until it finds DRV, which it will find in cell A5. Then it reads across one column, and the result of the @VLOOKUP function will be the contents of cell B5, or $12, Tim's hourly wage rate.

BARRON'S BUSINESS LIBRARY

	A	B	C	D	E
1	Hourly Wage Table				
2	Class|Exp:	1	2	3	4
3	ACCT ↓	$14.50	$15.37	$16.29	$17.27
4	DISP ↓	$14.80	$15.69	$16.63	$17.63
5	DRV →	$12.00	$13.80	$15.87	$18.25
6	MGR	$14.90	$15.79	$16.74	$17.75
7	MRKT	$12.20	$12.93	$13.71	$14.53

Multiply by the number of hours Tim will work (given in cell K19) to calculate the amount that Tim will be paid: $24,996.

The v in @VLOOKUP stands for "vertical." There is another function (@HLOOKUP) that works the same except that it searches along the first row of the range; the third argument gives the number of rows to move down. Both these functions work differently with numerical data. In that case, the range to be searched needs to be in order and does not need to contain an exact match; the computer will select the largest item that is less than the item to be found.

Now copy the formula down. Note that it was important to include the dollar signs in the range $A$3..$E$7, because you don't want this range to change when you copy. The other items in the formula—the job class, experience, and hours—will all change when you move to a new employee; therefore, you did not include dollar signs there. For example, when you copy the formula down to cell L20 you will see:

@VLOOKUP(I20,$A$3..$E$7,J20)*K20

The final version of the personnel budget table is shown on page 85.

The budget estimates that 250,000 miles is the total capacity of this office without anyone working overtime. The figure for hours in column K is based on this figure. However, the budget plan estimates that the actual total will be 260,000 miles. The budget estimates that these 10,000 extra miles will require a total of 333 hours of overtime, which will cost an average wage of $22. The total wage budget is found by the formula @SUM(L19..L27).

SPREADSHEETS: BUDGET DEVELOPMENT

	G	H	I	J	K	L
15	Personnel Budget—Next Year		Capacity Miles			Total Mile
16	South Hill Office		250,000			260,000
17						
18	Name	SS NUM	Class	Exp	Hrs	Pay
19	Tim	123-45-6781	DRV	1	2,083	$24,996
20	Sue	123-45-6782	DRV	4	2,083	$38,015
21	Joe	123-45-6783	DRV	2	1,040	$14,352
22	Joan	123-45-6784	DISP	1	2,080	$30,784
23	Bill	123-45-6785	ACCT	3	1,040	$16,944
24	Mary	123-45-6786	MRKT	2	2,080	$26,899
25	VACANT		DRV	1	2,083	$24,996
26	VACANT		MGR	1	2,080	$30,992
27	Overtime				333	$7,333
28						
29				Total Wages		$215,311
30				Soc Sec		$17,268
31	Ovrt.Wge:	$22.00		Benefits		$43,062
32	SS Rate	8.02%				
33	Ben Rate	20.00%		Total Personnel		$275,641

Then you also need to add an extra 8.02 percent for social security and another 20 percent for other benefits, giving the total personnel budget. Note that cells H32 and H33 are formatted using the percent format.

At the same time the South Hill office is developing its budget, all the other offices are working on their budgets. The wage table will be the same for all of them. However, next year it will change. If the changes are made at the central office, it should be possible for the changes to be made automatically for all of the offices. This suggests that there should be a way to link the different spreadsheets so that changes in one are automatically reflected in others. After the personnel budget has been determined for the South Hill office, this figure should be linked to another spreadsheet that puts together the personnel budget for the whole organization. Then that spreadsheet must be linked to the spreadsheet that develops the entire budget. You also need a way to link computers at the different locations. These issues will be discussed later.

You may have realized that you need to keep track of much more information about each individual than is shown in the personnel budget spreadsheet. However, there is no need to keep all of that information in the budget spreadsheet. You need a data base that stores information about all of the personnel in the organization, along with a way for other systems in the company to obtain access to this information as needed. There are many times like this when you will need to keep track of information that will be used for more than one purpose. When a data item changes it is very helpful if this change could be entered into the data base once and then be reflected automatically in all of the other systems that use this data. The issue of data base management is covered in Chapter 9.

CHAPTER PERSPECTIVE
Spreadsheet programs are the perfect tool for budget development. You need to consider many different variables, including variations in the activity level of the business and the cost of the inputs. The spreadsheet can be designed so that changes in any one of these variables are automatically reflected in the budget amounts.

REFERENCES
Matthews, Lawrence, *Practical Operating Budgeting* (New York: McGraw Hill), 1977.

Macros

CHAPTER 5

INTRODUCTION AND MAIN POINTS

As we mentioned earlier, there is a trade-off between a general-purpose program and a special-purpose program. Lotus 1-2-3 is a general-purpose program, which makes it applicable for many different types of businesses, but which also means that a lot of work may be required to set up a Lotus 1-2-3 spreadsheet to solve your particular problem. Once you have done this, you won't have to keep redoing it, and then you will have some of the advantages of a special-purpose program—that is, you will have a Lotus 1-2-3 spreadsheet tailored for your particular business.

The Lotus 1-2-3 macro structure provides a way to save a set of commands that you can then call whenever you need them. At the simplest level, a macro is simply a set of keystrokes that have been saved so they can be called by a single key; at more complicated levels, the macro command structure is a type of computer programming language.

After studying this chapter:

— You will be able to plan a sequence of keystrokes that you wish to execute as a macro.

— You will understand the power and flexibility of interactive macros.

MACROS AS KEYSTROKE SEQUENCES

There are four steps to running a macro. First, *plan the macro*. Think of a command sequence that you use often; for example, suppose you frequently want to format a cell into currency format. Think of the key sequence you must type:

/ (to call the command menu)

R (Range)

F (Format)

C (Currency)

2 (number of decimal places)

RETURN key (to signal you are done entering the number of decimal places)

(Then the computer will ask you for the range to format. You can type the range; however, if you wish to format the current cell, you can simply hit the RETURN key because the program is guessing that the current cell is the one you want to format):

RETURN key

Therefore, the keystroke sequence you want is:

/RFC2 (RETURN) (RETURN)

Second, *type the keystrokes in the macro* by finding an empty cell in the worksheet and typing in the keys. There are a couple things to be careful of. First, if you hit the / key, the command menu will immediately appear; this is not what you want at the moment. Therefore, you need to type the single quote key, ', first; the program will treat this cell as a label so it will not call up the command menu until you are ready for it. You can't simply type the RETURN key, since the computer will think you are done entering data into this cell as soon as you do. Therefore, in all macro keystrokes, the tilde symbol, ~, is used to represent the RETURN key. Therefore, type these characters into the open cell:

'/RFC2 ~~

Third, *give the macro a name*. Use the /RNC (Range Name Create) command to name the cell containing the macro. Macro names must start with a backslash, \, and then consist of a letter of the alphabet. (Note that the backslash, \, is not the same as the forward slash, /). In this case call the macro \ c, since the c will remind you that the macro will format a cell in the currency format.

Fourth, you can now *execute the macro anytime that you want*. In order to execute it, press the ALT key and the letter in the macro name. The ALT key is similar to the SHIFT key and the CONTROL key; it has no action when pressed by itself, but, when pressed simultaneously with another key, it changes the meaning of that other key. In this case, if you press the ALT key and the c key simultaneously, the macro will be executed, causing the current cell to be formatted to currency format.

There are several keys in addition to the RETURN key that cannot be typed directly into a macro:

Key	Symbol used in Macros
RETURN	~
DOWN ARROW	{DOWN}
UP ARROW	{UP}
LEFT ARROW	{LEFT}
RIGHT ARROW	{RIGHT}
HOME	{HOME}
PAGE UP	{PGUP}
PAGE DOWN	{PGDOWN}
GOTO (F5)	{GOTO}
ESCAPE	{ESC}

See the reference manual for the complete list.

Here's an example of a more complicated macro. Suppose that you need to format the cell in currency format and then change the width to 12 characters. Here is the sequence of keys to enter into the macro cell:

'/RFC2~/WCS12~

INTERACTIVE MACROS

Suppose there were some columns that you wished to set to width 10. You could write another macro to accomplish that; however, if you had several different column widths to set, you would end up with an awkward number of macros. What you need is a way to write one macro that will work for any column width you wish to set. Of course, such a macro must then ask which column width you wish to use. This type of macro is called an *interactive macro,* because it can interact with the user while it is being executed.

The expression {?} is put into a macro when you want the program to stop and wait for the person at the keyboard to type something. Here is a new version for the currency format macro:

'/RFC2~/WCS{?}~

The computer will execute all of the keystrokes before the {?} just as before. When it reaches the {?}, it will stop. The screen will show the prompt asking for the column width, since this was the point at which the macro was interrupted.

At this point you need to type the value you want for the column width. As soon as you press the RETURN key, the computer will resume executing the macro at the point after the {?}. In this case, the macro has only one more character, ~, and then it is finished.

The use of interactive macros greatly increases the flexibility of Lotus 1-2-3. In Chapter 7, you will see how an interactive macro can be used to automate the data entry process.

Here is another example. Suppose you need to format a group of cells to currency format, but you want to be able to specify the cells at the time the macro is executed, not when it is written. Use this macro:

/RFC2~{?}~

Now the computer will hit the {?} at the point at which it is asking for the range to format. At this point you may either type the corners of the range (such as A2..B20) or use the 1-2-3 point feature (that is, use the arrow keys to highlight the correct range). In either case, press the RETURN key after entering the range.

There will be times when you wish to enter a value in a cell and give it a descriptive name and then also label the cell so you know what it means. However, you may have noticed one annoying feature in the last chapter: We needed to type each name twice, once as the label in the adjacent cell and once again when you used the Range Name Create command to create the name. It would be nice to be able to have the computer assign the name automatically from the adjacent cell. Again, a macro comes to the rescue:

{?}~{RIGHT}{?}{LEFT}/RNLR~

To operate this macro, move the cell pointer to the cell that will contain the name. When you execute the macro, this is what will happen:

{?} ~	the computer will wait for you to type in the name the name will be stored in the cell you started at
{RIGHT}	move the pointer to the adjacent cell to the right
{?}~	the computer will wait for you to type in the value
{LEFT}	move the cell pointer to the cell containing the name
/RNLR~	call the Range Name Label command. This command will automatically take the label in a given cell and give that name to an adjacent cell. You have four choices for the adjacent cell: the R indicates to assign the name to the cell to the right. You could also use /RNLD~ to assign the name to the cell directly below it.

MACROS

In Chapter 7, we will see examples of some longer macros. When the macro becomes too long to fit in a single cell, move down to the cell directly below the first cell and continue the macro there. When the computer is executing a macro it will keep working down until it comes to an empty cell.

Long macros can be very powerful tools, but they do present a potential problem: you may make a mistake while typing the macro so that the result does not work out as you had intended. The computer will do exactly what you tell it to do, not what you meant it to do. In computer programming this type of error is called a *bug*, and the process of fixing it is known as *debugging*. For purposes of debugging, it would help to slow the macro down so that you can see it operate one keystroke at a time. To accomplish this, enter Step mode. Step mode is invoked by pressing the ALT key simultaneously with the F2 key. The word STEP will appear at the bottom of the screen as a reminder to you. When in Step mode, the computer will execute one key in the macro, then wait for you to press a key before going on to execute the next macro keystroke. It doesn't matter which key you press; the space bar is a convenient choice. In this way you will be able to see the macro execute in slow motion, and you should be able to see where it starts to go wrong and figure out how to fix it. When you are ready for the macro to execute at normal speed again, press ALT-F2 again and the STEP indicator will disappear from the bottom of the screen.

At other times, you may want the macro to operate faster than normal. There are two commands you can use to accomplish this: {WINDOWSOFF} and {PANELOFF}. {WINDOWSOFF} suspends the updating of the main worksheet screen, saving the computer time; however, you will not be able to see what is happening while the macro is being executed. {PANELOFF} suspends the display of the control panel at the top of the screen; this is helpful if your macro involves a lot of menu commands, because it means that the screen will not have to constantly update the menus at the top of the screen. Don't use these commands until you have tested the macro and know that it is operating correctly. The commands {WINDOWSON} and {PANELON}, respectively, undo the effects of the previous commands.

LOTUS 1-2-3; STRONG POINTS AND WEAK POINTS

Now that you have had some experience with Lotus 1-2-3, you can begin to appreciate some of the good features of this program. Unfortunately, there are also a few weak points that we will look at later. Here are some general principles for effective computer/user interaction that are illustrated by Lotus 1-2-3.

■ Menu structure. There are several appealing features of the Lotus 1-2-3 menu structure. First, the fact that it is arranged in a hierarchy makes it easier for people to use. If the menu displayed a list of every single command all at once, it would fill up much of the screen and it would be awkward to work with; by arranging the commands in a hierarchy, the menu screen at any particular level never displays more than twelve choices. This hierarchical arrangement means that when you enter a command you see only the choices relevant to that command and not those relevant to others. For example, when you enter the Range Name command, you will see only choices relevant to the Name command on the screen.

Menus are very helpful for computer users because they mean that people needn't memorize all the commands. By looking at the menu you can be instantly reminded of your choices. However, menus do have one disadvantage: if there is a command that you use frequently, you will memorize the keystroke sequence and find it unnecessary and cumbersome to look at the menus. Fortunately, 1-2-3 provides you with a choice. The menus are available for those who want them, but experienced users can type the keystrokes directly (for example, /RNC). In general, it is good for a program to provide this type of choice so that new users aren't required to memorize the commands and experienced users are not slowed down by the help provided for new users. In a way, the menus are like training wheels—use them as you need them, and take them off when you no longer do.

■ Computer guesses. As we have seen, the 1-2-3 program tries as much as possible to guess what you want to do. This makes it easier to use the program, because you simply have to type the RETURN key when it has guessed correctly. If it has not guessed correctly, then you type in the specific result you want. In some cases, the guessing process works well; for example, the Name command guesses that you want to name the current cell, and the Print Range command guesses that you want to print the same range as was printed last time. At other times the program cannot guess what you want but displays choices on the screen. For example, when you use the File Retrieve command, the program displays a list of the worksheet files available on your disk; you may use the arrow keys to highlight the choice you want.

- Choice of entry mode. Allowing users to choose between typing ranges explicitly (such as A2..E5) and using the arrow keys recognizes individual preferences in how to interact with the machine.

- Protection from losing data. Whenever you call for a command that will lose a significant amount of data, such as the worksheet erase command or the quit command, the program asks you for confirmation before it proceeds. This is a good principle that all programs should follow: Don't make it easy to accidentally lose data.

- On-screen help. Pressing the F1 key presents information about the program on the screen. This help is context-sensitive, meaning that the computer tries to present help on a topic that you are likely to need at the moment, based upon what you seem to be trying to do. There is also a menu of choices for the help screens, so you should be able to find the topic you want if the computer has not guessed correctly. Press ESCAPE to return to where you were before you called for help. As a general rule, programs are easier to use if help is available on the screen (although a program still needs an old-fashioned paper manual, too).

- Built-in procedures for many common tasks. You should not have to write your own instructions for a task that is commonly needed. The @ functions provide a wide variety of commonly needed capabilities; consult the reference manual. One common task is sorting a group of data items; 1-2-3 comes with a built-in sorting procedure (as part of the Data command; see Chapter 9).

- Graphics capabilities. The 1-2-3 graphics commands provide easy ways to create many different types of graphs to illustrate your data.

- Transportability of the data. A program should be able to read data from other formats and present data in a form that can be used by other programs as well. The File Import command can be used to read a standard text (ASCII) file into a worksheet, and the Print File command writes a worksheet as a disk file that can be used by other programs, such as a word processing program.

Lotus 1-2-3 also has some pitfalls you should try to avoid. In addition, there are some difficulties inherent in the spreadsheet concept.

■ **Confusing or misleading appearance.** The appearance of the worksheet does not always clearly indicate what is going on. Even worse, the worksheet can give a misleading impression of what is happening. For example, consider these calls:

	A
1	100
2	36
3	56
4	45
5	═══
6	192

It appears that cell A6 contains the sum of cells A1 to A4. If you add the numbers up, though, you find that 192 = 100 + 36 + 56. If you look at the formula in cell A6, it turns out to be @SUM(A1..A3), not @SUM(A1..A4). This type of mistake is one of the most treacherous problems with spreadsheets. You have to be particularly careful if you insert a new row at the end of the range to be summed. Imagine how tricky this problem can be in a large worksheet. There is a story that a major building contractor once severely underbid for a job because of precisely this problem: their spreadsheet left out a cell when it calculated the sum of all of the costs, and the company was stuck with working on a contract at a price too low for it to make a profit.

There are times when you would like to use a formula to calculate a value in a cell and then store the value, not the formula. This can be done with the Range Value command, but the problem of potentially misleading appearances remains. Unless you move the cell pointer to a cell, you cannot tell whether it contains a value or a formula.

■ **The giant 2-D spreadsheet.** People long ago realized that organizing work on one giant sheet (as in a scroll) was less efficient than organizing it in a book consisting of many small pages. Large spreadsheets would be easier to deal with if they consisted of separate pages instead of one giant page. In fact, that is the new trend in spreadsheets; Release 3 of Lotus 1-2-3 provides for three-dimensional spreadsheets (that is, separate pages). The advantages of this design will be discussed in Chapter 12.

It is awkward to move around a giant two-dimensional spreadsheet. You can make this problem easier by naming cells at different locations and then using the GOTO key (F5) to reach those locations. The biggest danger occurs with the insert and delete operations; these effectively become unusable for large spreadsheets because deleting a row in one location may affect many other locations in the spreadsheet that are also located along that row. Again, the 3D design will take care of this problem.

▬ Confusing proliferation of versions. Recent versions of Lotus 1-2-3 include Release 2.2, 3.0, 3.1, 1-2-3/G for OS/2 Presentation Manager, and a Macintosh version. Check carefully with your dealer to make sure that the version you obtain has the features you need.

▬ Awkward printing requirements. The use of the separate printgraph program requires the user to leave 1-2-3.

▬ Cumbersome requirements for naming. In one respect, spreadsheets represent a step backward in the process of giving instructions to computers. One lesson that computer programmers have learned is that computer instructions should be understandable by people as well as by the computer. In particular, this means that variables should be given names that provide some indication of their meaning. For example, "p" or "price" are much better names for price than is a generic cell reference such as "A2." We have seen how the 1-2-3 naming feature allows you to give meaningful names to cells, but this involves an extra step that people may be tempted to skip. As a result, you may see formulas such as this:

$$((1+\$K\$14)^{\wedge}\$k\$13+1)/(1+\$K\$14)^{\wedge}A3*C5$$

The computer has no trouble figuring out what this means, but it is very difficult for a person.

▬ Difficulty in reading macros. The macro feature provides a powerful, flexible programming capability for users of 1-2-3, but complicated macros are difficult for people to understand. This is also a step backward in view of what has been learned about computer programming in recent years.

CHAPTER PERSPECTIVE

It is not possible for the makers of a general purpose program such as Lotus 1-2-3 to provide one-key commands for all of the tasks you need for your particular business, but neither is it necessary for you to keep retyping the same keystroke sequence for a task that you need to execute often. The solution is to set up a macro, which allows you to add to 1-2-3 new commands that are customized for your needs.

Accounting

CHAPTER 6

INTRODUCTION AND MAIN POINTS

You can trust the computer to handle the calculations required by an accounting system. However, you still should learn the principles of accounting so that you understand what is happening to your business. As a general rule, you should understand what your computer is doing. It may be too boring to do yourself, but you should at least have an idea what the machine is doing; otherwise, you run the risk that you will be presented with results that look as if they must be right because they came from a computer without having any idea how they were developed.

After studying the material in this chapter:

— You will review (or learn) the basic concepts of accounting: balance sheets and income statements.

— You will know some ways in which computers can gather the data needed by an accounting system.

BRIEF INTRODUCTION TO ACCOUNTING

There are very precise rules for double-entry bookkeeping that determine how a transaction is to be recorded. These rules provide that each transaction must be entered in two places, since each transaction involves two actions—for example, giving up money to obtain goods. In a manual bookkeeping system, one common error is a failure to enter a transaction properly in both places, causing the accounts to be out of balance when their totals are calculated. Fortunately, this type of error can be avoided with a computer accounting system, since you only need to enter the transaction once and the computer automatically makes sure that the double entry recording takes place. Of course, you still can go wrong if you enter the wrong amount for the transaction or if you enter the wrong account numbers.

The fundamental accounting equation is as follows:

$$\text{assets} = \text{liabilities} + \text{equity}$$

ACCOUNTING

Owners' equity is defined as assets − liabilities. Both assets and liabilities are entered on a balance sheet, a statement that lists your total for each type of asset and liability for a particular date.

For example, if you used to run a baby-sitting business in which your only asset consisted of $20 cash in a shoe box and you didn't owe anything to anybody else, then your total equity was equal to $20.

Balance Sheet—Baby-sitting Business
January 12

Assets	Liabilities and Equity
Cash $20	Equity $20

If the next day you borrowed $30 from your parents and put it in the shoebox, your assets became $50 but your equity was still only $20 because the $30 showed up as a liability.

Balance Sheet—Baby-sitting Business
January 13

Assets	Liabilities and Equity
Cash $50	owed to parents $30
	Equity $20

If your baby-sitting business earned $12 the next night, your cash increased $12, as did your equity. Notice how each transaction affects two places on the balance sheet.

Balance Sheet—Baby-sitting Business
January 14

Assets	Liabilities and Equity
Cash $62	owed to parents $30
	Equity $32

If you paid $5 the next day for some signs to advertise the business, then cash and equity both decreased by $5.

However, you would not have a very good idea of what was going on if you simply recalculated your balance sheet every day. You need to keep track of the different categories of income and expenses. Therefore, you report two types of statements: a balance sheet giving your condition at the end of the period and an income statement (also called a profit-and-loss statement) that summarizes your income and expenditure activity during the period. This means that for your day-to-day accounting, instead of immediately adding each revenue item to the equity account, you instead add it to a temporary account labeled revenue, and, instead of immediately subtracting each expenditure item from your equity, you instead add it to a temporary account labeled expenditure. The temporary version of the fundamental equation is:

$$\text{assets} = \text{liabilities} + \text{equity} + \text{revenue} - \text{expenditure}$$

which is normally written in this form:

$$\text{assets} + \text{expenditure} = \text{liabilities} + \text{equity} + \text{revenue}$$

In a manual accounting system you keep track of each transaction in a book called a journal. For complicated businesses you need more than one journal. Here is the journal for the baby-sitting business:

Date Description	Amount	To: (Debit)	From (Credit)
1/13 borrowed from parents	$30	assets: cash	liability: borrowing
1/14 earned from Smith family	$12	assets: cash	revenue: babysitting
1/15 advertising signs	$5	expense:advrt.	assets:cash

Note that each transaction affects two different accounts. When you earn income, then the money comes from an income account and goes to an asset account (cash); when you spend money, the money comes from an asset account (cash) and goes to an expenditure account. In technical accounting terms, the account the money comes from is said to be the account to *credit;* the account the money goes to is said to be the account to *debit.*

By adding up all of the transactions that affect either revenue or expense, you can calculate an income statement:

Income Statement—Baby-sitting Business
Week of January 13 to 19

Revenue
  babysitting   12
Expense
  advertising signs   5
Profit   7

We can also calculate the new balance sheet:

Balance Sheet—Baby-sitting Business
January 19

Assets	Liabilities and Equity	
Cash $57	Owed to parents	$30
	Equity	$27

There are two ways to calculate the value of the equity on Jan 19. You could use the values of the assets and liabilities for that date:

equity = assets − liabilities
  27   =   57   −   30

Alternatively, you could look at the total income and expenditures during the period:

equity at end = equity at beginning + revenue − expenditure
    27   =   20   +   12   −   5

As you became older you probably became involved in a more complicated type of business in which you had more than one type of asset, more than one type of liability, more than one type of expenditure, and more than one type of revenue. You need to keep track of each type of account separately, and each should have its own account number. Page 103 shows the sample Chart of Accounts for the Easy Van Commuting Service.

Here is a summary of some different types of transactions and how they are accounted for:

- use cash for a business expense

add *to* appropriate expense account, subtract *from* cash account

[*debit* expense, *credit* cash]

- collect cash from the sale of a service

add *to* cash account; list amount coming *from* appropriate revenue account

[*debit* cash, *credit* revenue]

- transfer from one asset to another (for example, collecting cash while selling an item out of inventory, paying cash for an item that you store in inventory, paying cash for a capital asset, depositing currency in a bank deposit, withdrawing currency from a bank deposit, collecting cash from someone who owes you money, that is, who was listed under assets as accounts payable)

add *to* asset that increases, subtract *from* asset that decreases

[*debit* asset that increases, *credit* asset that decreases]

- borrow money *to* cash account, *from* liability account

[*debit* cash, *credit* liability]

You should make sure that you understand the principles for each of these types of transactions. The bracketed expression in each case gives the use of the technical accounting terms "debit" and "credit"; see an accounting book for more information on those terms.

DATA ENTRY

In a manual accounting system the bookkeeper collects all the journals and goes through the process of "posting" the entries to the correct accounts. This is precisely the type of operation with which the computer can help. First, however, you need to figure out how the data will get into the computer. There are several possibilities.

First, a person may read the paper copies of the original journals and type the data into the computer. This is probably the best way if the number of transactions per day is relatively small. During the 1950s and 1960s, many clerks made their living keypunching transactions data onto punched cards. However, for businesses with a large number of transactions, this is a very boring job; it is preferable for the information on the transactions to be converted into machine-readable form at an earlier stage of the process.

Some other options for posting the data exist. One possibility is a computer check-writing system. To use this, you need the appropriate software, which may come with a computerized accounting package. Then you need to obtain checks for your organization on continuous sheets that can be fed through a printer. If you write a lot of checks, you should have one printer dedicated to this purpose so you do not need to keep loading and unloading the check paper in the printer. You need an accounts payable clerk with a computer connected to the check-writing printer and an authorization system so that the clerk knows when to write checks. The authorization might come from an electronic mail system, saving the clerk the need to retype the check information, or it might come on paper, in which case the clerk needs to type the information into the computer to have the check printed. At the same time the check is printed, the information can be entered automatically into an appropriate journal in the computer accounting system. If your business has more than one computer, you need a network system to connect the accounts payable computer to the computer that performs the accounting. By contrast, if you write the checks by hand, you need to duplicate your work when you enter that same data into the accounting system.

A second option is an electronic funds transfer system, which eliminates the need to use paper checks at all. An example is the direct deposit of paychecks and social security checks, which is becoming more common. The business prepares the payroll data as before but does not send the data to the check printer. Instead, it ships the data (typically, a reel of magnetic tape) directly to the bank. The bank arranges for the proper accounts to be credited and debited, just as it would with a paper check-clearing process. The difference is that work is saved since all of the data are originally in machine-readable form. The company keeps a copy of the payroll data for use by its accounting system.

Another option is a cash register to total cash transactions. At a grocery store, the number of individual items sold during a day is enormous, and would take untold hours of tedium for the bookkeeper to look at the record of every individual transaction. Fortunately, a cash register is designed to calculate totals automatically. The cashier must enter the data once (at the time of the sale), but it need not be entered again. After entering the amount, the cashier types a key indicating the general category for that item (such as groceries, produce, or medicine), and the cash register is able to calculate the total sales for each category. The cash register also prints a paper tape showing the detail of each transaction.

Still another option is a bar code system that keeps track of the items as they are sold. The traditional cash register just described has the disadvantages of requiring considerable concentration for the clerk to enter each price correctly fast enough to keep the customers satisfied and of being unable to keep track of the sales of each individual item; this could only be done if the clerk typed in a code number for each item, which is clearly out of the question at a busy store. In addition, the prices must be placed on little stickers on each item; changing the prices is a big job.

A bar code system solves all of these difficulties. It does have one disadvantage—a high initial cost. However, once the system is set up—and most grocery stores switched to a bar code system during the 1980s—the advantages become clear. Of course, the system is feasible only if the producer of each product puts the code on the package at the time of production and if there is national agreement on the coding system. The coding system in use in the United States is called the Universal Product Code. You can see an example of the UPC by looking at the back of this book. The pattern of dark bars on a white background is read by a scanner built into the cashier's table or by a wand that the cashier waves over the code. The code number is then sent to the cash register, which looks in its memory to find the price of the item. It adds this amount to the customer's bill, prints a receipt showing the specific item, and then stores the record of the item purchased so it can be sent to the inventory system. (Since no one can grow lettuce that comes with bar codes, the clerk still needs to type in codes for greens, fruits, and other produce.)

CHART OF ACCOUNTS

Before you begin using an accounting system, you need to establish a chart of accounts. We will use as an example the chart of accounts for the Easy Van commuting service. Each account is given a four-digit account number. The accounts are divided into five major (first-level) categories: assets (with numbers between 1000 and 1999), liabilities (2000–2999), equity (3000–3999), revenue (4000–4999), and expense (5000–5999). The accounts are then arranged in a hierarchy:

Acct.#	Title	Level
1000	ASSETS	1
1100	Cash	2
1110	Currency*	3
1120	Bank Checking*	3
1200	Time Deposit*	2
1300	Securities*	2
1400	Accounts Receivable*	2
1500	Capital Assets	2
1510	Van	3
1511	Original Value*	4
1512	Accum. Deprec.*	4
2000	LIABILITIES	1
2100	Accounts Payable*	2
2200	Bank Loan*	2
2300	Services Due*	2
3000	OWNER'S EQUITY*	1
4000	REVENUE	1
4100	Earned fr.Services*	2
4200	Interest*	2
5000	EXPENSE	1
5100	Wages*	2
5200	Fuel*	2
5300	Maintenance	2
5310	Tires*	3
5320	Oil Change*	3
5330	Transmission*	3
5340	Brakes*	3
5350	Steering*	3
5360	Washing*	3
5370	Other Maint.*	3
5400	Insurance*	2
5500	Depreciation*	2
5600	Office Expense	2
5610	Paper*	3
5620	Phone	3
5621	Local*	4
5622	Long Distance*	4
5630	Other Office*	3
5700	Interest Expense*	2

There are seven different expense categories: wages, fuel, maintenance, insurance, depreciation, office expense, and interest. These are all second-level categories, because they are subdivisions of a first-level category (expense). Some of these categories have third-level subcategories; for example, the office expense category has three subcategories: paper, phone, and other office. This can be extended even further to fourth-level subcategories; in our case, the only accounts divided into fourth-level subcategories are the phone account, divided into local and long distance, and the van account, divided into original value and accumulated depreciation. The level for each account is the same as the number of nonzero digits in the account number.

The principle of arranging information hierarchically is very important for managerial decisionmaking, as you will see in the next chapter. Sometimes you need to look at the whole "forest"; too much detail about each individual account makes it difficult to see the whole picture. Other times you need to look at the individual "trees," so you need to be able to break down the data in detail. For example, if you are writing a check from a bank account, you need detailed information about the balance of that particular account. If you are trying to assess your liquidity position, you need only the sum of your cash assets, no matter what bank account or till they might be located in.

You also need to divide accounts into detail accounts and general accounts. Any account that does not have any subcategories is a detail account; the others are general accounts. You enter transactions only into detail accounts. Then the totals for the general accounts are calculated by adding up the appropriate detail accounts. In the chart of accounts, detail accounts are marked with a *.

In the next chapter we will discuss how the Lotus 1-2-3 program can be used to enter transactions data and then update the balances in each account.

CHAPTER PERSPECTIVE

A business needs to keep track of its transactions according to the rules for double entry bookkeeping. You should understand enough accounting so that you can understand how different types of transactions are entered, but you can let the computer perform the tedious computational tasks needed to maintain the accounting system.

Advanced 1-2-3 Macros for Accounting

CHAPTER 7

INTRODUCTION AND MAIN POINTS

Now that you have some familiarity with the general principles of accounting, we turn to the specific process by which a computer can perform accounting calculations. A computer accounting system requires three steps: 1) the user must enter the chart of accounts (this needs to be done only once); 2) the user must enter transaction data on a regular basis; 3) the computer automatically updates the accounts. In this book, we use Lotus 1-2-3 macros as a simple accounting system, but in reality, you will likely wish to obtain a specialized accounting program. There are two main reasons for studying the Lotus 1-2-3 macros in this chapter: to learn the principles on which a computer accounting system works; and to learn how to write advanced Lotus 1-2-3 macros. This chapter is the most difficult in the book because much of the information presented is technical; your reward for completing it will be a greatly increased ability to design powerful 1-2-3 macros.

After studying the material in this chapter:

— You will know the procedures followed by a computer accounting system.

— You will be familiar with several more 1-2-3 @ functions: @IF, @ISERR, @INDEX, and @NOW.

— You will know several advanced macro commands: {GETNUMBER, {GETLABEL, {IF, {BRANCH, {LET, {PUT, AND {BEEP.

— You will understand how to use a macro subroutine.

CHART OF ACCOUNTS

Consider the Easy Van Commuting Service, which is simple enough that all transactions can be entered manually into a general journal. First, you need to enter your chart of accounts into the computer (see pages 106–107).

Column N gives the account title, and column L gives the account number. (See the chart of accounts in the previous chap-

K	L	M	N	O	P	Q	R	S	T
ABBREV	ACCT#		TITLE		BALANCE			DEBIT	CREDIT
x	1000		ASSETS	0	10000.00	D	1		
x	1100		Cash	1	10000.00	D	2		
CU	1110		Currency	2	0.00	D	3	$0.00	
CH	1120		Bank Checking	3	10000.00	D	3	$10,000.00	
TD	1200		Time Deposit	4	0.00	D	2	$0.00	
SE	1300		Securities	5	0.00	D	2	$0.00	
AR	1400		Accounts Receivable	6	0.00	D	2	$0.00	
x	1500		Capital Assets	7	0.00	D	2		
x	1510		Van	8	0.00	D	3		
VAN	1511		Original value	9	0.00	D	4	$0.00	
ACDP	1512		Accum. Deprec.	10	0.00	C	4	$0.00	
x	2000		LIABILITIES	11	0.00	C	1		
AP	2100		Accounts Payable	12	0.00	C	2		$0.00
LOAN	2200		Bank Loan	13	0.00	C	2		$0.00
SDUE	2300		Services Due	14	0.00	C	2		$0.00
EQU	3000		OWNER'S EQUITY	15	-10000.00	C	1		$10,000.00
x	4000		REVENUE	16	0.00	C	1		
E	4100		Earned fr.Services	17	0.00	C	2		$0.00
INT.I	4200		Interest	18	0.00	C	2		$0.00
x	5000		EXPENSE	19	0.00	D	1		
WAGE	5100		Wages	20	0.00	D	2	$0.00	
FUEL	5200		Fuel	21	0.00	D	2	$0.00	

x						
TIRE	5300	Maintenance	22	0.00	D	2	$0.00
OIL	5310	Tires	23	0.00	D	3	$0.00
TRAN	5320	Oil Change	24	0.00	D	3	$0.00
BRAKE	5330	Transmission	25	0.00	D	3	$0.00
STEER	5340	Brakes	26	0.00	D	3	$0.00
WASH	5350	Steering	27	0.00	D	3	$0.00
O.MNT	5360	Washing	28	0.00	D	3	$0.00
INSUR	5370	Other	29	0.00	D	2	$0.00
DEPR	5400	Insurance	30	0.00	D	2	$0.00
x	5500	Depreciation	31	0.00	D	2	$0.00
PAP	5600	Office Expense	32	0.00	D	3	
x	5610	Paper	33	0.00	D	3	$0.00
LOCPH	5620	Phone	34	0.00	D	4	$0.00
LDPH	5621	Local	35	0.00	D	4	$0.00
O.OFF	5622	Long Distance	36	0.00	D	3	$0.00
INT.E	5630	Other Office	37	0.00	D	3	$0.00
	5700	Interest Expense	38	0.00	D	2	$0.00
							$10,000.00
							$10,000.00

ter.) Column K gives an abbreviation for each detail account that can be used in the data entry process. Each abbreviation must be unique. No transactions will be entered directly into a general account, so all of the general accounts are marked with an X in this column.

Accounts can be classified into debit accounts (asset and expense accounts) or credit accounts (liability, equity, and revenue accounts). See a book on accounting for more details. Column Q contains a letter indicating the type of account.

Column R gives the level of the account—that is, whether the account is at the top of the hierarchy (level 1) or further down. Column M is an example of a column that is left empty as a separator. Column O gives the row number for the account, with the first account being row 0. You may think it is confusing to call the first account row 0, but you will see that the @INDEX function expects the first row of a range to be row 0. You may also find it confusing that the row number in the table is not the same as the row number in the spreadsheet. This commonly happens with spreadsheets; because the first row of the spreadsheet should contain labels, the first row of a table will not be the same as the first row of the spreadsheet.

Column P gives the balance in each account. Suppose that you have just started the business and have made a $10,000 contribution from your own money to the business. Then the balance sheet should look like this:

ASSETS	LIABILITIES AND EQUITY
Cash 10,000	Equity 10,000

In Column P, debit accounts show up as positive numbers and credit accounts show up as negative numbers. It also helps to present the account information in the form of a trial balance, with debit accounts in the left column and credit accounts in the right column.

In order to create the debit and credit columns, you need a function that acts as follows: If this row represents a debit account, then put the amount in the debit column; otherwise leave it blank. Lotus 1-2-3 provides the @IF function for this purpose. Enter this formula into cell S4:

$$@IF(Q4="D",P4," ")$$

The IF function contains three parts (called *arguments*): The first argument is a logical expression that can be either true or false. In this case, the logical expression is Q4="D". The computer checks cell Q4 to see if it really is equal to "D." If it is, then the program uses the second argument; if it is false, then it uses the third argument. In our case, cell Q4 does equal "D" and the logical expression is true, so the program turns to the second argument: P4. and writes the formula +P4 into cell S4. In other words, the value in cell S4 is the same as the value in cell P4 (in this case, zero). Now copy this formula down to all of the cells in column S. You then need to go back and erase the cells that correspond to general accounts. You would like to be able to sum the total of all of the debits, and you would have horrendous double and triple counting if you added the total of all of the general accounts as well as all of the detail accounts. To erase a cell use the /RE (Range Erase) command.

If you move the pointer to cell S14, you will see the formula:

$$@IF(Q14="D",P14," ")$$

Because we did not use absolute addresses (with dollar signs) the program changed the formula when it was copied down. In this case cell Q14 is not equal to "D" because this is a credit account, so the program chooses the third argument: " ", and cell S14 is set to be a blank cell.

The general form of @IF is:

@IF *(condition, formula to use if true, formula to use if false)*

To create the column with the credit accounts, enter this formula into cell T4:

$$@IF(Q4="C",-P4," ")$$

Since Q4 does not equal "C" (since row 4 corresponds to a debit account), the program puts a blank space in cell T4. Copy the formula down to the other cells in column T and then erase the cells for general accounts. If you move the pointer to cell T14, you will see:

$$@IF(Q14="C",-P14," ")$$

Since Q14 does equal "C," the program chooses the second argument and puts the formula −P14 into cell T14. (The negative sign is needed to cancel the fact that credit accounts show up with negative signs in column P.)

MACRO FOR JOURNAL ENTRIES

In manual accounting systems, the records of day-to-day transactions are kept in books called journals. In a computerized accounting system the same information that goes into the journals is put into the computer. The Easy Van Commuting Service is simple enough that all transactions can be entered into a single general journal; for each transaction, you should record the date, a description, the amount, the account where the money is going to (the account to debit), and the account where the money is coming from (the account to credit). You could enter this information into the worksheet, using the arrows to move around. However, you can make the process easier by writing a data entry macro that makes sure that each data item is entered into the appropriate cell.

The macro will need:

▬ a prompt to the user for each piece of information. It does no good if the user isn't sure what information to type at a particular point. You cannot use the {?} command, as you did in Chapter 5, because {?} provides no prompt. However, you can use the GETNUMBER and GETLABEL commands provided by 1-2-3.
▬ put the data value in the appropriate cell.
▬ return to the beginning to repeat the process.

You can also add two more helpful features: having the program number the transactions automatically and display the account number for each account. (You will type in the account abbreviation when you enter the data.) The computer uses the @VLOOKUP command to find the correct account number.

To use the journal entry macro, first enter the column headings as follows:

	A B C	D	E	F G	H	I
1	General Journal – Easy Van Commuting					
2				DEBIT	CREDIT	
3	DATE│DESCRIPTION	AMOUNT		(TO)	(FROM)	
4						

ADVANCED 1-2-3 MACROS FOR ACCOUNTING

Format column E to currency format with two decimal places, and change the column widths as needed. For example, column C should be only one space wide, since it contains nothing but the vertical line. Column D should be 30 spaces wide so the descriptions will fit.

Move the cursor to cell A4 (the start of the first transaction), and then press ALT E to begin the entry macro. Here is what the macro will do:

- put the transaction number (in this case, 1) in cell A4
- ask you to enter the date
- ask you to enter the description of the transaction (2 lines)
- ask you to enter the amount of the transaction
- ask you to enter the abbreviation of the account to debit
- ask you to enter the abbreviation of the account to credit

After you have entered the data, the macro will display the information for that transaction on the screen. Here is an example:

```
      A B C    D           E        F       G    H       I
 1   General Journal – Easy Van Commuting

 2                                  DEBIT    CREDIT

 3      DATE|DESCRIPTION  AMOUNT    (TO)     (FROM)

 4   1  2-Jan|bank loan   $21,000.00 1120    CH 2200 LOAN

 5          |
```

Then the macro will move to cell A6 and repeat the entire process.

On page 112 is the macro itself. It is much more complicated than the macros we looked at earlier; refer to the explanation that follows it so you will be able to understand how it works.

The macro is placed in column AD, far to the right of the rest of the work in the worksheet. (Column AA comes after column Z, column AB is next, and so on.) The macro occupies several cells in this column; recall that when a macro finishes with one cell, it starts executing the cell immediately below. Use the /RNC (Range Name Create) command to assign the name \E to cell AD43. Then move the pointer to the location of the first

	AD	AE
42	JOURNAL ENTRY MACRO \E	{CPDEFINE}
43	{PANELOFF}/RNCCP~~	/RNDCP~/RNCCP~~
44	{WINDOWSOFF}/C{ESC}{UP 2}~	
45	{CPDEFINE} {LET CP,CP+1}~{RIGHT}	
46	{CPDEFINE} {GETLABEL "Date:",CP}~	
47	{RIGHT}'|{DOWN}'|{RIGHT}{UP}	
48	{CPDEFINE} {GETLABEL "Description line 1:",CP}~{DOWN}	
49	{CPDEFINE} {GETLABEL "Description line 2:",CP}~{RIGHT}{UP}	
50	{CPDEFINE} {GETNUMBER "Amount,",CP}~{RIGHT 2}	
51	{CPDEFINE} {GETLABEL "Account to debit:",CP}~{LEFT}	
52	@VLOOKUP(CP,K2..R40,1)~	
53	{CPDEFINE} {IF @ISERR(CP)}{RIGHT}{BEEP}{BRANCH AD51}	
54	/RV~~{RIGHT 3}	
55	{CPDEFINE} {GETLABEL "Account to credit:",CP}~{LEFT}	
56	@VLOOKUP(CP,K2..R40,1)~	
57	{CPDEFINE} {IF @ISERR(CP)}{RIGHT}{BEEP}{BRANCH AD55}	
58	/RV~~	
59	{WINDOWSON}	
60	{LEFT 7}{DOWN 2}{BRANCH AD44}	

ADVANCED 1-2-3 MACROS FOR ACCOUNTING

transaction to be entered and activate the macro by pressing ALt-E. Note that cell AD42 contains a heading for the macro that is not part of the macro itself.

The data are actually entered with these commands: GETLABEL and GETNUMBER. They work the same except that, as you might expect, GETLABEL reads in a label and GETNUMBER reads in a number. The general form of GETLABEL is:

{GETLABEL *prompt string, location*}

When the program reaches the GETLABEL command, the prompt string will be displayed. You then type in a label, which will be stored at the indicated location. *location* can be either a range name or a cell address. You want to store the result at the current pointer location, so you should define the name CP to refer to the current cell pointer location. This means that you need to redefine it each time that the pointer moves. The keystroke sequence to do this is:

/RNDCP~/RNCCP~~

The first sequence: Range Name Delete CP causes the old definition for CP to be erased; the next sequence / Range Name Create CP creates a new definition for CP at the current pointer location.

You can create a macro *subroutine* to execute a sequence of commands that is frequently used. A macro subroutine is like a regular macro, except that it is called by another macro, instead of by a keystroke. The macro subroutine has been entered in cell AE43 and given the range name {CPDEFINE}. Now, whenever you include the command {CPDEFINE} in your main macro, the macro subroutine will be executed and CP will be defined to be the current cell pointer location.

You can see how lines 46, 48, 49, 50, 51, and 55 in the macro work: first, the CPDEFINE subroutine is called; then the GETLABEL or GETNUMBER command is used to read in the appropriate data item from the keyboard; and then the arrow keys {UP}, {DOWN}, {LEFT} and {RIGHT} are used to move the pointer to the next location.

Here is the explanation for the rest of the macro, starting at the top:

Line 43: The command {PANELOFF} is used to prevent the control panel at the top of the screen from being updated with each macro keystroke. This causes the macro to execute more quickly. The sequence /RNCCP~~ gives an initial definition to the name CP; otherwise the first call to {CPDEFINE} would result in an error message as the program tried to delete the nonexistent name CP.

Line 44: The command {WINDOWSOFF} stops 1-2-3 from updating the worksheet screen after each cell entry. Again, this allows execution to proceed more quickly. The command is undone with {WINDOWSON}; this command is included in line 59 so you will be able to see the complete transaction after it has been entered.

The sequence /C{ESC}{UP 2}~~ causes the cell that is two cells up to be copied down into the current cell. (Try this key sequence manually to see how it works. Whenever you are unsure how to write a macro to accomplish a particular task, try to do it manually first, carefully recording each key that you press.) The cell that is two cells up is the transaction number for the previous cell (it will be a blank cell, which will be treated as zero, if you are about to enter the first transaction).

Line 45: The LET command allows you to put a specific value in a specified cell. The general form is:

{LET *location, value*}

In this case the location is CP, the current cell pointer location; the formula CP+1 causes the value to become one more than its old value. This allows you to number the transactions automatically. Note that the LET command evaluates the formula CP+1 and stores only the value; it does not store the formula itself.

Line 47: This sequence causes a vertical line to be entered to separate the date from the transaction description. You could have entered more vertical lines to separate other columns if you had wanted to.

Lines 52 and 56: The @VLOOKUP formula is used to find the account number for the account that is entered.

@VLOOKUP(CP,K2..R40,1) means:

CP, that is, the contents of the current pointer location, is the value that you are looking for; K2..R40 is the table range you are searching. The first column contains the account abbreviations, which is the column to be searched. Once the program finds an abbreviation that matches the one located in CP, it will move one column to the right (to column L) and find the value in that location—in this case, the account number. (If you add more accounts, you will have to adjust the range K2..R40 to make sure that it includes all of the accounts.)

Lines 53 and 57: You could have a problem if you incorrectly enter an abbreviation that does not fit any of the accounts. In that case you should stop and re-enter the value. You can use the macro IF command to accomplish this. The general form of the IF command is:

{IF *condition*}*commands to be done if condition is true*

If the given condition is true, the program follows the commands in the rest of that cell; otherwise it skips directly to the next cell down. In this case, use this condition:@ISERR(CP) The @ISERR command is very simple: it has the value TRUE if the given cell has the value ERR (for error); otherwise it has the value FALSE. If you have typed an account abbreviation that does not exist, the @VLOOKUP command will not be able to find a match and will return the value ERR. The @ISERR command will then return the value TRUE. In that case, you will want the program to do three things:

{RIGHT}—that is, move back to the cell where the account abbreviation is to be entered

{BEEP}—this command causes the computer to beep. This is important because it alerts you that an error has been made.

{BRANCH AD51}—the BRANCH command changes the order of execution of the macro. Normally, when the macro has completed the execution of one cell, it moves down one cell and continues execution there. However, when it comes to a BRANCH command the macro jumps to the given cell, in this case AD51, and begins executing there. When BRANCH is used along with IF, the macro writer has considerable power to write macros that can respond differently to different conditions. The BRANCH command is not like the GOTO command; the GOTO command causes the cell pointer to move to the specified location, while the BRANCH command causes the execution of the macro to continue at the specified location.

If you enter a valid account abbreviation, the last part of the IF command will be ignored and the macro will proceed to execute the next line. However, if the account abbreviation is invalid, the macro will be sent back to the line that asks for that information. You are sentenced to keep returning to that line until a valid account abbreviation is entered.

This example illustrates another important general principle of computer systems: The system should be designed to catch input that is obviously wrong and to request a correction. If input is wrong in a nonobvious way (for example, you might enter an account abbreviation that is valid but isn't the correct one for a particular transaction), there is not much the computer system can do to catch such an error.

Lines 54 and 58: The @VLOOKUP(CP,K2..R40,1) formula has been written into the cell for the account number. However, a problem will occur when you move to a new cell and CP changes; the result of the @VLOOKUP formula changes as the worksheet is updated. In order to prevent that, you need to change the formula into the value. In order to do this, use the /RV~~ (Range Value) command, which will look at a cell, evaluate the formula contained there, and then store the value instead of the formula.

Line 60: The command {BRANCH AD44} causes macro execution to return to cell AD44, the second line of the program. Note that there is no (IF) before this Branch command, so the Branch will be executed every single time the program reaches this point. A loop has been created. Loops are very common in computer programming because they provide a way for the computer to execute the same set of instructions again and again. Recall that computers are most helpful when they are able to perform the same operation many times. In fact, this loop is an infinite loop, because there is no way for the macro ever to get out of it. Fortunately, 1-2-3 provides a way out: pressing the CONTROL key and the BREAK key simultaneously interrupts the execution of any macro. That is how to get out of this one.

Some entries for the journal for the Easy Van Commuting Service appear on pages 117 and 118.

You can add more transactions later as needed. Move the pointer to cell A38 (the start of the next transaction) and press ALT E to execute the journal entry macro again. If you discover that you made a mistake while you are in the middle of entering, press Control Break to stop the macro, use the arrow keys to move back to the location of the mistake, and fix it. Then move back to the start of the next transaction and press ALT E, and the macro will resume.

These sample transactions are not intended to represent completely the activity of the business during a typical month, but they do illustrate some of the transactions that businesses typically undertake. The accounting framework developed here can handle all types of accounting transactions, but accounting becomes complicated when the entry of some transactions requires judgment instead of simply writing down a number. Also, in reality matters can become more complicated if the business needs to keep a separate set of books with entries for depreciation, etc., for tax purposes.

MACRO FOR POSTING TO ACCOUNTS
The next step in the accounting process is to take the entries from the journal and post the amounts to the correct accounts.

General Journal—Easy Van Commuting

	DATE	DESCRIPTION	AMOUNT	DEBIT (TO)	CREDIT (FROM)
1	2-Jan	bank loan	$21,000.00	1120 CH	2200 LOAN
2	2-Jan	purchase van	$30,000.00	1511 VAN	1120 CH
3	2-Jan	fuel purchase (on credit card)	$30.65	5200 FUEL	2100 AP
4	3-Jan	cash receipts	$120.00	1110 CU	4100 E
5	10-Jan	cash receipts	$300.00	1110 CU	4100 E
6	10-Jan	bank deposit	$420.00	1120 CH	1110 CU
7	17-Jan	cash receipts	$432.00	1110 CU	4100 E
8	17-Jan	sell ticket book	$200.00	1120 CH	2300 SDUE
9	18-Jan	oil change	$92.56	5320 OIL	1120 CH
10	24-Jan	tickets redeemed	$30.00	2300 SDUE	4100 E

11	24-Jan	cash receipts	$360.00	1110 CU	4100 E
12	31-Jan	loan: principal repay	$5.00	2200 LOAN	1120 CH
13	31-Jan	loan: interest payment	$200.00	5640 INT.E	1120 CH
14	31-Jan	pay fuel bill	$30.65	2100 AP	1120 CH
15	31-Jan	purchase fuel	$29.85	5200 FUEL	2100 AP
16	31-Jan	pay wages	$378.00	5100 WAGE	1120 CH
17	31-Jan	depreciation – van	$312.50	5500 DEPR	1512 ACDP

ADVANCED 1-2-3 MACROS FOR ACCOUNTING

This is the process for which the computer is most helpful, because it can complete the process automatically. Again we use a 1-2-3 macro, and you can learn more about how macros work as you go along.

As with any complicated macro, the first step is to determine your general strategy. Conceptually, the process is simple: For each transaction, subtract the amount *from* one account (the one to *credit*) and add the amount *to* another account (the one to *debit*). Under this framework, each credit account ends up with a negative balance, but you have already seen how to handle this. (See page 108).

The general strategy for processing each transaction is as follows:

First, use the @VLOOKUP function to find the account number to debit and the old value of that account. Add the amount of this transaction and store the result in the cell giving the balance for that account. Then follow the same strategy for the account number to credit, except that you subtract the transaction amount from the old account balance. See pages 120–121 for the macro.

This macro uses some cells for temporary storage. The macro itself is in column X, and some explanatory cells are included in column Y, so column Z is used for the temporary storage. The first cell Z1 is simply a counter that is set to 1 initially (line 2) and then increases by one after every transaction is processed (line 13). The {LET} command is used to accomplish this.

Line 3: Move the pointer to cell Z2, which stores the amount of the transaction. To find the amount, use the @INDEX function. The general form is:

@INDEX(*range, column location, row location*).

The @INDEX function looks in the given range for the value of the cell given by the column location and the row location. However, there is one tricky feature: The first column of the range is called column 0, and the first row of the range is called row 0. For example, suppose that you have these cells:

	H	I	J
12	100	115	140
13	210	230	250
14	330	360	370
15	480	490	498

	X	Y
1	Posting Macro \P	
2	{WINDOWSOFF}{PANELOFF}{LET Z1,1}	store counter value in Z1
3	{GOTO}Z2~@INDEX(E4..E200,0,(2*Z1-2))~{DOWN}	Z2=amnt. of transaction
4	{IF Z2=0}{BRANCH X14}	If amnt=0 start addition
5	@INDEX(F4..F200,0,(2*Z1-2))~{DOWN}	Z3=acct.# to debit
6	@INDEX(H4..H200,0,(2*Z1-2))~{DOWN}	Z4=acct.# to credit
7	@VLOOKUP(Z3,L2..P40,3)~{DOWN}	Z5=row # of acct. to debit
8	@VLOOKUP(Z3,L2..P40,4)~{DOWN}	Z6=old amnt.-acct. to debit
9	{PUT P2..P40,0,Z5,Z6+Z2}	update balance-acct.to deb.
10	@VLOOKUP(Z4,L2..P40,3)~{DOWN}	Z7=row # of acct. to credit
11	@VLOOKUP(Z4,L2..P40,4)~{DOWN}	Z8=old amnt.-acct. to credit
12	{PUT P2..P40,0,Z7,Z8-Z2}~	update balance-acct.to cred.
13	{LET Z1,Z1+1}{BRANCH X3}	increase counter/repeat proc
14	{LET Z1,38}	start addition section
15	{GOTO}M2~@IF(K2="x",0,P2)~/CM2~M2..M40~	set general accounts to zero
16	/RVM2..M40~P2..P40~/REM2..M40~	
17	{GOTO}Z2~@INDEX(P2..R40,2,Z1)~{DOWN}	Z2=level
18	@INDEX(P2..R40,0,Z1)~{DOWN}	Z3=amount
19	{IF Z2=1}{BRANCH X25}	
20	/CZ1~~{DOWN}	set Z4 equal to Z1

21	`{LET Z4,Z4-1}~`	decrease Z4 to next higher l
22	`{IF @INDEX(P2..R40,2,Z4)<>(Z2-1)}{BRANCH X21}`	
23	`@INDEX(P2..R40,0,Z4)~`	Z5=old amnt.at n.h.level
24	`{PUT P2..R40,0,Z4,Z3+Z5}`	update amnt.at n.h.level
25	`{LET Z1,Z1-1}`	decrease counter until
26	`{IF Z1>0}{BRANCH X17}`	all accts. processed
27	`{GOTO}A2~'Posted:~`	put current date at
28	`{GOTO}D2~@NOW~`	top of journal to
29	`/RFD1~/RV~~`	indicate posting is done

The function @INDEX(H12..J15,0,0) will return 100; @INDEX(H12..J15,1,0) will return 115; @INDEX(H12..J15,0,1) will return 210; and @INDEX(H12..J15,1,2) will return 360.

In this macro, the given range (E4..E200) has only one column, so you have to use 0 as the column location. (Otherwise an error will occur.) The expression 2*Z1−2 gives the row location for the transaction you are currently processing. For the first transaction, Z1 = 1 and 2*Z1−2 = 0, so the element in the first row of the range will be returned. (Recall that 1-2-3 designates the first row of the range as row 0.) For the second transaction, Z1 = 2 and 2*Z1−2 = 2; for the third transaction, 2*Z1−2 = 4, and so on. The range E4..E200 must be modified if you have entered a large number of transactions that extend beyond this range.

Line 4: If the amount of the transaction stored in Z2 is zero, you know that you have reached the end of the journal. Use the BRANCH command to proceed to the next part of the program (the addition section which starts in cell X14).

Line 5 and 6: Again the @INDEX function is used, first to find the account number of the account to debit (stored in cell Z3) and then to find the account number of the account to credit (stored in cell Z4).

Line 7, 8, 10, and 11: Use the @VLOOKUP function to find the row number of the account to debit (note that on our original chart of accounts on page 106, the row number is given in column O, which is 3 columns to the right of the account number. That accounts for the three in the function @VLOOKUP(Z3,L2..P40,3). Then you need to look up the old balance in the account to debit, which is four columns to the right of the account number, so use @VLOOKUP(Z3,L2..P40,4). Note that the range L2..P40 has to be designed so that the first column contains the item that you are looking up (in this case, the account number). Then lines 10 and 11 repeat the same process for the account to credit.

Lines 9 and 12: To update the balance for each account, use the PUT macro command. The general form is:

{PUT *range, column location, row location, new value*}

The first three arguments of the PUT command work exactly the same as they do with @INDEX: you need to specify the range, the column location, and the row location (recalling that the first column is known as column 0 and the first row is known as row 0). However, the @INDEX function returns the value that it finds in the indicated cell, whereas the PUT command stores the specified value in the indicated cell. The new value may be a formula, as it is in this case: z6+z2. The PUT command stores the value that results from the formula, not the formula itself.

That is all it takes for the macro to update the account balances. Line 13 causes the counter in cell Z1 to increase by 1, and the macro execution returns to the beginning (with the command BRANCH X3).

Whenever a macro uses temporary storage, such as this one does, it helps to include comments in the adjacent cell to remind you what the contents of each cell mean (see column Y). Also, you must make sure that the macro's temporary storage does not overwrite any other values that you may have already stored in that location of the worksheet.

There is one more task that your posting macro should perform: It should calculate the totals for each of the general accounts. (Recall that a general account is any account that has some other accounts below it in the hierarchy.) To do this, it needs to add together the totals in each of the accounts one level below. The macro accomplishes this task starting at cell X14; the BRANCH command in cell X4 sends the macro execution to this point when it has finished processing the accounts.

Before starting the addition, you need to set the value of each general account at zero. The macro accomplishes this in lines 15 and 16, using column M as temporary storage. The @IF function in line 15 puts a 0 in any cell with an "x" in the abbreviation column—i.e., all general accounts. In all other accounts, the value in column M is the same as the corresponding value in column P. Copy these values from column M to column P, using the /RV (Range Value) command instead of the /C (Copy) command to avoid copying the @IF formulas themselves; you want only the values copied. Finally, the /RE (Range Erase) command is used to erase the temporary values in column M. (As with all of these macro operations, you need to try it yourself to fully understand how it works.)

Here is the general strategy for the addition section of the macro: Start at the bottom. If the account is at level 1, you do not need to add its total to any other account; however, if the account is below level 1, read up the chart until you find the first account at a higher level. For example, the bottom account (interest expense) is at level 2, so read up the table until you come to an account at level 1 (the account EXPENSE). Add the total of the lower level account to the total of the higher level account. Then return to the account that is second from the bottom and keep repeating the process until you reach the top of the chart of accounts.

Here is the explanation of how the addition section of the macro accomplishes this:

Line 14: Again, cell Z1 is a counter. However, this time it starts at 38, the row number of the last account, and counts down. (The value 38 must be changed if you change the number of accounts.) Line 25 causes the value in Z1 to be decreased by 1. In the rest of the discussion, the account located in the row whose number is stored in cell Z1 will be called the current account. This becomes quite complicated; we mean not the row containing cell Z1 but the row whose row number is stored in cell Z1.

Line 17 and 18: Using the @INDEX function, the level of the current account is stored in cell Z2 and the amount stored in cell Z3.

Line 19: If the current account is at level 1, you don't need to do anything (since there is no higher account to add the value to). In that case you can proceed to process the next account, so branch to cell X25.

Line 20 to 21: Copy the value in cell Z1 (the row number for the current account) down to cell Z4. Z4 is a counter that represents the account you are looking at. Your mission now is to search up the chart of accounts until you find the first account that is one level above the current account.

Line 22: The expression @INDEX(P2..R40,2,Z4) gives you the level of the account you are looking at. This result is built into the logical expression in the IF command:

$$\{IF\ @INDEX(P2..R40,2,Z4)<>(Z2-1)\}$$

The expression <> stands for "not equal"; you can think of it as "greater than or less than." Z2-1 gives the level for the account that is one level above the current account, which is the one you are looking for. If the account given by Z4 does not equal this, you have to keep looking; in that case, the condition in the IF command is true, so execute the rest of the cell: BRANCH X21. BRANCH X21 causes the macro to return to cell X21, subtract one from the value in cell Z4, and then repeat the process.

Lines 23 and 24: Once you finally find the account at the next higher level, store its value temporarily in cell Z5 (this is accomplished by the @INDEX function in line 23), then add the amount of the current account (from cell Z3) and store the result in the balance for the n.h. level account (n.h. stands for next higher). This is accomplished by the PUT command in line 24.

Line 26: If the counter Z1 is greater than zero, there are more accounts to process, so the BRANCH X17 command returns you to the start of the addition loop. You do not need to perform any addition for the account in row 0, since that account must be at level 1. Therefore, when the counter Z1 reaches zero, move on to the next section of the macro in cell X27.

Lines 27 to 29: The Posting macro performs one more function: It displays the date of the posting at the top of the journal. First it moves the pointer to cell A2, writes the label posted, and uses the 1-2-3 function @NOW to calculate the current date. The @NOW function returns the serial number of the current date, where all dates are counted from the beginning of the century. That serial number is not too meaningful, but you can convert it into standard date notation by using the Range Format Date command to format that cell in date format. This is accomplished by the command sequence /RFD1˜. Finally, use the /RV (Range Value) command to convert the @NOW formula into the value of the current date. (Otherwise, the @NOW function would be updated to the current date whenever you use the spreadsheet again, so it would be of no help in letting you know when the posting took place.)

The result of the posting macro appears on pages 126–127.

Total debits equal total credits, as they must. The computer can make sure that this happens automatically, so some of the errors that can occur with manual accounting systems are no longer possible. However, you may have problems, of course, if the transaction data in the journal are wrong. The information in this table is called a trial balance. You can use this information directly to prepare an income statement and a balance sheet. At the end of the fiscal year, "clear" the revenue and expense accounts—that is, set all of their values to zero and adjust the owner's equity account by adding the revenue and subtracting the expense amount. You can also add some more accounts under the owner's equity accounts in order to trace the changes that occur in the equity, but you should turn to an accounting book for more detail on that.

CHAPTER PERSPECTIVE

A computer accounting system can spare you from the drudgery of accounting (such as worrying about everything adding up

	K	L M	N	O	P	Q	R	S DEBIT	T CREDIT
1	ABBREV	ACCT#	TITLE		BALANCE		L		
2	x	1000	ASSETS	0	31393.29	D	1		
3	x	1100	Cash	1	1705.79	D	2		
4	CU	1110	Currency	2	792.00	D	3	$792.00	
5	CH	1120	Bank Checking	3	913.79	D	3	$913.79	
6	TD	1200	Time Deposit	4	0.00	D	2	$0.00	
7	SE	1300	Securities	5	0.00	D	2	$0.00	
8	AR	1400	Accnts Receivable	6	0.00	D	2	$0.00	
9	x	1500	Capital Assets	7	29687.50	D	2		
10	x	1510	Van	8	29687.50	D	3		
11	VAN	1511	Original Value	9	30000.00	D	4	$30,000.00	
12	ACDP	1512	Accum. Deprec.	10	-312.50	D	4	($312.50)	
13	x	2000	LIABILITIES	11	-21194.85	C	1		
14	AP	2100	Accounts Payable	12	-29.85	C	2		$29.85
15	LOAN	2200	Bank Loan	13	-20995.00	C	2		$20,995.00
16	SDUE	2300	Services Due	14	-170.00	C	2		$170.00
17	EQU	3000	OWNER'S EQUITY	15	-10000.00	C	1		$10,000.00
18	x	4000	REVENUE	16	-1242.00	C	1		
19	E	4100	Earned-f.sales	17	-1242.00	C	2		$1,242.00
20	INT.1	4200	Interest	18	0.00	C	2		$0.00
21	x	5000	EXPENSE	19	1043.56	D	1		
22	WAGE	5100	Wages	20	378.00	D	2	$378.00	
23	FUEL	5200	Fuel	21	60.50	D	2	$60.50	

ADVANCED 1-2-3 MACROS FOR ACCOUNTING

24	x						
25	TIRE	5300	Maintenance	22	92.56	D	2
26	OIL	5310	Tires	23	0.00	D	3
27	TRAN	5320	Oil Change	24	92.56	D	3	$92.56
28	BRAKE	5330	Transmission	25	0.00	D	3	$0.00
29	STEER	5340	Brakes	26	0.00	D	3	$0.00
30	WASH	5350	Steering	27	0.00	D	3	$0.00
31	O.MNT	5360	Washing	28	0.00	D	2	$0.00
32	INSUR	5370	Other	29	0.00	D	2	$0.00
33	DEPR	5400	Insurance	30	0.00	D	2	$0.00
34	x	5500	Depreciation	31	312.50	D	3	$312.50
35	PAP	5600	Office Expense	32	0.00	D	3
36	x	5610	Paper	33	0.00	D	3	$0.00
37	LOCPH	5620	Phone	34	0.00	D	4
38	LDPH	5621	Local	35	0.00	D	4	$0.00
39	O.OFF	5622	Long Distance	36	0.00	D	4	$0.00
40	INT.E	5630	Other Office	37	0.00	D	3	$0.00
41		5700	Interest Expense	38	200.00	D	2	$200.00
42								$32,436.85 $32,436.85

127

correctly) and free your mind to think about the interesting accounting judgment calls.

The macro structure of 1-2-3 provides powerful abilities to customize the computer so that it performs precisely the tasks that are helpful for your business. In this chapter you have seen how this can be done.

Budget Monitoring

CHAPTER 8

INTRODUCTION AND MAIN POINTS
We have seen how computers can help in the budget development process (Chapter 4) and in keeping track of actual financial transactions (Chapter 7). Now we consider the process of monitoring budget performance—that is, comparing the actual results with the budget plan. A significant difference between the two calls for an analysis of the situation and, possibly, corrective action.

After studying the material in this chapter:
- You will understand the concept of a budget performance report.
- You will understand the value of arranging budget data hierarchically, permitting you to examine the budget both in fine detail and in broad categories.
- You will see some more examples of applications of 1-2-3 macros.

BUDGET PERFORMANCE REPORTS
A key tool in the budget monitoring process is the budget performance report. A budget performance report should be sent on a regular basis (perhaps monthly) to the manager of each division, who should have the authority to take action to keep within budget (it is pointless to send the report if the managers can't do anything about it) and the responsibility for the performance of their unit (it doesn't do any good to send the report if the managers ignore it).

Before beginning to think about how to use the computer for a particular task, you need to determine the information needed. Consider an organization that expects to repair a few broken windows during the year. It has no way of knowing in advance how much it will need to spend on broken windows; the best it can do is develop an estimate based on past data.

The budget performance report compares the projected expense with the actual figure for a specific period of time:

Year to Date—January to August

Account	Budget	Actual	Variance
Window repair	$40.00	$37.50	$2.50

The term *variance* is used to describe the difference between the planned spending and the actual spending. A positive variance is "good"; it means the actual spending is below the budget. A negative variance means actual spending exceeds the budget.

The budget for a large organization can become very complicated because there is a large number of line items, and it may not be feasible to prepare budget estimates for every single item. For example, instead of developing a budget line item for window repair, it may be more helpful to have a line item for general building repair. The window repair amount could come out of this item. The decision to use a more or less detailed budget, which must be made during the budget planning process, involves a trade-off: A more detailed budget helps with the planning process but requires more work to develop. Note that even if you do not have a specific budget amount for window repair, it is still a good idea to record the actual amount spent on window repair so that you can analyze the budget performance of the overall repair category and see where your estimates were off. For example, the budget performance report for the repair category might look like this:

Year to Date—January to August

Account	Budget	Actual	Variance
building repair	200.00	172.10	27.90
window repair	x	37.50	x
plumbing repair	x	98.20	x
electrical repair	x	7.95	x
roof repair	x	0	x
other repair	x	28.45	x

Knowing the actual amount spent on each repair subcategory helps analyze the spending in the overall category, even if you have decided not to develop specific budget amounts for each subcategory.

The budget allowances should be flexible, varying with a measure of the business activity level, such as sales revenue. For example, suppose your business suffers a severe slump and you close your facilities four days per week. The repair bill will be low because of reduced wear and tear. If the repair budget is a fixed number, it will be easy to outperform that target; you should not congratulate the repair crew for coming in under budget if the facilities have been closed. On the other hand, if business is booming and the facilities are open overtime hours, the repair bill will likely increase. The budget allowance should also increase, and you should not blame the repair crew for failing to meet the initial budget; the organization should instead be celebrating the fact that business is good.

The task of developing budget allowance formulas is complicated; they need to be worked out by the central budget office and each individual division working together, looking at past data. Once the formula has been developed, it is easy for the computer to perform the calculations. Note that the budget for fuel for the Easy Van Commuting Service in Chapter 4 varies depending on the number of passengers given door-to-door service; on the other hand, some costs are budgeted as fixed amounts because they do not change as the activity level of the business changes.

Once you have identified those budget items that have significant variances, either positive or negative, you need to determine if corrective action is necessary. This task requires judgment, and the computer cannot help with that part. However, the computer may be able to provide useful information. For example, if window repair spending exceeds budget, one obvious question is whether the price of windows has gone up or if windows have been breaking at an unusually high rate. Clearly, the corrective action would be different in these two different circumstances.

The budget monitoring process is a kind of art; it is necessary for the managers to treat the budget monitoring process seriously without feeling that they are confined in a straitjacket by a central office that is ignorant of the situation on the front lines.

EXAMPLE: COMMUTING VAN SERVICE BUDGET REPORT

For the rest of this chapter we consider the simple case of the Easy Van Commuting Service, which has only one budget performance report for the entire organization. Later we investigate the case of larger organizations with more than one budget unit.

The budget monitoring system takes information from two sources: the budget planning spreadsheet (see Chapter 4) and the accounting system (see Chapter 7). The 1-2-3 File Combine command can be used to read in a portion of one worksheet into another worksheet.

Once you combine this information into a single budget performance spreadsheet you have what appears on page 133.

For this purpose look at only the revenue and expense accounts (account numbers beginning with 4 and 5.)

Column A gives the account number, column C gives the account title, Column D gives the row number for the account, and Column E gives the budgeted amount for that category, taken from the budget development worksheet. The budget does not include separate line items for the subcategories for office expenditures; these have been marked with x. Column F gives the actual spending amounts, taken from the accounting system. Column G gives the variance. In cases where there is no line item budget amount, the variance should also be given as x. In order to do that, use the @IF function. Enter this formula into cell G2:

@IF(E2 = "x", "x", E2-F2)

If the condition E2="x" is true, then the first option is chosen, and cell G2 contains "x". If the condition is false, then the second option is chosen and cell G2 becomes E2-F2, the variance. By now you are experienced enough with 1–2–3 to realize you can copy this formula down to all of the other cells in the column.

Note that you can consider the budget as giving spending, which means that revenue is listed as negative amounts. (This is the way that the numbers come from the accounting system in Chapter 7.) If actual revenue in a given category falls short of planned revenue, then you should record this as a negative variance. In this way you can be consistent: Negative variances always mean "bad" and positive variances always mean "good."

DETAILED AND SUMMARY VIEWS OF BUDGET PERFORMANCE

Sometimes you want to see the budget in full detail, looking at all of the line items with a magnifying glass. Other times you wish to look only at the big picture. It would be convenient if you could design your budget reporting system so that you could

BUDGET MONITORING

A	B	C	D	E	F	G	H	I	J
ACT#		TITLE	ROW	BUDGET	ACTUAL	VARIANCE	LV	SL	UP
4000		REVENUE	1	($5,101.00)	($5,050.00)	($51.00)	1	3	0
4100		Earned fr.Services	2	($5,076.00)	($5,048.00)	($28.00)	2	1	1
4200		Interest	3	($25.00)	($12.00)	($13.00)	2	0	1
5000		EXPENSE	4	$5,044.00	$5,066.00	($22.00)	1	0	0
5100		Wages	5	$1,494.00	$1,494.00	$0.00	2	1	4
5200		Fuel	6	$625.00	$700.00	($75.00)	2	1	4
5300		Maintenance	7	$512.00	$480.00	$32.00	2	8	4
5310		Tires	8	$170.00	$140.00	$30.00	3	1	7
5320		Oil Change	9	$137.00	$132.00	$5.00	3	1	7
5330		Transmission	10	$30.00	$26.00	$4.00	3	1	7
5340		Brakes	11	$40.00	$32.00	$8.00	3	1	7
5350		Steering	12	$40.00	$98.00	($58.00)	3	1	7
5360		Washing	13	$50.00	$40.00	$10.00	3	1	7
5370		Other	14	$45.00	$12.00	$33.00	3	0	7
5400		Insurance	15	$430.00	$430.00	$0.00	2	1	4
5500		Depreciation	16	$1,250.00	$1,250.00	$0.00	2	1	4
5600		Office Expense	17	$133.00	$112.00	$21.00	2	5	4
5610		Paper	18	x	$45.00	x	3	1	17
5620		Phone	19	x	$65.00		3	3	17
5621		Local	20	x	$35.00	x	4	1	19
5622		Long Distance	21	x	$30.00		4	1	19
5630		Other Office	22	x	$2.00	x	3	0	17
5700		Interest Expense	23	$600.00	$600.00	$0.00	2	0	4

133

easily switch between these situations. The chart on page 133 shows everything in full detail. Now we present a macro that allows you to change your perspective on the budget. Actually, we present three macros. The first displays only the top level accounts (in this case, only revenue and expense). Name this macro \A. When you execute the macro (by pressing ALT-A), you will see:

	Z AA	AB	AC	AD	AE	AF
1	ACT#	TITLE	ROW	BUDGET	ACTUAL	VARIANCE
2	4000	REVENUE	1	($5,101.00)	($5,050.00)	($51.00)
3	5000	EXPENSE	4	$5,044.00	$5,066.00	($22.00)

The second macro allows you to select any account and see the detail for that account. Suppose that you have just executed the \A macro, so that the screen display is as shown above. Now move the cell pointer to cell Z3, so the account number 5000 (Expense) is highlighted and execute the second macro, called \D (for detail). This is the result:

	Z AA	AB	AC	AD	AE	AF
1	ACT#	TITLE	ROW	BUDGET	ACTUAL	VARIANCE
2	5000	EXPENSE	4	$5,055.00	$5,066.00	($22.00)
3	5100	Wages	5	$1,494.00	$1,494.00	$0.00
4	5200	Fuel	6	$625.00	$700.00	($75.00)
5	5300	Maintenance	7	$512.00	$480.00	$32.00
6	5400	Insurance	15	$430.00	$430.00	$0.00
7	5500	Depreciation	16	$1,250.00	1,250.00	$0.00
8	5600	Office Expense	17	$133.00	$112.00	$21.00
9	5700	Interest Expense	23	$600.00	$600.00	$0.00

Now you can see the detail of all of the expense categories at level 2. Suppose you want to look at the maintenance category in more detail. Move the cell pointer to cell Z5, so that it highlights account number 5300 (for maintenance). Execute the second macro \D again and the screen will display:

	Z AA	AB	AC	AD	AE	AF
1	ACT#	TITLE	ROW	BUDGET	ACTUAL	VARIANCE
2	5300	Maintenance	7	$512.00	$480.00	$32.00
3	5310	Tires	8	$170.00	$140.00	$30.00
4	5320	Oil Change	9	$137.00	$132.00	$5.00
5	5330	Transmission	10	$30.00	$26.00	$4.00
6	5340	Brakes	11	$40.00	$32.00	$8.00
7	5350	Steering	12	$40.00	$98.00	($58.00)
8	5360	Washing	13	$50.00	$40.00	$10.00
9	5370	Other	14	$45.00	$12.00	$33.00

Now you can see the detail of this category. In this case, none of these categories has any further subcategories, but in a large organization with a complicated hierarchy of accounts, it is very helpful to be able to move up or down the hierarchy toward greater aggregation or toward greater detail as you need to. You need one more macro to move up; call it \U. If you move the cell pointer to cell Z2 to highlight the account number for maintenance and then execute the \U macro, you will move one step back up the account hierarchy and the screen will show the same table it showed previously (page 134).

Note the similarity to the hierarchical structure of the 1-2-3 menu system. The / key moves you to the top of the menu tree, just as the \A macro moves you to the top of the account tree. Moving the cell pointer to the choice you want and pressing RETURN moves you down the menu tree, just as moving the cell pointer to the account number you want to detail and pressing ALt-D moves you down the account tree. The ESCAPE key moves you back up the menu tree, and the \U macro moves you back up the account tree.

All of the commands used in the macros have been introduced before. These macros use two additional columns in the spreadsheet: column I (labeled SL for same level), which gives the number of rows you need to go down in order to reach the next account at the same level, and column J (labeled UP), which gives the row number of the account immediately above. It would be a lot of work to type in the numbers in that column, particularly if there were a long chart of accounts. You should instantly think of the solution: using a macro to generate those numbers. The macro to accomplish this task is given on page

#	P	Q
1	MACRO TO CREATE TOP LEVEL REPORTS \A	
2	{PANELOFF} {WINDOWSOFF}	
3	/RNCNXTSL~	create name NXTSL
4	/REZ2..AI250~	erase range for report
5	/RNCALOC~A2..I2~	ALOC: top line of accounts
6	{GOTO}Z1~{DOWN}	move to range where report
7	{WINDOWSON}	will be shown
8	/CALOC~~	copy ALOC to report location
9	{WINDOWSOFF}	
10	/RNDNXTSL~	delete NXTSL and assign
11	/RNCNXTSL~{ESC} {RIGHT 8}~	to new value
12	{IF NXTSL=0} {GOTO}Z1~{QUIT}	quit if no more accts. this level
13	/RNCALOC~{ESC} {DOWN NXTSL}.{RIGHT 10}~	move ALOC down to next acct.
14	{DOWN} {BRANCH P8}	repeat process with next acct.
15		
16		
17		
18	MACRO TO SHOW DETAIL \D	
19	{WINDOWSOFF} {PANELOFF}	
20	/RNCROWNUM~~/RNDROWNUM~	ROWNUM is assigned to the cell
21	/RNCROWNUM~{ESC} {RIGHT 3}~	3 spaces right of pointer,
22	/RNCALOC~{ESC} {HOME} {DOWN ROWNUM}.{RIGHT 10}~	then ALOC is assigned to
23	/REZ2..AI250~	the account in that row
24	{GOTO}Z1~{DOWN}	erase range for report
25	/CALOC~~	move to report location
26	/RNDROWNUM~/RNCROWNUM~{ESC} {RIGHT 3}~	copy ALOC to report location
27	/RNCALOC~{ESC} {HOME} {DOWN ROWNUM} {DOWN}.{RIGHT 10}~	assign new value of ROWNUM
28	{DOWN} {BRANCH P8}	now use previous macro to
29		display rest of accounts
30	MACRO TO MOVE ONE LEVEL UP \U	
31	{WINDOWSOFF} {PANELOFF}	
32	/RNCROWNUM~~/RNDROWNUM~	this is the same as the
33	/RNCROWNUM~{ESC} {RIGHT 9}~	previous macro, except that
34	/RNCALOC~{ESC} {HOME} {DOWN ROWNUM}.{RIGHT 10}~	it first looks up the row
35	/REZ2..AI250~	
36	{GOTO}Z1~{DOWN}	number of the account
37	/CALOC~~	one level up
38	/RNCALOC~{ESC} {DOWN}.{RIGHT 10}~	
39	{DOWN}/CALOC~~	
40	{BRANCH P11}	

BUDGET MONITORING

1	MACRO TO FILL IN NXTSL AND NXTUP COLUMN \R	
2	{WINDOWSOFF} {PANELOFF}	
3	/RNCX~I1~	create name X in cell I1
4	{GOTO}X~{LEFT} {DOWN}	move pointer to column H (level of account)
5	/C~N1~	copy current cell to cell N1 (temp.storage)
6	{IF N1=0} {BRANCH L16}	if level is zero, finished with this part
7	/RNCX~{DOWN}~	move range X one cell down
8	{PUT N2,0,0,1}~	put value 1 in cell N2; to use as counter
9	{DOWN}	move cell pointer to next account
10	/C~N3~	copy level of this account to cell N3
11	{IF N3=N1} {PUT X,0,0,N2} {GOTO}X~{LEFT} {DOWN} {BRANCH L4}	
12	{IF N3<N1} {PUT X,0,0,0} {GOTO}X~{LEFT} {DOWN} {BRANCH L4}	
13	{LET N2, N2+1} {BRANCH L9}	
14		
15	FILL IN NXTUP COLUMN	this segment works up the account table
16	{UP}	starting at the bottom
17	/RNCX~{RIGHT}~	create name X in NXTUP column
18	/C~N1~	copy level of this account to N1
19	{IF N1=0} {QUIT}	reached end of account table
20	{IF N1=1} {PUT X,0,0,N1-1} {BRANCH L25}	
21	{PUT N2,0,0,N1-1}~	N2 will equal the level of the NXTUP acct.
22	{UP}/C~N1~	keep searching up the account table until
23	{IF N1 <> N2} {BRANCH L22}	finding an account at the next higher lev.
24	/C{ESC} {LEFT 4}~X~	copy the row number to location X
25	/RNCX~{UP}~	move X up one cell
26	{GOTO}X~{LEFT 2}	repeat the process with the next account
27	{BRANCH L18}	

137. You might also wish to write a short macro that would automatically print the report that shows on the screen.

The three macros that control the amount of detail that is presented are shown on page 136.

CHAPTER PERSPECTIVE
Computers are servants whose ultimate goal is to provide helpful information. Decide on the information that your budget monitoring process will need and determine how the computer can provide that information. You should have the option of looking at the budget in fine detail or in broad categories.

Data Base Management

CHAPTER 9

INTRODUCTION AND MAIN POINTS
The word datum refers to a single fact; its plural, data, refers to a set of factual information. So far we have used the computer primarily to keep track of numerical data. There are many other types of data that can be stored and processed by computers. Again the tremendous advantage of an alphabet becomes clear: as long as the computer can store a small number of symbols to represent letters, it can store the text of anything.

Businesses are likely to need to keep track of a variety of data items, including employees, customers, vendors, inventory items, and equipment.

After studying the material in this chapter:
- You will know how to create a data base in Lotus 1-2-3.
- You will understand three fundamental operations to perform on data bases: sorting, selecting, and tabulation.

FIELDS, RECORDS, AND FILES
Consider a list of employees. The information for each individual employee is called a *record;* each record consists of several data items, such as the name of the employee, the social security number, and so on. Each of these data items is called a *field.* A collection of records is organized into a *file,* and a collection of files forms a *data base.*

The goal of data base management is to extract useful information from the data. Often you need to connect items located in more than one file. For example, the personnel file contains detailed information for each individual employee, which need not be duplicated in the work schedule file. As long as each employee in the scheduling file is identified by a unique code, such as the social security number, the data base system can obtain any other information about that employee from the personnel file. The term *relational data base* is used to refer to a data base in which items in one file can be related to items in another file in this manner.

The data in a computer data base must be stored in a computer storage medium, such as a hard disk, a mainframe disk pack, or a reel of magnetic tape. The user needs to have data base management software available. Ideally, the user should not have to worry about the physical location of a data item in the data base; the software should allow the user to access the data according to the characteristics of the data themselves. Although mainframe data base systems have been in use since the early days of computers, several software packages dedicated to data base management have become popular since the introduction of microcomputers.

When Lotus 1-2-3 was introduced, one feature that contributed to its popularity was the inclusion of some data management facilities. As a data base manager 1-2-3 is not as powerful as a program dedicated to that purpose (in most cases a special purpose program can beat a general purpose program in its own field). The size of a 1-2-3 data base is limited (although still large enough for many purposes), and early versions did not provide facilities for linking different data files as is done in data base programs, although Release 3 provides some of this ability. However, if you are already using 1-2-3 as a spreadsheet, there is a big advantage in using it also as a data base because you are already familiar with the general structure of the program.

If your business is large enough, you will need to store data on a mainframe computer or minicomputer and to hire professional programmers to maintain the system. Even in that case, however, individual users can have their own microcomputers networked together and access to data management software.

Microcomputers are powerful enough to handle all of the data management needs of a small business, such as a doctor's office. Mailing labels can be printed from a list of customers maintained on the hard disk if you wish to send a mailing to all customers or those that meet specific conditions. You can even use a word processing program that automatically types the name and address of the recipient on the letter.

If you are just starting your business you can start using 1-2-3 as a data manager, since you should obtain a spreadsheet program anyway. If your data files become too large to fit in 1-2-3, or the relational data base calculations you need to perform become too complicated for 1-2-3 to handle, you can obtain a dedicated data base program and transfer the data to that program.

DATA BASES IN 1-2-3
When you set up a data base in Lotus 1-2-3, each row corresponds to a record and each column represents a field in that record. The top row gives the name for each field.

Suppose that the Easy Express Shipping Service creates a data base on the eighteen large U.S. cities where it maintains offices. The record for each city contains six fields: the name of the city, the region of the country where it is located, the population of the metropolitan area containing the city in thousands (1988), its average high temperature, its average low temperature, and a code classifying its location: whether it is by an ocean (OCN), a bay (BAY), a lake (LAKE), a river (RIV), an artificial channel (CHAN), or not on a major body of water (X) (see page 142).

SORTING
There are three types of processing operations that are often performed on data bases: sorting, selecting, and tabulating. 1-2-3 provides commands to perform each of these functions.

To sort the cities according to their population, type /D to see the menu of data commands at the top of the screen: Fill Table Sort Query Distribution Matrix Regression Parse

Choose the Sort option, and you will see:

DATA-RANGE PRIMARY-KEY SECONDARY-KEY RESET GO QUIT

Select the Data-Range option (by pressing D or by highlighting Data-Range and then pressing RETURN). The screen will show this prompt:

ENTER DATA-RANGE:

The data range is the range containing the complete data base (except the field names in the top row). Enter A2..F19 (or use the arrow keys) to indicate the location of the data base.

Next, tell the program which item you wish to sort along. This item is known as the primary key. Move the pointer to the Primary Key option, press RETURN, and you will see:

PRIMARY SORT KEY:

In order to sort by population, set the primary key to be the column containing population; therefore, enter the range

	A	B	C	D	E	F
1	CITY	REGION	POP	HIGHTEM	LOWTEM	LOCATION
2	Atlanta	SE	2737	97	15	X
3	Baltimore	NE	2342	105	-7	BAY
4	Boston	NE	4110	98	1	OCN
5	Chicago	MW	8181	99	-22	LAKE
6	Cleveland	MW	2769	90	-17	LAKE
7	Dallas	SE	3766	106	10	X
8	Detroit	MW	4620	96	-21	RIV
9	Houston	SE	3641	98	20	CHAN
10	Los Angeles	SW	13770	96	41	OCN
11	Miami	SE	3001	96	44	OCN
12	Minneapolis	MW	2388	94	-25	RIV
13	New York	NE	17918	96	8	OCN/RIV
14	Philadelphia	NE	5963	94	-7	RIV
15	Pittsburgh	NE	2284	91	-15	RIV
16	San Francisco	SW	6042	100	34	OCN/BAY
17	Seattle	NW	2421	91	20	BAY
18	St. Louis	MW	2467	107	-6	RIV
19	Washington DC	NE	3734	97	3	RIV

DATA BASE MANAGEMENT

C2..C19. The computer will ask whether you wish to sort the items in ascending order or descending order. In order to show the populations with the largest city listed first, choose descending order (D); if you wish to alphabetize a list of words, choose ascending order (A) so the beginning of the alphabet will be listed first.

To execute the sorting process, select option Go. You will see what appears on page 144.

One note about the Sort command: Numbers are not sorted in the same manner as labels; the number 2 comes before the number 10, but the label "2" comes after the label "10". When sorting words, the program automatically adds blank spaces to the end of each word: for example, "cat" comes before "catalog"; when sorting numbers, the program automatically adds blank spaces to the left side of each word: _2 comes before 100.

Sometimes the computer comes across a tie during the sorting process. If you have specified a secondary key, the computer will break the tie (if possible), depending on the order of items in the secondary key.

SELECTION

There are times when you wish to look at specific records. Enter the command /DQ (Data Query) to choose the Query subcommand from the data menu. The screen will show:

Input Criterion Output Find Extract Unique Delete Reset Quit

First, specify the input range, which is the entire data base range, including the field names (A1..F19).

Second, specify the criterion for the selection. Find an open area of the worksheet. To select cities in the northeast region, enter this criterion into cells H1 and H2:

	H
1	REGION
2	NE

Cell H1, which contains the field name, must be at the top of the criterion list. The cell below it contains the specific element that you wish to look for. (If you wish to look at all cities that are *not* in the northeast, enter ~NE into cell H2.)

	A	B	C	D	E	F
1	CITY	REGION	POP	HIGHTEM	LOWTEM	LOCATION
2	New York	NE	17918	96	8	OCN/RIV
3	Los Angeles	SW	13770	96	41	OCN
4	Chicago	MW	8181	99	-22	LAKE
5	San Francisco	SW	6042	100	34	OCN/BAY
6	Philadelphia	NE	5963	94	-7	RIV
7	Detroit	MW	4620	96	-21	RIV
8	Boston	NE	4110	98	1	OCN
9	Dallas	SE	3766	106	10	X
10	Washington DC	NE	3734	97	3	RIV
11	Houston	SE	3641	98	20	CHAN
12	Miami	SE	3001	96	44	OCN
13	Cleveland	MW	2769	90	-17	LAKE
14	Atlanta	SE	2737	97	15	X
15	St. Louis	MW	2467	107	-6	RIV
16	Seattle	NW	2421	91	20	BAY
17	Minneapolis	MW	2388	94	-25	RIV
18	Baltimore	NE	2342	105	-7	BAY
19	Pittsburgh	NE	2284	91	-15	RIV

DATA BASE MANAGEMENT

At this point you have two options: extracting all records meeting this criterion and creating a new data base, or browsing through the original data base with the records meeting the criterion highlighted. After you have set the input range and the criterion range, choose the Find option. The screen will look like what is shown on page 146.

The first record meeting the criterion is highlighted—in this case, New York. If you now press the down arrow, the highlight bar will jump down to the next record meeting the criterion. Keep using the down arrow to highlight more records meeting the criterion. However, once you reach the last record meeting the criterion the down arrow key will not move the highlight bar down any further. You may also use the up arrow key to move up to the previous record matching the criterion. The find option is particularly important if you need to edit records meeting a certain criterion. A small marker will appear within the highlighted area to indicate which cell is active. You may move this marker to the left or the right with the arrow keys to edit the active cell.

Now suppose you wish to create a new data base containing only these selected records. First choose a blank area of the worksheet to contain the new data base, and then copy the row containing the record titles down to this area; in this case, copy the record titles to row 25, columns A to F. Now return to the submenu for the Data Query command:

Input Criterion Output Find Extract Unique Delete Reset Quit

You do not need to reenter the input range and the criterion range because they stay the same. Choose the Output command and enter A25..F25 in response to the prompt: Enter Output Range.

Now chose the Extract command, and the computer will copy the selected records with the result (see page 147).

You could have written this command sequence as a macro:

/CA1..F1~A25..F25~	copy record headings to output range
/DQ	enter data query command
IA1..F19~	set input range
CH1..H2~	set criterion range
OA25..F25~	set output range
E~	extract data meeting criterion

	A	B	C	D	E	F
1	CITY	REGION	POP	HIGHTEM	LOWTEM	LOCATION
2	New York	NE	17918	96	8	OCN/RIV
3	Los Angeles	SW	13770	96	41	OCN
4	Chicago	MW	8181	99	-22	LAKE
5	San Francisco	SW	6042	100	34	OCN/BAY
6	Philadelphia	NE	5963	94	-7	RIV
7	Detroit	MW	4620	96	-21	RIV
8	Boston	NE	4110	98	1	OCN
9	Dallas	SE	3766	106	10	X
10	Washington DC	NE	3734	97	3	RIV
11	Houston	SE	3641	98	20	CHAN
12	Miami	SE	3001	96	44	OCN
13	Cleveland	MW	2769	90	-17	LAKE
14	Atlanta	SE	2737	97	15	X
15	St.Louis	MW	2467	107	-6	RIV
16	Seattle	NW	2421	91	20	BAY
17	Minneapolis	MW	2388	94	-25	RIV
18	Baltimore	NE	2342	105	-7	BAY
19	Pittsburgh	NE	2284	91	-15	RIV

DATA BASE MANAGEMENT

	A	B	C	D	E	F
25	CITY	REGION	POP	HIGHTEM	LOWTEM	LOCATION
26	New York	NE	17918	96	8	OCN/RIV
27	Philadelphia	NE	5963	94	-7	RIV
28	Boston	NE	4110	98	1	OCN
29	Washington DC	NE	3734	97	3	RIV
30	Baltimore	NE	2342	105	-7	BAY
31	Pittsburgh	NE	2284	91	-15	RIV

This macro is not very general; it will work only if you have exactly the same cells in the input, criterion, and output range each time. Here is a more general macro:

/C{?}~{?}~	copy record headings to output range
/DQ	enter data query command
I{?}~	set input range
C{?}~	set criterion range
O{?}~	set output range
E~	extract data meeting criterion

Now, whenever the computer reaches the {?} during macro execution, it will wait for the user to enter the appropriate range (which can be done either by typing the coordinates of the range or by using the point feature). For this macro to work, you must have already defined the cells in the criterion range.

In some cases, you might not need to see all of the fields for the records that you copy. Choose which fields you wish to see, and copy those field names down to the first row of the output range. If you wish only to see the CITY, REGION, and POP fields, enter A25..C25 for the output range and call the Extract command; the screen will show:

	A	B	C
25	CITY	REGION	POP
26	New York	NE	17918
27	Philadelphia	NE	5963
28	Boston	NE	4110
29	Washington DC	NE	3734
30	Baltimore	NE	2342
31	Pittsburgh	NE	2284

What if you want to look at all the cities in either the northeast or the southeast? In that case you need to specify two different criteria connected by the word OR: select either northeast OR southeast. Add SE to the criterion range below NE:

	H
1	REGION
2	NE
3	SE

DATA BASE MANAGEMENT

Now change the criterion range to H1..H3. You do not have to reenter the input range as long as it has not changed. Erase the data base you created with the previous step by using this command sequence: /REA25..F31. (You should always erase the old data base range if you are planning to extract some new data cells into that range so they don't become mixed up with each other.) Call the Extract command as shown on page 150.

There are several other ways of combing criteria. If you wish to extract midwestern cities located on rivers, set up the selection criteria this way:

	H	I
1	REGION	LOCATION
2	MW	RIV

Enter the criterion range as H1..I2, call the Extract command, and the cities Detroit, St. Louis, and Minneapolis will be extracted.

Note the difference between arranging the criteria sideways and vertically. When the criteria are arranged sideways, they act as if they are connected by the word AND; thus, the criteria range above means: "Select records that meet both of these two conditions: the region is MW, AND the location is RIV."

When the criteria are arranged vertically, they act as if they are connected by the word OR. Thus, the criteria range

	H
1	REGION
2	NE
3	SE

means: "Select records that meet either one of these two conditions: the region is NE, OR the region is SE."

Suppose you wish to select cities that are either in the northeast or located along rivers. Set up the criteria range H1..I3 as follows:

	H	I
1	LOCATION	REGION
2		NE
3	RIV	

	A	B	C	D	E	F
25	CITY	REGION	POP	HIGHTEM	LOWTEM	LOCATION
26	New York	NE	17918	96	8	OCN/RIV
27	Philadelphia	NE	5963	94	-7	RIV
28	Boston	NE	4110	98	1	OCN
29	Dallas	SE	3766	106	10	X
30	Washington DC	NE	3734	97	3	RIV
31	Houston	SE	3641	98	20	CHAN
32	Miami	SE	3001	96	44	OCN
33	Atlanta	SE	2737	97	15	X
34	Baltimore	NE	2342	105	-7	BAY
35	Pittsburgh	NE	2284	91	-15	RIV

DATA BASE MANAGEMENT

Because RIV and NW are not on the same line, the computer will treat these criteria as if they are separated by OR (instead of AND). It will therefore select New York, Philadelphia, Detroit, Boston, Washington, D.C., St. Louis, Minneapolis, Baltimore, and Pittsburgh.

If you had put the criteria on the same line:

	H	I
1	LOCATION	REGION
2	RIV	NE

the computer would have selected only Philadelphia, Washington, D.C., and Pittsburgh, since those are the only cities that meet the criteria of being both in the northeast and located along rivers.

However, you should note that New York also meets the criterion of being on a river. In some cases a record fits into more than one category for a particular field. In this database, there are two cities that fit into two location categories: New York is by both a river and an ocean, and San Francisco is by both a bay and an ocean. Both applicable location entries have been included in the data base for these cities. In order to locate all cities on oceans, you need to set up the criteria so that the computer looks through the records to see if the characters OCN occur anywhere in the field. To do that, you can use the @FIND function, which searches through one string to determine the location of another given string. The expression @FIND("OCN",F2,0) looks for the string OCN within cell F2, starting at character position 0. If it does not find that string, then the result is ERR. If you write this expression:

@ISERR(@FIND("OCN",F2,0))

the result is the logical value TRUE if the @FIND function fails to find OCN within cell F2, and FALSE otherwise. This is the reverse of what you want, so you need to include #NOT# at the start of the logical expression. Therefore, enter the criteria range as follows:

	H
1	LOCATION
2	#NOT#@ISERR(@FIND("OCN",F2,0))

When you enter a logical formula such as this as a criterion, use a cell reference to the field in the first record when you wish to refer to a particular field. In this case, cell F2 is used to represent the location field. In order to see the display of the logical formula instead of the logical value 1 or 0 that is the result of the formula evaluation, use the Range Format Text command to format cell H2 to text mode and the Worksheet Column Set-Width command to increase the width of this column.

Enter the criteria range as H1..H2, call the Extract command, and all records containing the characters OCN in column F will be extracted (see page 153).

You will often want to select records according to whether their field value is greater or less than a specified value. Suppose, for example, you wish to look at all cities where the low temperature is greater than zero. Set up the criteria range as follows:

	H
1	LOWTEM
2	+E2>0

Again, cell H2 must be formatted to text format for the formula to be displayed. E2 is the first cell in the column containing the low temperature data. This cell reference must be entered as a relative address. If you wish to select cities whose low temperature was greater than a value specified in another cell, such as J3, enter that cell in the formula as an absolute address: +E2>$J$3.

Now when the Extract command is called, the cities with low temperatures greater than zero will be selected: New York, Los Angeles, San Francisco, Boston, Washington, D.C., Houston, Dallas, Miami, Atlanta, and Seattle.

You may use these symbols when entering criteria: = equal; < less than; <= less than or equal; > greater than; >= greater than or equal; <> not equal (less than or greater than).

Suppose you wish to look at all cities whose metropolitan

DATA BASE MANAGEMENT

	A	B	C	D	E	F
25	CITY	REGION	POP	HIGHTEM	LOWTEM	LOCATION
26	New York	NE	17918	96	8	OCN/RIV
27	Los Angeles	SW	13770	96	41	OCN
28	San Francisco	SW	6042	100	34	OCN/BAY
29	Boston	NE	4110	98	7	OCN
30	Miami	SE	3001	96	44	OCN

area population is between three million and six million. Enter the criteria as follows:

```
     H
1  | POP
2  | (C2>3000)#AND#(C2<6000)
```

Call the Extract command, and the cities Philadelphia, Detroit, Boston, Dallas, Washington, D.C., Houston, and Miami will be selected.

The specific criteria to use when analyzing a data base depend on the question you are investigating. Data base management operations provide a powerful, flexible way for you to get the information that you need.

FREQUENCY DISTRIBUTION TABLE

Suppose you would like to know how many cities are very cold, how many are medium cold, and so on. You need to tabulate a frequency distribution table. To do this, imagine that you have a series of bins corresponding to each category that you are interested in. For example, one bin consists of all temperatures less than -20, another consists of all temperatures from -20 to -10, and so on. Then imagine that you throw each record into the appropriate bin. When you are done, you count the number of records in each bin. That is what a frequency table does. To create the frequency table, move to a blank area of the worksheet and enter the upper value for each bin:

```
        A
22  |  -20
23  |  -10
24  |    0
25  |   10
26  |   20
27  |   30
28  |
```

Enter this command: /DATA DISTRIBUTION
The computer will show this prompt:

DATA BASE MANAGEMENT

ENTER VALUES RANGE:

Type E2..E19, since that is the range containing the low temperature data. Next, the computer will prompt:

ENTER BIN RANGE:

Type A22..A27, the range containing the upper limit for each bin. The result is:

	A	B
22	-20	3
23	-10	2
24	0	3
25	10	4
26	20	3
27	30	0
28		3

The computer counted three cities with temperatures less than or equal to -20 (Chicago, Detroit, and Minneapolis); two cities with temperatures greater than -20 and less than or equal to -10 (Cleveland and Pittsburgh), and so on. Note that the last entry gives the number of records whose values were larger than the largest bin limit (in this case, Los Angeles, San Francisco, and Miami have temperatures higher than 30).

CHAPTER PERSPECTIVE

A data base contains an organized collection of facts. Fields are arranged in records, which are arranged in files. A computer data base program can process data to present you with useful information. Three common operations performed on data bases are sorting, selecting, and tabulating.

Investment Decisions

CHAP 10

INTRODUCTION AND MAIN POINTS

Many business decisions require spending money now in order to receive benefits in the future. Examples are the purchase of a capital asset and the purchase of a product to be held in inventory for sale at a later date. Business decision makers need to evaluate amounts of money received at different times. It should be clear that one dollar today is worth more than one dollar received in the future; if you had the dollar today, you could put it in the bank and end up with more than one dollar in the future. This comes about not because of some magic of banking but because capital goods today can produce goods now and so are worth more than capital goods in the future.

However, if you had a choice between one dollar today and two dollars one year from now, it would be better to choose the two dollars one year from now. Where do you draw the line? You need to be able to compare the value of amounts of money arriving at different times, using the concept of *present value*.

After studying the material in this chapter:

— You will understand the formula for present value, and you will see how a spreadsheet can be used to calculate present values for investment projects.

— You will know how to calculate the internal rate of return for an income stream.

— You will know how to calculate the present value of an annuity.

— You will know how to create a table for home mortgage payments.

PRESENT VALUE

Suppose interest is compounded once each year at a rate of $r = .08$ (8 percent). This means that $100 today is worth the same as $108 one year from now; more generally, X dollars today is worth $X(1 + r)$ dollars one year from now. You can reverse that equation to show that X dollars one year from now is worth $X/(1 + r)$ today. The formula $X/(1 + r)$ gives the present value of that future amount. (Note that one dollar in the future is worth less than one dollar today even if there is no inflation. If there is inflation, the interest rate will tend to increase, magnifying the effect.)

If you put $100 in the bank and leave it for two years, you will have $108 at the end of the first year and $108(1 + .08) = 100(1 + .08)^2 = 116.64$. at the end of the two years. After three years, you will have $100(1 + r)^3$. In general, the amount at the end of each year will be $(1 + .08)$ times the amount you had at the end of the previous year. Therefore, $100 today is worth the same as $100(1 + r)^n$ at a period of time n years in the future.

The general formula for present value is:

Present value of X dollars received n years in the future:

$$\frac{X}{(1 + r)^n}$$

If the present value of the future earnings from an investment project is greater than the amount you must pay initially, then the investment is profitable. This type of calculation is conveniently performed on a spreadsheet program.

Suppose you have the opportunity to buy $50,000 worth of merchandise today to store in inventory. You will be able to sell this merchandise for $55,000 one year from now. In order to determine whether this is a good investment, you need to calculate the present value of the $55,000 worth of future earnings. Here is a spreadsheet:

	A	B	C	D	E
1	Yrs in Future	Amount	Present Value		Int Rate
2		1 $55,000.00	$50,925.93		0.08

Enter the amount received in cell B2, and enter the interest rate into cell E2 either as a decimal fraction (0.08) or as a percent (8%). The display of the interest rate on the screen depends on how you format the cell. If you format the cell using percent format the rate will be shown as a percentage; otherwise, it will be shown as a decimal fraction. After entering the value, use the /RNC command to assign the name R to this cell.

Enter this formula into cell C2:

$$+B2/(1+\$R)$$

The screen will display the present value amount: $50,925.93. This means that it is a good investment to obtain this merchandise today at a cost of $50,000. If the cost of the merchandise rises above $50,925.93, you would not wish to purchase it because you would do better putting the money in the bank and collecting the 8 percent interest.

What if you don't have $50,000 today but can borrow that amount at 8 percent? It would still be profitable to purchase the merchandise at any price less than $50,925.93, because you will earn enough to pay back the interest on the loan and still have some left over. The general rule for an investment project is the same whether you must borrow the money or spend money you already have: If the present value of the future earnings is greater than the initial cost, it is a profitable project. If you are borrowing the money, then the interest rate to use in the present value formula is the rate that you will be charged on the borrowed money; if you already have the money, use the interest rate that you could obtain on your best alternative investment, such as purchasing securities. In reality, the rate you must pay when you borrow is almost certainly higher than the interest rate you may obtain by lending your funds.

Suppose that you suddenly discover that the interest rate will be 12 percent, instead of 8 percent. Again you can see the power of spreadsheets, since you merely change the number in the cell containing the interest rate; the computer will automatically calculate the new present value: 55,000/1.12 = 49,107.14. In this case you would not want to purchase the merchandise at a price of $50,000. A higher value of interest rate always reduces the attractiveness of an investment project that requires an initial expenditure with earnings in the future.

Although an investment project is profitable if the present value of the future earnings exceeds the initial cost, this does not mean that business decision making is simple. The future earnings figures (as well as the future interest rates) are only estimates. The hard part of decision making comes when you

INVESTMENT DECISIONS

need to form these estimates. You should be careful to avoid being misled by the precise numbers that come from the spreadsheet program; the results are no better than the estimates that were used. Still, you should understand the present value rules so you at least know the right criterion to use for judging a project.

In the case of a more complicated investment project, you receive amounts spread out over more than one period. Suppose you are considering the purchase of an ice cream factory at a cost of $75,000. This factory lasts six years before it self-destructs with no salvage value. You have estimated the profits that you will make from the sale of ice cream produced by the machine during each of the next six years: 12,000, 15,000, 17,000, 18,000, 18,500, and 20,000. You have entered these numbers into the spreadsheet:

	A	B	C	D	E
1	Yrs in Future	Amount			Int Rate
2	1	$12,000.00			0.08
3	2	$15,000.00			
4	3	$17,000.00			
5	4	$18,000.00			
6	5	$18,500.00			
7	6	$20,000.00			

You could add up the total amount of the future earnings, but this would yield an erroneous result, since amounts further into the future are worth less (or, put another way, need to be discounted more). In order to calculate the present value of each of these future amounts, assign the name N to cell A2 and enter this formula into cell C2: +B2/(1+$R)^N. (The ^ symbol represents exponentiation.) Copy this formula down to cells C2 to C7. You now understand 1-2-3 well enough to predict that the formula in cell C3 will be +B3/(1+$R)^A3. To find the present value for the complete stream of future earnings, add together each of these present value amounts by entering this formula into cell C9: @SUM(C2..C7). The computer displays the result: $75,891.06. You can see that the $75,000 ice cream factory is a profitable investment.

	A	B	C	D	E
1	Yrs in Future	Amount	Present Value		Int Rate
2		1 $12,000.00	$11,111.11		0.08
3		2 $15,000.00	$12,860.08		
4		3 $17,000.00	$13,495.15		
5		4 $18,000.00	$13,230.54		
6		5 $18,500.00	$12,590.79		
7		6 $20,000.00	$12,603.39		
8			————————		
9			$75,891.06		

Since you will often perform this type of calculation in business, you would expect Lotus 1-2-3 to provide an @ function to accomplish this task. The function @NPV requires two arguments. The first argument is the value of the interest rate (in this case, you have assigned the name R to this quantity). The second argument gives the range of cells that represent the future earnings. The first cell in the range gives the amount that you will be receiving at the end of the first year, the second cell gives the amount at the end of the second year, and so on. The easy way to calculate the present value of the investment project is to design the spreadsheet like this:

	A	B	C	D	E
1	Yrs in Future		Amount			Int Rate
2		1 $12,000.00			0.08
3		2 $15,000.00			
4		3 $17,000.00			
5		4 $18,000.00			
6		5 $18,500.00			
7		6 $20,000.00			
8					
9	Present Value of earnings:	$75,891.06			
10	Initial cost:	$75,000.00			
11	Net present value:	$891.06			

Enter this formula into cell B9:

@NPV($R,B2..B7)

INVESTMENT DECISIONS

Note that the result 75,891.06 is the same when you did it the long way. It is common to refer to the difference between the present value of the future earnings and the initial cost as the *net present value* (which is 891.06 in this example). There is one unfortunate feature of the Lotus 1-2-3 notation; the @NPV function in 1-2-3 gives only the present value of the future earnings (since the first cell in the range gives the earnings at the end of the first year); the net present value can be easily calculated by entering the value of the initial cost into a cell (B10 in this example) and then creating a new cell to give the net present value (B11 in this example).

In the examples so far, we have assumed that the interest is compounded once per year. The same formulas work if the compounding period is different than one year, provided that you make the proper adjustments. If the interest rate is compounded each month, you must use the monthly interest rate (equal to the annual interest rate divided by 12), and the cells in the @NPV range must give the amount that you will earn at the end of each month.

INTERNAL RATE OF RETURN

Sometimes you wish to know the maximum interest rate that you could pay to borrow money and still make a profit on a project. The answer is given by a quantity called the *internal rate of return* of the investment project. If the interest rate equals the internal rate of return, you will just break even by investing in the project; if the internal rate of return is greater than the interest rate, the project is profitable. Technically, the internal rate of return is the value of the interest rate that would make the net present value of the investment project equal to zero.

You could find the internal rate of return by trial and error. Using the spreadsheet shown above, you could test different values of the interest rate until you find one that causes the net present value to be zero. For an investment project where you pay money now and receive money in the future, a higher interest rate always lowers the net present value. Therefore, if you insert a value for the interest rate and find the net present value is positive, you know that the internal rate of return is greater than that value; if the value you insert for the interest rate causes the net present value to be negative, you know the internal rate of return is less than that value. (If the income stream includes some negative values in the future, it is possible for there to be more than one value for the interest rate that causes the net present value to be zero. In that case, the internal rate of return does not provide a reliable guide for decision making.)

The trial-and-error process for finding the internal rate of return can be time-consuming, but again the 1-2-3 program anticipates a common task and provides a built-in procedure for doing the calculation. The @IRR function requires two arguments: an initial guess for the internal rate of return and the range of cells containing the future income receipts. The first cell in the range represents the amount of the initial payment, which must be entered as a negative number. (This is different from the @NPV function, where the first cell in the range is the amount of the earnings at the end of the first year.) The computer requires you to enter an initial guess because it will in fact use a trial-and-error procedure to find the result; there is no formula that can be used. In some cases the computer is unable to find a result after a certain number of repetitions of the trial-and-error process, in which case it reports ERR as the result of the function. However, that does not happen for well-behaved investment projects with a negative amount for the first cell and positive amounts thereafter. And, as mentioned above, you should not use the internal rate of return in other cases.

Here is the spreadsheet for this case:

	A	B
1	Yrs in Future	Amount
2	0	($75,000.00)
3	1	$12,000.00
4	2	$15,000.00
5	3	$17,000.00
6	4	$18,000.00
7	5	$18,500.00
8	6	$20,000.00
9		
10		
11	IRR:	8.36%

Enter this formula into cell B11: @IRR(0.1,B2..B8). 0.1 is the value of your initial guess. The result for the internal rate of return is 8.36 percent. You previously found that this investment project has a small positive present value when the interest rate is 8 percent, so you know that the internal rate of return must be slightly greater than 8 percent.

THE PRESENT VALUE OF AN ANNUITY

Consider a simpler case where the future receipts are all the same (as is the case with a security paying a constant amount). The term *annuity* applies to such a stream of constant payments. For example, enter the amount 18,000 into cells B2 to B7 in the spreadsheet from page 160. The computer will calculate the present value: $83,211.83. There is an easier way to perform the calculations in the case where the future earnings are all the same: using the @PV function. The @PV function requires three arguments: the first gives the amount of the constant payment received each period, the second gives the interest rate, and the third gives the number of periods that you will receive this amount. Set up the spreadsheet as follows:

	A	B
1	Amount of payment:	$18,000.00
2	Interest rate:	0.08
3	Number of periods:	6
4	Present Value:	$83,211.83

Assign the name AMT to cell B1, the name R to cell B2, and the name N to cell B3. Enter this formula into cell B4:

@PV(AMT,R,N)

and the computer will automatically calculate the result.

HOME MORTGAGE PAYMENTS

Another common problem is calculating payments on a loan taken for a fixed period with fixed payments. Home mortgage payments are an example of such a situation, where the payments are typically made monthly for a period of 30 years. 1-2-3 provides the @PMT function that calculates the payment on a loan. The function requires three arguments: the initial principal amount (that is, the amount borrowed), the monthly interest rate, and the number of months to pay off the loan (360 for the case of a 30-year mortgage).

Set up this spreadsheet:

BARRON'S BUSINESS LIBRARY

	A	B
1	Principal:	$100,000
2	Years:	30
3	N:	
4	Annual Rate:	10.50%
5	R:	
6	Payment:	

To know the monthly payment if you borrow $100,000 on a 30-year fixed rate loan at 10.5 percent, enter the formula +B2*12 into cell B3. Assign the name PRINC to cell B1 and N to cell B3. Enter the annual interest rate into cell B4. Since the interest rate is compounded monthly you need to use the monthly interest rate in the formula for the payment. Enter this formula into cell B5: +B4/12. Then adjust the value of the annual interest rate, and the spreadsheet will calculate automatically the correct value for the monthly interest rate. Assign the name R to cell B5. Enter this formula into cell B6: @PMT(PRINC,R,N). The resulting value for the monthly payment is $914.74.

	A	B
1	Principal:	$100,000
2	Years:	30
3	N:	360
4	Annual Rate:	10.50%
5	R:	0.00875
6	Payment:	$914.74

To double-check the result, multiply the monthly interest rate times the principal amount ($875 in this example). The monthly payment figure should be slightly bigger than this figure, which it is in this case. In general, if there is an easy way to calculate an approximate result, you should do that in order to make sure that the result from your precise calculation is close to the true figure. In this way you can be sure that you are not off by a factor of 100 or some other such devastating amount.

You might wish to create a table showing how the monthly payment figure will vary for different values of the interest rate an the principal payment. Set up the spreadsheet as shown on page 165.

INVESTMENT DECISIONS

	A	B	C	D	E	F	G
1	N:	360	Home Mortgage Payment Table				
2					Principal		
3	Ann Rate	r	$100,000	$125,000	$150,000	$175,000	$200,000
4	8.00%	0.0067					
5	8.50%	0.0071					
6	9.00%	0.0075					
7	9.50%	0.0079					
8	10.00%	0.0083					
9	10.50%	0.0088					
10	11.00%	0.0092					
11	11.50%	0.0096					
12	12.00%	0.0100					
13	12.50%	0.0104					
14	13.00%	0.0108					
15	13.50%	0.0113					

Assign the name N to cell B1, the number of months. Enter the various values for the principal amount as shown in row 3, and enter the values for the annual interest rate as shown in column A. The monthly interest rate is calculated in column B. Enter the formula +A4/12 into cell B4 and copy that formula down to the other cells in column B. We have shown the values for the monthly interest rate formatted with four decimal places, but you should remember that the computer's memory keeps track of more decimal places than it displays. (The resulting figures would not be as accurate if the computer used only four decimal places during the course of its calculation.)

Enter this formula into cell C4: @PMT(C$3,$B4,$N). Note carefully the placement of the dollar signs; this formula is trickier than those used previously. The $ before the N means that the third argument always refers to the value of N in cell B1, no matter where you copy the formula to. The first argument of the @PMT function is the principal amount, which always comes from row 3, so you need to put the dollar sign in front of the 3. However, the principal amount does not always come from column C (you take the principal amount from column D, E, F, or G). Therefore, do not put a dollar sign in front of the C.

The second argument of the @PMT function gives the interest rate amount. Since this value always comes from column B, put the dollar sign in front of B. However, since it does not always come from row 4, do not put the dollar sign in front of the 4.

Copy the formula in cell C4 to the range C4..G15. The result is on page 167.

Move the pointer to cell D4, and you will see this formula: @PMT(D$3,$B4,$N). Move to cell C5, and you will see this formula: @PMT(C$3,$B5,$N).

1-2-3 provides another way to create a two-way table such as this. Set up the labels for the rows and columns (see page 168).

Enter this formula into cell B3 (the upper left-hand corner of the table: @PMT(A2,B2,$N). A2 and B2 represent temporary storage locations. Now execute this command: /DT2 (Data Table 2). The computer will ask:

ENTER TABLE RANGE:

INVESTMENT DECISIONS

360 Home Mortgage Payment Table
Principal

	A	B	C	D	E	F	G
	Ann Rate	r	$100,000	$125,000	$150,000	$175,000	$200,000
1	8.00%	0.0067	$733.76	$917.21	$1,100.65	$1,284.09	$1,467.53
2	8.50%	0.0071	$768.91	$961.14	$1,153.37	$1,345.60	$1,537.83
3	9.00%	0.0075	$804.62	$1,005.78	$1,206.93	$1,408.09	$1,609.25
4	9.50%	0.0079	$840.85	$1,051.07	$1,261.28	$1,471.49	$1,681.71
5	10.00%	0.0083	$877.57	$1,096.96	$1,316.36	$1,535.75	$1,755.14
6	10.50%	0.0088	$914.74	$1,143.42	$1,372.11	$1,600.79	$1,829.48
7	11.00%	0.0092	$952.32	$1,190.40	$1,428.49	$1,666.57	$1,904.65
8	11.50%	0.0096	$990.29	$1,237.86	$1,485.44	$1,733.01	$1,980.58
9	12.00%	0.0100	$1,028.61	$1,285.77	$1,542.92	$1,800.07	$2,057.23
10	12.50%	0.0104	$1,067.26	$1,334.07	$1,600.89	$1,867.70	$2,134.52
11	13.00%	0.0108	$1,106.20	$1,382.75	$1,659.30	$1,935.85	$2,212.40
12	13.50%	0.0113	$1,145.41	$1,431.77	$1,718.12	$2,004.47	$2,290.82

	A	B	C	D	E	F	G
1	N:	360	Home Mortgage Payment Table				
2					Principal		
3	Ann Rate		$100,000	$125,000	$150,000	$175,000	$200,000
4	8.00%	0.0067					
5	8.50%	0.0071					
6	9.00%	0.0075					
7	9.50%	0.0079					
8	10.00%	0.0083					

Type in B3..G15; this is the entire range for the table, including the row and column headings. Next, the computer will ask:

ENTER INPUT CELL 1:

Type in B2. The computer will look through the range of the row labels (.0067, .0071, and so on), copy each value one at a time to cell B2, and then calculate the result of your formula (where B2 is given as the second argument to the @PMT function—that is, the interest rate). Next, the computer will ask:

ENTER INPUT CELL 2:

Type in A2. The computer will copy each of the column headings one at a time to cell A2, which is used as the first argument of the @PMT function in your formula—that is, the initial principal amount. When the computer has paired each of the given interest rate values with each of the given principal values and displayed the result in the correct cell, it will have constructed a table identical to the one on page 167.

The monthly payment on a home mortgage is divided into two parts: the interest payment and the principal reduction payment. The interest payment is equal to the interest rate times the remaining principal balance. After the interest payment is calculated, the remaining payment amount is used to reduce the principal. In the early years of the mortgage, the interest payment consumes almost all of the payment amount, and the remaining principal balance declines very slowly. As time passes, the interest payment lessens and the principal payment increases, so the remaining balance declines at a faster rate. If you have borrowed money for a home, it can be depressing to see how slowly the remaining balance declines in the early years, although there is a silver lining since the interest payment is tax deductible.

On page 170 you will find an example of a spreadsheet that shows the amount of the principal reduction each month.

Assign the name N to cell A2 (the number of months the loan will last), PRINC to cell B4 (the initial principal balance—that is, the amount borrowed), and R to cell D2 (the monthly interest rate, found by dividing the annual interest rate by 12). Enter these formulas into the appropriate cells:

E2: @PMT(PRINC,R,N) the amount of the monthly payment (assign the name PAY to cell E2)

	A	B	C	D	E
1	Months	Int Rate:	Annual:	0.105	Payment
2	360		Monthly:	0.00875	$914.74
3					
4	Month	Princ.Bal	Int.Paym.	Princ.Pay.	
5	1	$100,000.00			
6	2				

INVESTMENT DECISIONS

	A	B	C	D	E
1	Months	Int Rate:	Annual:	0.105	Payment
2	360		Monthly:	0.00875	$914.74
3					
4	Month	Princ.Bal	Int.Paym.	Princ.Bal	
5		$100,000.00			
6	1	$99,960.26	$875.00	$39.74	$10,476.37
7	2	$99,920.17	$874.65	$40.09	
8	3	$99,879.74	$874.30	$40.44	
9	4	$99,838.94	$873.95	$40.79	
10	5	$99,797.80	$873.59	$41.15	
11	6	$99,756.29	$873.23	$41.51	
12	7	$99,714.42	$872.87	$41.87	
13	8	$99,672.18	$872.50	$42.24	
14	9	$99,629.57	$872.13	$42.61	
15	10	$99,586.59	$871.76	$42.98	
16	11	$99,543.23	$871.38	$43.36	
	12	$99,499.50	$871.00	$43.74	

BARRON'S BUSINESS LIBRARY

	A	B	C	D
552	348	$10,377.24	$97.95	$816.79
553	349	$9,553.30	$90.80	$823.94
554	350	$8,722.15	$83.59	$831.15
555	351	$7,883.73	$76.32	$838.42
556	352	$7,037.98	$68.98	$845.76
557	353	$6,184.82	$61.58	$853.16
558	354	$5,324.20	$54.12	$860.62
559	355	$4,456.05	$46.59	$868.15
560	356	$3,580.30	$38.99	$875.75
561	357	$2,696.89	$31.41	$883.41
562	358	$1,805.74	$23.69	$891.14
563	359	$906.80	$15.80	$898.94
564	360	($0.00)	$7.93	$906.80

172

C5: + $R*B4 the amount of the interest payment
D5: + $PAY-C5 the remaining payment available for principal reduction
B5: +B4-D5 the new value of the principal

Copy these formulas down for a total of 360 rows, and you will see the monthly decline in the principal balance. The first and last months of the complete table are shown on pages 171—172.

Just as it should, the principal balance is reduced to zero at the end of the 360 months.

It is also useful to calculate the total amount of interest paid during a year, since that amount is deductible from income taxes. Enter this formula into cell E5:

$$@SUM(C5..C16)$$

to find the interest payment for the first year (assuming that the loan started in January; if it started in another month you need to adjust the range so that it covers one complete calendar year).

DEPRECIATION

An important principle of accounting states that income and expenditures should be recorded at the time they actually affect the business, which is not necessarily the same time that cash changes hands. If you spend $1 million on a capital investment, it is very misleading to report a $1 million expense this year and no expense in the future when you are using the capital good. On the other hand, it is misleading to list the asset at its initial value during its entire life and then suddenly record it as vanishing at the end. A capital good wears out as it is used, and the amount that it wears out (called *depreciation*) should be recorded as an expense each year. In practice it is difficult to determine the precise amount by which a capital good has worn out during a year, so standard rules are used instead. Three possible methods are the straight-line method (which assumes that there is an equal amount of depreciation during the entire life of the good), the double-declining-balance method, and the sum-of-years-digits method (see a book on accounting for more information). Since depreciation calculations are commonly needed in spreadsheets, 1-2-3 provides built-in functions to perform these calculations. Here is a spreadsheet that shows alternative treatment of depreciation for a capital good that has

BARRON'S BUSINESS LIBRARY

an initial cost of $100,000 and a useful life of eight years, at which time it will be scrapped and sold for a $15,000 salvage value.

	A	B	C	D	E	F
1		Alternative depreciation methods					
2	Initial Cost:		$100,000.00		Life:	8
3	Salvage:		$15,000.00			
4						
5	Period		SLN	DDB	SYD	
6	1					
7	2					
8	3					
9	4					
10	5					
11	6					
12	7					
13	8					

Assign the name ICOST to cell C2, SALV to cell C3, and LIFE to cell F2. Column B gives the amount of depreciation each year using straight-line depreciation. Enter this formula to cell B6:

@SLN($ICOST,$SALV,$LIFE)

and copy it down to cells B6..B13. Note that the @SLN function requires three arguments: the initial cost of the capital good, the salvage value, and the useful life of the capital good. With this method the amount of depreciation is the same each year. Column C gives the depreciation figure each year using the double-declining-balance method. Enter this formula into cell C6:

@DDB($ICOST,$SALV,$LIFE,A6).

The @DDB function requires four arguments. The first three are the same as with @SLN; the fourth argument gives the period for which you wish to calculate the depreciation amount. (There is no need to specify the period with @SLN, because the depreciation is the same each period.)

Column D gives the depreciation figure using the sum-of-years-digits method. Enter this formula to cell D6:

	A	B	C	D	E	F
1	Alternative depreciation methods					
2	Initial Cost:		$100,000.00		Life: 8	
3	Salvage:		$15,000.00			
4						
5	Period	SLN	DDB	SYD		
6	1	$10,625.00	$25,000.00	$18,888.89		
7	2	$10,625.00	$18,750.00	$16,527.78		
8	3	$10,625.00	$14,062.50	$14,166.67		
9	4	$10,625.00	$10,546.88	$11,805.56		
10	5	$10,625.00	$7,910.16	$9,444.44		
11	6	$10,625.00	$5,932.62	$7,083.33		
12	7	$10,625.00	$2,797.85	$4,822.22		
13	8	$10,625.00	$0.00	$2,361.11		
14						
15		$85,000.00	$85,000.00	$85,000.00		

@SYD($ICOST,$SALV,$LIFE,A6)

The arguments are the same as with @DDB.

Note that the sum of the depreciation amounts is $85,000 in each case and the sum of the depreciation amounts plus the salvage value equals the initial cost (see page 175).

For tax purposes you need to calculate depreciation using the current rules set forth by the government. It is to the business's advantage to depreciate larger amounts earlier, since that has the effect of postponing the payment of taxes.

CHAPTER PERSPECTIVE

In order to make investment decisions, you need to be able to compare amounts of money received at different times using the formula for present value. This is the type of calculation for which computer spreadsheets are very helpful.

Budget Information for Large Organizations

CHAPTER
11

INTRODUCTION AND MAIN POINTS
Suppose your organization has been very successful and has grown much more complex. Budgeting is now more complicated, and it is no longer possible for one person to monitor the spending of the entire organization. The computer can help keep track of spending. As with any use of the computer, ask yourself what information you need to help you make your decisions and then figure out how the computer can help you process that information. For large organizations there are several different dimensions along which you might wish to classify budget data.

After studying the material in this chapter:
- You will recognize four different dimensions of budget data.
- You will be familiar with different ways of arranging budget data, depending on the question you need to investigate.

CLASSIFYING BUDGET DATA BY FUNCTION, TIME, LOCATION, AND OBJECT
In the example of a simple organization presented in Chapters 7 and 8, we looked at budget data classified according to one dimension: the function of the spending. For larger organizations additional information about each transaction should be recorded. These are:
- The function of the expenditure. In our previous work with simpler budgets, the function was indicated by the account number.
- The time that the expenditure occurred.
- The location where the spending took place. As your organization becomes larger, you will probably have more than one geographic location. Some of these may be copies of each other (as are the branches at a bank, where each location performs the same functions as the other branches). Other locations may be specialized (for example, you may have a factory to produce basic components at one location and a second location

that assembles the finished product). In either case, you will sometimes wish to analyze budget data separately for each location; at other times you will wish to consolidate data, combing all locations or having the various locations consolidated into regions. To do this, the locations need to be arranged in a hierarchy.

— The object being purchased. Each item is represented by an object code. For example, personnel, one example of an object category, may be broken down into a hierarchy (secretarial, production, administrative, and so on). Other object codes represent the purchase of supplies (which can be broken down further); electricity; and so on. You can also keep track of the vendor from whom the object was purchased; supplies bought from Brand X company would have a different object code than those from Brand Y.

Classifying expenditures by object is not the same as classification by function. If you hire an accountant for your retail division and an accountant for your manufacturing division, they perform different functions although they both fit into the same object code of personnel, that is, accountants.

EXAMPLE OF BUDGET CLASSIFICATION: THE U.S. GOVERNMENT

For an example of a very large, complicated organization, consider the U.S. government. Federal government expenditures are classified according to the following hierarchy of function and subfunction:

		Spending—Fiscal 1989 (millions)
050	National Defense	303,559
051	Military	294,880
053	Atomic energy defense activities	8,119
054	Defense-related activities	560
150	International Affairs	9,574
151	International development and humanitarian assistance	4,837
152	International security assistance	1,467
153	Conduct of foreign affairs	2,886

BUDGET INFORMATION FOR LARGE ORGANIZATIONS

154	Foreign information and exchange activities	1,106
155	International financial programs	-722
250	General Science, Space, and Technology	12,838
251	General science and basic research	2,642
253	Space flight	6,336
254	Space, science, applications, and technology	2,787
255	Supporting space activities	1,073
270	Energy	3,702
271	Energy supply	2,226
272	Energy conservation	333
274	Emergency energy preparedness	621
276	Energy information, policy, and regulation	521
300	Natural Resources and Environment	16,182
301	Water resources	4,271
302	Conservation and land management	3,324
303	Recreational resources	1,817
304	Pollution control and abatement	4,878
306	Other natural resources	1,890
350	Agriculture	16,948
351	Farm income stabilization	14,846
352	Agricultural research and services	2,102
370	Commerce and Housing Credit	27,719
400	Transportation	27,608
401	Ground transportation	17,946
402	Air Transportation	6,622
403	Water transportation	2,916
407	Other transportation	124
450	Community and Regional Development	5,361
451	Community development	3,693

452	Area and regional development	1,894
453	Disaster relief and insurance	-226
500	Education, Training, Employment, and Social Services	36,684
501	Elementary, secondary, and vocational education	9,193
502	Higher education	10,649
503	Research and general education aids	1,391
504	Training and employment	5,292
505	Other labor services	786
506	Social services	9,374
550	Health	48,390
551	Health-care services	39,164
552	Health research	7,325
553	Education and training of health-care work force	545
554	Consumer and occupational health and safety	1,356
570	Medicare	84,964
600	Income security	136,031
601	General retirement and disability insurance (except Social Security)	5,650
602	Federal employee retirement and disability	49,151
603	Unemployment compensation	15,616
604	Housing assistance	14,715
605	Food and nutrition assistance	21,192
609	Other income security	29,706
650	Social Security	232,542
700	Veterans Benefits and Services	30,066
750	Administration of Justice	9,422
751	Federal law enforcement activities	4,667

752	Federal litigative and judicial activities	3,255
753	Federal correctional activities	1,044
754	Criminal justice assistance	455
800	General government	9,124
801	Legislative functions	1,651
802	Executive direction and management	129
803	Central fiscal operations	5,570
804	General property and records management	-341
805	Central personnel management	134
806	General purpose fiscal assistance	2,061
808	Other general government	813
809	Deductions for offsetting receipts	-893
900	Net interest	169,137

Federal government spending is classified according to the following object codes:

10	Personal Services and Benefits
11	Personnel compensation
11.1	Full-time permanent
11.3	Other than full-time permanent
11.5	Other personnel compensation
12	Personnel benefits
13	Benefits for former personnel
20	Contractual Services and Supplies
21	Travel and transportation of persons
22	Transportation of things
23	Rental and miscellaneous
23.1	Rental payment to General Services Administration
23.2	Rental payment to others
23.3	Communication, utilities, and miscellaneous charges
24	Printing and reproduction
25	Other services

26	Supplies and materials
30	Acquisition of Capital Assets
31	Equipment
32	Land and structures
33	Investments and loans
40	Grants and Fixed Charges
41	Grants, subsidies, and contributions
42	Insurance claims and indemnities
43	Interest and dividends
44	Refunds

MULTIDIMENSIONAL BUDGET DATA

Consider a manufacturing firm that produces two products at four locations. Its budget data are classified according to three functions (111—manufacturing product one; 112—manufacturing product two; and 120—shipping); four locations (11—north; 12—south; 13—east; and 14—west); and five object codes (11—personnel; 12—raw materials; 13—fuel; 14—electricity; and 15—factory rental). Each item is identified by a number. An expenditure transaction is identified by an account number containing three segments (function, location, and object). For example, the journal entry

112–13–14 $256

means that $256 was spent on electricity (object code 14) at the east location (location code 13) for the manufacture of product two (function code 112).

We will look at budget data for only two time periods (the first and second quarters). When you summarize these data, you will have an array with four dimensions (function, time, location, and object). We have already looked at two-dimensional arrays (a traditional spreadsheet), with rows along one dimension and columns along the other dimension. In the next chapter we will see three-dimensional spreadsheets, which consist of several pages of two-dimensional worksheets and in which each cell is identified by three coordinates—row, column, and page number. We have an intuitive understanding of three-dimensional spreadsheets because we live in a three-dimensional world; it is much harder to picture a four-dimensional array. Think of a

BUDGET INFORMATION FOR LARGE ORGANIZATIONS

four-dimensional array as a bookcase full of books, each with its own number. Each book consists of page after page of spreadsheets. How would you find one particular cell? First, you would have to give the book number (dimension one), then you would have to give the page number (dimension two), then the row number (dimension three), and then the column number (dimension four).

Four-dimensional arrays tend to have a very large number of entries. For the example shown on pages 184–185, the complete array has $3 \times 2 \times 4 \times 5 = 120$ elements, which can be arranged in a series of six tables with four rows and five columns each.

Note that there is no spending on raw materials, electricity, or rent for the shipping function.

As we have noted before, a budget information system should be flexible so that you may look either at items in detail or at broad aggregates. Usually you will not want to look at the complete four-dimensional array at once because that would confront you with too much information. One of the major challenges of management today is to reduce the clutter of information overload and focus on the key issues. There are two ways to reduce the size of the array and rearrange the budget data to illustrate particular issues more clearly—either aggregate across one dimension or select only one specific item from one dimension. For example, suppose you wish to focus on the budget only in the first quarter. Then you have a three-dimensional array as appears on page 186.

You may also wish to change your view of the budget by rearranging the order of the dimensions. The best view depends on the question being investigated. If you wish to compare spending on the different objects among the different locations, the view above is the best. On the other hand, to compare spending on the different objects by the different functions, you should rearrange the data in this way (see pages 187–188).

If you wish to compare spending for the different functions at different locations without worrying about spending by object, you should aggregate across the object dimension. That will leave you with a two-dimensional array as follows on page 189.

Or, to compare spending by function and object without concentrating on the difference by location, aggregate across location and look at the two-dimensional array shown on page 190.

The task of rearranging the expenditure data array should be left to the computer. It cannot be done conveniently directly

QRT1

111:PROD1

11:PROD1	11:PERS	12:RWMTR	13:FUEL	14:ELECTR	15:RENT	TOTAL
11:NORTH	5423	2913	0	298	865	9499
12:SOUTH	2130	1987	0	175	216	4508
13:EAST	5188	2763	0	221	786	8958
14:WEST	4376	2333	0	433	112	7254
TOTAL	17117	9996	0	1127	1979	30219

111:PROD2

11:PROD2	11:PERS	12:RWMTR	13:FUEL	14:ELECTR	15:RENT	TOTAL
11:NORTH	5825	2456	0	233	846	9360
12:SOUTH	2330	1977	0	198	232	4737
13:EAST	5111	2463	0	213	745	8532
14,WEST	4678	2433	0	477	133	7721
TOTAL	17944	9329	0	1121	1956	30350

QRT2

112:PROD2

11:PROD2	11:PERS	12:RWMTR	13:FUEL	14:ELECTR	15:RENT	TOTAL
11:NORTH	9976	1914	0	458	234	12582
12:SOUTH	4555	1133	0	634	346	6668
13:WEST	6178	3743	0	321	454	10696
14:WEST	8766	1333	0	233	562	10894
TOTAL	29475	8123	0	1646	1596	40840

BUDGET INFORMATION FOR LARGE ORGANIZATIONS

112:PROD2	QRT2 11:PERS	12:RWMTR	13:FUEL	14:ELECTR	15:RENT	TOTAL
11:NORTH	3425	4456	0	253	876	9010
12:SOUTH	4530	1507	0	138	252	6427
13:EAST	7135	1562	0	253	645	9595
14:WEST	8600	2453	0	454	144	11651
TOTAL	23690	9978	0	1098	1917	36683

120:SHIP	QRT1 11:PERS	12:RWMTR	13:FUEL	14:ELECTR	15:RENT	TOTAL
11:NORTH	833	0	345	0	0	1178
12:SOUTH	754	0	211	0	0	965
13:EAST	978	0	398	0	0	1376
14:WEST	587	0	278	0	0	865
TOTAL	3152	0	1232	0	0	4384

120:SHIP	QRT2 11:PERS	12:RWMTR	13:FUEL	14:ELECTR	15:RENT	TOTAL
11:NORTH	825	0	375	0	0	1200
12:SOUTH	430	0	257	0	0	687
13:EAST	843	0	346	0	0	1189
14:WEST	367	0	258	0	0	625
TOTAL	2465	0	1236	0	0	3701

```
BUDGET QRT1
111:PROD1

            11:PERS  12:RWMTR  13:FUEL  14:ELECTR  15:RENT  TOTAL
11:NORTH     5423     2913       0        298       865    9499
12:SOUTH     2130     1987       0        175       216    4508
13:EAST      5188     2763       0        221       786    8958
14:WEST      4376     2332       0         43       112    7254
TOTAL       17117     9995       0       1127      1979   30219

BUDGET QRT1
112:PROD2

            11:PERS  12:RWMTR  13:FUEL  14:ELECTR  15:RENT  TOTAL
11:NORTH     9976     1914       0        458       234   12582
12:SOUTH     4555     1133       0        634       346    6668
13:EAST      6178     3743       0        321       454   10696
14:WEST      8766     1333       0        233       562   10894
TOTAL       29475     8123       0       1646      1596   40840

BUDGET QRT1
120:SHIP

            11:PERS  12:RWMTR  13:FUEL  14:ELECTR  15:RENT  TOTAL
11:NORTH      833       0      345         0         0    1178
12:SOUTH      754       0      211         0         0     965
13:EAST       978       0      398         0         0    1376
14:WEST       587       0      278         0         0     865
TOTAL        3152       0     1232         0         0    4384
```

BUDGET INFORMATION FOR LARGE ORGANIZATIONS

```
BUDGET QRT1
11:NORTH    11:PERS   12:RWMTR   13:FUEL   14:ELECTR   15:RENT   TOTAL
111:PROD1     5423      2918         0         298       865      9499
112:PROD2     9976      1914         0         458       234     12582
120:SHIP       833         0       345           0         0      1178
TOTAL        16232      4827       345         756      1099     23259

BUDGET QRT1
12:SOUTH    11:PERS   12:RWMTR   13:FUEL   14:ELECTR   15:RENT   TOTAL
111:PROD1     2130      1987         0         175       216      4508
112:PROD2     4555      1133         0         634       346      6668
120:SHIP       754         0       211           0         0       965
TOTAL         7439      3120       211         809       562     12141

BUDGET QRT1
13:EAST     11:PERS   12:RWMTR   13:FUEL   14:ELECTR   15:RENT   TOTAL
111:PROD1     5188      2763         0         221       786      8958
112:PROD2     6178      3743         0         321       454     10696
120:SHIP       978         0       398           0         0      1376
TOTAL        12344      6506       398         542      1240     21030
```

BUDGET QRT1 14:WEST	11:PERS	12:RWMTR	13:FUEL	14:ELECTR	15:RENT	TOTAL
111:PROD1	4376	2333	0	433	112	7254
112:PROD2	8766	1333	0	233	562	10894
120:SHIP	587	0	278	0	0	865
TOTAL	13729	3666	278	666	674	19013

BUDGET INFORMATION FOR LARGE ORGANIZATIONS

```
BUDGET QRT1 all OBJECT
             11:NORTH    12:SOUTH    13:EAST    14:WEST    TOTAL
111:PROD1       9499        4508       8958       7254     30219
112:PROD2      12582        6668      10696      10894     40840
120:SHIP        1178         965       1376        865      4384
TOTAL          23259       12141      21030      19013     75443
```

```
BUDGET QRT1 all LOCATION
            11:PERS   12:RWMTR   13:FUEL   14:ELECTR   15:RENT   TOTAL
111:PROD1   17117      9996         0       1127       1979      30219
112:PROD2   29475      8123         0       1656       1596      40840
20:SHIP      3152         0      1232          0          0       4384
TOTAL       49744     18119      1232       2783       3575      75443
```

with a spreadsheet program, but a programmer could write a program that performs these three functions:
- rearranging the order of the dimensions in an array
- aggregating across the last dimension
- selecting only one item from a particular dimension

Note that the last two options cause the number of dimensions in the array to be reduced by one.

You of course want to analyze the data using the spreadsheet program as you have done before; therefore, the program should be designed so that its results can be incorporated directly into the Lotus 1-2-3 worksheet. You will also want to compare actual spending with budget amounts, as discussed in Chapter 8. In fact, you could arrange the budget data as a five-dimensional array, with one dimension comprising the budget/actual/variance classification the remaining dimensions comprising function, time, location, and object. However, as we pointed out earlier, usually you will not want to develop budget amounts for every single detailed object code or function; instead, the budget amounts will focus on broader categories, so your comparisons of actual figures to budget figures will not occur at the fully detailed level that has been discussed in this chapter. See a book on budgeting systems for more information.

CHAPTER PERSPECTIVE
The record of a transaction should include at least function, time, location, and object. The budgetary information system should be sufficiently flexible so that a manager may look at the data in either aggregate form or in fine detail, and it should be possible to rearrange the presentation of the data depending on the issue currently being investigated.

REFERENCES
Budget of the United States Government, Fiscal Year 1991 (Washington, D.C.: Office of Management and Budget), 1990.

Three-Dimensional Spreadsheets

INTRODUCTION AND MAIN POINTS

If you have worked with large spreadsheets, you have probably noticed that it is awkward to know where to put things. If you were working on paper you would not put all your work on one gigantic sheet of paper; instead, you would use many different sheets and collect them in a notebook. It would help if you could use the same principle when working with electronic spreadsheets. Fortunately, software is constantly improving. Lotus 1-2-3 Release 3, along with some other new programs, allows you to create three-dimensional spreadsheets that contain several pages (also called sheets or worksheets); each page is similar to a worksheet in a two-dimensional spreadsheet, with data arranged in rows and columns. You can move up and down and left and right along each individual page, and you can move forward and backward to different pages.

After studying the material in this chapter:

— You will know how to create a multiple page spreadsheet in Lotus 1-2-3 Release 3.

— You will know how the group command can be used when you want all of the pages to have the same format.

— You will understand how to use Release 3 to link data from different files.

MULTIPLE WORKSHEET FILES

When you first start 1-2-3 Release 3, the screen will look like this:

THREE-DIMENSIONAL SPREADSHEETS

```
A:A1                                              READY
```

A	A	B	C	D	E	F	G	H
1								
2								
3								
4								
5								
6								
7								
8								
9								
10								
11								
12								
13								
14								
15								
16								

Notice that it looks very similar to the traditional two-dimensional spreadsheet; letters label each column and numbers label each row. The difference is that there are now letters to identify each page. The coordinates of an individual cell are written with the page letter first, followed by a colon, the column letter, and the row number. The top line of the screen gives the coordinates of the current cell: A:A1. The page letter A appears above the indicator for row 1.

If you use the arrow keys to move two columns right and three rows down, the indicator at the top of the screen will change to A:C4 (page A, column C, row 4). You can move around a single page in the same manner that you move around a two-dimensional spreadsheet.

Imagine that you have put one page of paper on your desk. This is similar to the situation when you first start 1-2-3 Release

3. To use additional pages, you must add more pages to the one on your desk. Similarly, in order to use a multiple-page spreadsheet in 1-2-3, you need to insert more pages. The command menu structure for Release 3 works in the same manner as in previous versions (although some new choices appear on the menu). When you press /WIS (for Worksheet Insert Sheet), the computer will prompt you to state whether you wish to add sheets before or after the current sheet. Choose after. Then the computer will ask you how many sheets to insert. Choose two. You have now created a three-page 1-2-3 spreadsheet.

Press the CONTROL key and the page up key simultaneously to move to the next sheet (in this case, sheet B). The screen will show:

B:A1   READY

B	A	B	C	D	E	F	G	H
1								
2								
3								
4								
5								
6								
7								
8								
9								

The coordinates of the current cell are now given as B:A1, and the page letter above the indicator for row 1 has now changed to B. Press CONTROL-PAGE DOWN if you wish to move back to the previous page.

You can use Release 3 the same as previous versions by putting everything on one giant page. However, it makes more sense to put different items on different pages. For example, if there is more than one table in a worksheet each table should

THREE-DIMENSIONAL SPREADSHEETS

be placed on a different page, particularly if you will be inserting or deleting rows or columns. These can be treacherous operations in a large two-dimensional spreadsheet—deleting a row deletes all cells in that row in the entire spreadsheet, so it affects any other information located in that same row anywhere else in the worksheet. Even worse, you will not even notice the problem until you happen to look at that other section of the worksheet.

EXAMPLE: ICE CREAM SHOP

In Chapter 3 we set up a spreadsheet to represent information about an ice cream shop. The different sections of the spreadsheet were located at different locations in the two-dimensional worksheet. Now we will look at the way this spreadsheet could have been arranged using Release 3, including additional information that allows you to determine whether this ice cream shop is likely to be a profitable investment (see Chapter 10).

Set up the cost information on page A as follows:

A	A	B	C	D	E	F
			Cost			
1						
2	Variable Cost		Labor Cost		Fixed Cost	
3	ice cream	0.50	wage	5.9	elect	200
4	cone	0.10	workers	2	phone	50
5	napkin	0.01	hours	360	insur.	75
6	AVC	0.61	LC	4248	FC	325

In cell B6 enter the formula @SUM(B3..B5); in cell D6 enter +D3*D4*D5; in cell F6 enter @SUM(F3..F5). Formulas can be entered in the same manner as in previous versions of 1-2-3. If all cells in the given range are on the same page as the formula, you need not include the page letter although you can if you want to, in which case the formula in cell B6 would have been written @SUM(A:B3..A:B5).

Page B contains the figures for revenue and profit:

BARRON'S BUSINESS LIBRARY

B	A	B	C	D	E
1		Revenue and Profit			
2	Price	Quantity	Revenue	Cost	Profit
3	$0.8				
4	$0.9				
5	$1.0				
6	$1.1				
7	$1.2				
8	$1.3				
9	$1.4				
10	$1.5				
11	$1.6				
12	$1.7				
13	$1.8				
14	$1.9				
15	$2.0				

Enter the values of the slope and intercept on page C:

C	A	B
1	Decision Making Variables	
2	Demand Function	
3	Slope:	−6200
4	Intcp:	16000

Now fill in the formulas on page B. To calculate the quantity, enter this formula into cell B:B3: +$C:$B$4+$C:$B$3*A3, where C:B4 is the cell containing the intercept and C:B3 is the cell containing the slope. The dollar signs are included to indicate absolute addresses. Note that no dollar sign is included with the cell reference to A3, since that cell will change when it is copied down to the other cells in the column. Also, note that it is not necessary to write B:A3 in the formula, since the computer automatically assumes that the cell is on the current page if it receives no indication to the contrary. Of course, the formula would be much easier to understand if the names SLOPE and INTCP had been assigned to the appropriate cells, as was done in Chapter 3. In this example we did not use names in formulas so you can see how cell coordinates are given for a three-dimensional spreadsheet.

THREE-DIMENSIONAL SPREADSHEETS

To calculate the cost column, enter this formula into cell B:D3:

+$A:$F$6+$A:$D$6+$A:$B$6*B3

Cell A:F6 represents the fixed cost; A:D6 represents the labor cost; and A:B6 represents the average variable cost. (Compare with the similar formula in Chapter 3.) B3 represents the quantity.

The columns for revenue and profit can easily be calculated from these formulas:
revenue: enter into cell B:C3: +A3*B3
profit: enter into cell B:E3: +C3−D3

The result after you have copied the formulas down to the remaining cells in each column is shown on page 198.

The remaining variables needed to make the decision about whether to do this investment are entered into page C (see page 199).

You must enter the values for slope, intercept, annual interest rate, number of years, and initial cost. The monthly interest is the annual interest rate divided by 12, and the number of months that the ice cream shop will be in business its life in years multiplied by 12. To calculate the maximum monthly profit, use the @MAX function. The range B:E3..B:E15 includes the profit figures on page B. Assuming that the monthly profits will be constant for the entire useful life of the project, you may use the @PV(AMNT,R,N) function (the present value of an annuity). Because the present value of the future earnings from this ice cream shop exceeds the initial cost, the net present value is positive and the shop would be a profitable investment.

If you wished to include macros in the spreadsheet; it would be convenient to put them on page D. For example:

D	A
1	Macros
2	Macro to format to currency format \C
3	/RFC{?}~{?}~

Several short macros can be put on the same page; a long macro can be put on a page by itself.

Revenue and Profit

	A	B	C	D	E
	Price	Quantity	Revenue	Cost	Profit
1	$0.8	11040	$8,832	$11,307.4	($2,475.4)
2	$0.9	10420	$9,378	$10,929.2	($1,551.2)
3	$1.0	9800	$9,800	$10,551.0	($751.0)
4	$1.1	9180	$10,098	$10,172.8	($74.8)
5	$1.2	8560	$10,272	$9,794.6	$477.4
6	$1.3	7940	$10,322	$9,416.4	$905.6
7	$1.4	7320	$10,248	$9,038.2	$1,209.8
8	$1.5	6700	$10,050	$8,660.0	$1,390.0
9	$1.6	6080	$9,728	$8,281.8	$1,446.2
10	$1.7	5460	$9,282	$7,903.6	$1,378.4
11	$1.8	4840	$8,712	$7,525.4	$1,186.6
12	$1.9	4220	$8,018	$7,147.2	$870.8
13	$2.0	3600	$7,200	$6,769.0	$431.0

THREE-DIMENSIONAL SPREADSHEETS

	A	B
1	Decision Making Variables	
2	Demand Function	
3	Slope:	-6200
4	Intcp:	16000
5		
6	Annual interest rate:	0.11
7	Monthly interest rate:	0.009167 <-enter formula: +B6/12
8		
9	Number of Years:	8
10	Number of Months:	96 <-enter formula: +B9*12
11		
12	Monthly Profit:	$1,446 <-enter formula: @MAX(B:E3..B:E15)
13		
14	Present Value of earnings:	$92,065 <-enter formula: @PV(B12,B7,B10)
15	Initial Cost:	$80,000
16	Net Present Value:	$12,065 <-enter formula: +B14-B15

BUDGETING FOR MULTIPLE DIVISIONS

Three-dimensional spreadsheets are even more helpful if your data are arranged in three dimensions. In the previous chapter we discussed how to arrange budget data into multiple dimension arrays. Now consider how to use a three-dimensional spreadsheet to develop the fuel budget of the expanded Easy Van Commuting Service, which now has three divisions. In our three-dimensional array, the pages represent the different divisions, the columns represent different months, and the rows represent different quantities needed in the calculation.

Use the /WISA (Worksheet Insert Sheet After) command to add four additional sheets to our spreadsheet. On page A, enter data that apply to the complete company (see page 201).

Assign the name CAP to cell A:B4; MPG to cell A:B5; and PRICE to cell A:B6.

Now develop the budget for the East division on page C as shown on page 202.

The basic structure of the worksheet is similar to the one in Chapter 4. Enter the numbers into cells B3 to B6. For cell C9, enter this formula: +$A:B$9. (The number of business days in January is given on page A, column B, row 9.) Copy this formula to cells D9..N9. Move the pointer to cell D9, and you will see the formula +$A:C$9. (The dollar signs work the same as before: A dollar sign means "do not change this part of the address no matter where you copy the formula.") By designing the worksheet in this manner you ensure that the number of business days per month on page C will be the same as that given on page A. This is important because the number of business days per month changes slightly each year. When you develop the budget for next year, you will need to change the relevant numbers on page A; the rest of the spreadsheet will reflect the changes automatically.

The rest of the formulas for column C are: cell C10: +C9*$B$3*$CAP (no. of days × no. of vans × van capacity)
cell C11: the estimated occupancy fractions are typed in
cell C12: +C10*C11 (capacity × occupancy fraction)
cell C13: +$PRICE*C12
          (price per ride × actual ridership)
cell C14: +2*$B$5*$B$3*C9+$B$6*C12
          (2 × highway miles × no. of vans × no. of days)
          + extra miles per passenger × actual ridership)
cell C15: +C14/$MPG

THREE-DIMENSIONAL SPREADSHEETS

	A	B	C	D	E	F	G	H	I	J	K	L	M
1		Easy Van Commuting Service Budget
2		Company Wide Data
3	
4	Capacity per van:	12
5	Fuel Use (MPG:)	14
6	Price per ride:	6
7	
8	Business Days:	Jan	Feb	Mar	Apr	May	Jun	Jly	Aug	Sep	Oct	Nov	Dec
9		21	19	22	21	22	21	21	23	19	23	21	20

Capacity per van:

201

	A	B	C	D	E	F	G
1			Budget—East Division				
2							
3	Number of Vans:	4					
4	Fuelcost-$/gal:	$1.30					
5	Highway Miles:	39					
6	Ext.m.per.pass:	1					
7							
8			Year	Jan	Feb	Mar	Apr	May
9	Days:						
10	Capacity:						
11	Occupancy		0.80	0.80	0.85	0.85	0.85
12	Actual:						
13	Revenue:						
14	Miles:						
15	Fuel Used:						
16	Fuel Cost:						

                    (total miles / miles per gallon)
cell C16: +$B$4*C15
                    (price of fuel × fuel used)

Use the Copy command to copy these formulas to the cells for the remaining months. Use the @SUM function to calculate the yearly totals for each row (the formula in cell B11 is B12/B10; you do not calculate the yearly occupancy fraction by adding the occupancy fraction from each month; instead, you divide the year's actual ridership by the year's capacity). The result appears on page 204.

Use /WGPE (Worksheet Global Protection Enable) to turn protection on and then unprotect cells C2 (the division name), B3..B6 (the data specific to this division), and cells C11..N11 (the occupancy fraction for this division). So far, everything is almost the same as it was in Chapter 4. Now you will see the power of the three-dimensional spreadsheet as you copy the page for this division to the pages for the other divisions and then enter the data specific for each of those divisions into the unprotected cells on those pages. The formulas and labels remain the same, so there is no need to reenter them; the protection feature prevents us from accidentally writing over one of the formulas.

The Copy command works almost the same as before. You may either type the ranges explicitly or use the point feature, although the point feature is more complicated because you cannot see the complete three-dimensional range on the screen. In this case, copy *from* C:A1..C:N16; copy *to* B:A1..E:N16, causing pages B, D, and E to become copies of page C. In order to make the appearance of each page identical, change the format for each of the other sheets. You are probably thinking that that will be a lot of work, since there are several different formats in use on the sheet and that it would be nice if the program automatically formatted all of the pages in the same way. With a little more thought, you may realize why you don't want 1–2–3 to format all pages the same way automatically—one of the advantages of the three-dimensional design is that the different pages can operate independently of each other. However, there are times when you would like the appearance of each page to be the same. In that case, use the /WGGE (Worksheet Global Group Enable) command, which causes every page to take on all of the formatting features of the current page. As long as the

	A	B	C	D	E	F	G
1		Budget—East Division					
2							
3	Number of Vans:	4					
4	Fuelcost-$/gal:	$1.30					
5	Highway Miles:	39					
6	Ext.m.per.pass:	1					
7							
8		Year	Jan	Feb	Mar	Apr	May
9	Days:	253	21	19	22	21	22
10	Capacity:	12,144	1,008	912	1,056	1,008	1,056
11	Occupancy:	0.80	0.80	0.80	0.85	0.85	0.85
12	Actual:	9,665	806	730	898	857	898
13	Revenue:	$57,989	$4,838	$4,378	$5,386	$5,141	$5,386
14	Miles:	88,601	7,358	6,658	7,762	7,409	7,762
15	Fuel Used:	6,329	526	476	554	529	554
16	Fuel Cost:	$8,227	$683	$618	$721	$688	$721

group command is in effect, operations such as inserting or deleting rows or columns affect every page.

You do not actually want page A to take on all of the formatting features of the remaining pages; therefore, turn group mode off (with /WGGD Worksheet Global Group Disable) and then format page A.

Press CONTROL-PAGE UP to move from page C to page D, and then enter the data for the West division into the unprotected cells. Then press CONTROL-PAGE UP to move to page E, and enter the data for the South division. Move the pointer around each of these pages so you can see how the copy command has affected the cell references. Note that most of the formulas entered into page C did not contain explicit page letters, so the spreadsheet automatically assumed that you meant to refer to the current page. When you copy these formulas to a new page, the computer assumes that the cell references refer to cells on that new page.

Now move to page B and change the label in cell C2 to "Complete Company." Most of the cells on this page consist simply of the @SUM function to total the results from the three divisions. Move to cell B:B10 and enter this formula: @SUM(C:B10..E:B10). Picture how the three-dimensional range specification works: C:B10..E:B10 refers to the range consisting of C:B10, D:B10, and E:B10. This formula combines the capacity from each division to calculate the total capacity for the company. Now use the Copy command to copy the formula from B10 to the complete range B10..N16. Move around the page to see how the cell references have been affected by the Copy command.

You are almost done. Enter the formula @SUM(C:B3..E:B3) into cell B3, since the total number of vans for the company is the sum of the vans from each division. Adjust those cells where the companywide result does not consist of the sum of the figures for the different divisions. Move to cell B11 (the occupancy fraction) and enter the formula +B12/B10; copy this formula to the range B11 to N11. Enter this formula into cell B4: +B16/B15. Note that the fuel cost per gallon of the company is found not by adding the fuel cost per gallon of each division but by dividing the total amount spent on fuel by the total amount of fuel purchases. Some of the divisions have a fuel cost higher than this figure, while others have a lower cost. (Rows 5 and 6 of the company page have been blanked out, since there is no companywide equivalent to these quantities.)

Pages B to E of the budget development spreadsheet are shown on pages 207–210.

Each page is too wide to fit on the screen. To save space, we will not display the rest of each page in this book. You can use the occupancy fraction figures that were used for the remaining months to reconstruct the entire spreadsheet on your own computer:

Division	Jun	Jly	Aug	Sep	Oct	Nov	Dec
East	0.70	0.70	0.70	0.80	0.85	0.85	0.80
West	0.70	0.70	0.60	0.70	0.90	0.90	0.80
South	0.60	0.60	0.60	0.60	0.85	0.85	0.70

Now you should protect all of the cells on the page for the company data. The spreadsheet is now ready for the budget development process. Each year, after you change certain data in the pages for each division, the spreadsheet will calculate the totals for the whole company automatically.

LINKING INFORMATION IN MORE THAN ONE FILE

Another powerful feature of 1-2-3 Release 3 is the ability to refer to data in more than one file. In Chapter 4 we saw how the South Hill office of the Easy Express shipping service could develop its personnel budget. Now, suppose that each location develops its budget in a separate file. We need to link these files to calculate the complete budget for the company.

Changes in the central file containing the companywide salary table are reflected automatically in the budget figures for each location. Enter this worksheet:

A	A	B	C	D	E
1		Salary Table			
2	Class|Exp:	1	2	3	4
3	ACCT	$14.50	$15.50	$16.29	$17.27
4	DISP	$14.80	$15.69	$16.63	$17.63
5	DRV	$12.00	$13.80	$15.87	$18.25
6	MGR	$14.90	$15.79	$16.74	$17.75
7	MRKT	$12.20	$12.93	$13.71	$14.53

THREE-DIMENSIONAL SPREADSHEETS

	A	B	C	D	E	F	G
1		Budget—Complete Company					
2							
3	Number of Vans:	9					
4	Fuelcost-$/gal:	$1.24					
5							
6							
7							
8		Year	Jan	Feb	Mar	Apr	May
9							
10	Days:	253	21	19	22	21	22
11	Capacity:	27,324	2,268	2,052	2,376	2,268	2,376
12	Occupancy:	0.78	0.82	0.83	0.86	0.86	0.86
13	Actual:	21,428	1,852	1,699	2,046	1,953	2,046
14	Revenue:	$128,567	$11,113	$10,192	$12,276	$11,718	$12,276
15	Miles:	195,492	16,300	14,771	17,182	16,401	17,182
16	Fuel Used:	13,964	1,164	1,055	1,227	1,172	1,227
17	Fuel Cost:	$17,357	$1,447	$1,311	$1,525	$1,456	$1,525

Budget—East Division

	A	B	C	D	E	F	G
1		Budget—East Division					
2							
3	Number of Vans:	4					
4	Fuelcost-$/gal:	$1.30					
5	Highway Miles:	39					
6	Ext.m.per.pass:	1					
7							
8		Year	Jan	Feb	Mar	Apr	May
9	Days:	253	21	19	22	21	22
10	Capacity:	12,144	1,008	912	1,056	1,008	1,056
11	Occupancy:	0.80	0.80	0.80	0.85	0.85	0.85
12	Actual:	9,665	806	730	898	857	898
13	Revenue:	$57,989	$4,838	$4,378	$5,386	$5,141	$5,386
14	Miles:	88,601	7,358	6,658	7,762	7,409	7,762
15	Fuel Used:	6,329	526	476	554	529	554
16	Fuel Cost:	$8,227	$683	$618	$721	$688	$721

THREE-DIMENSIONAL SPREADSHEETS

	A	B	C	D	E	F	G
1			Budget—West Division				
2							
3	Number of Vans:	2					
4	Fuelcost-$/gal:	$1.19					
5	Highway Miles:	40					
6	Ext.m.per.pass:	1					
7							
8		Year	Jan	Feb	Mar	Apr	May
9							
10	Days:	253	21	19	22	21	22
11	Capacity:	6,072	504	456	528	504	528
12	Occupancy:	0.80	0.80	0.85	0.90	0.90	0.90
13	Actual:	4,885	403	388	475	454	475
14	Revenue:	$29,311	$2,419	$2,326	$2,851	$2,722	$2,851
15	Miles:	45,365	3,763	3,428	3,995	3,814	3,995
16	Fuel Used:	3,240	269	245	285	272	285
17	Fuel Cost:	$3,856	$320	$291	$340	$324	$340

Budget—South Division

	A	B	C	D	E	F	G
1							
2							
3	Number of Vans:	3					
4	Fuelcost-$/gal:	$1.20					
5	Highway MIles:	36					
6	Ext.m.per.pass:	1					
7							
8		Year	Jan	Feb	Mar	Apr	May
9	Days:	253	21	19	22	21	22
10	Capacity:	9,108	756	684	792	756	792
11	Occupancy:	0.76	0.85	0.85	0.85	0.85	0.85
12	Actual:	6,878	643	581	673	643	673
13	Revenue	$41,267	$3,856	$3,488	$4,039	$3,856	$4,039
14	Miles:	61,526	5,179	4,685	5,425	5,179	5,425
15	Fuel Used:	4,395	370	335	388	370	388
16	Fuel Cost:	$5,274	$444	$402	$465	$444	$465

THREE-DIMENSIONAL SPREADSHEETS

Use the /RNC command to assign the name TABLE to the range A3..E7. Save this worksheet with the file name SALTAB.

Here is a part of the personnel budget worksheet for the South Hill office:

A	A	B	C	D	E	F
1		South Hill Office				
2	Name	Class	Exp	Hrs	Wage	Total Pay
3	Tim	DRV	1	2083	12	$24,996
4	Others					$250,645
5					Total	$275,641

We have entered the data for Tim, one of the employees. Recall that you used the @VLOOKUP function in Chapter 4 to determine the wage rate for a particular worker from the salary table. The principle is exactly the same here, except that now the salary table is in a different file. If you wish to reference a cell in another file using Release 3, include the file name surrounded by double brackets ≪ ≫ before you give the range name. Enter this formula into cell E3:

@VLOOKUP(B3,≪SALTAB≫TABLE,C3)

The expression ≪SALTAB≫TABLE refers to the range of cells named TABLE in the file SALTAB. If the name TABLE had not been assigned by using the Name command, you could have written the reference like this: ≪SALTAB≫A3..E7. If the file SALTAB is in a different directory, you need to add the path specification for its directory. If the file is on the hard disk of a different computer, obviously you have no way of accessing that data unless the computers are connected through a network (see Chapter 13).

Assign the name TOTAL to cell F5, and then save this worksheet using the file name SOUTH. Create the personnel budget worksheets for the West and North divisions. Now link all of these figures together into one spreadsheet giving the personnel budget for the entire organization:

A	A	B
1		Personnel Budget
2	Division	
3	West	$235,996
4	North	$220,996
5	South	$275,641
6		————
7	Total	$732,633

Enter this formula into cell B5:

+≪SOUTH≫TOTAL

The computer will look in the file SOUTH, find the cell that was given the name TOTAL, and return that value to cell B5. The equivalent formulas for the other cells are +≪WEST≫TOTAL and +≪NORTH≫TOTAL, assuming that in each case the name TOTAL has been defined to represent the total personnel budget for the division.

Assign the name TOTAL to cell B7, and save this spreadsheet under the file name PERBUD. Now you can create a worksheet for the total budget for the organization and link this figure into it:

A	A	B
1	Total Budget—Easy Express Shipping Service	
2		
3	Personnel	$732,633
4	Fuel	$456,397
5	Other	$395,200
6		————
7	Total	$1,584,230

The formula in cell B3 is +≪PERBUD≫TOTAL. Use equivalent formulas for the other categories after you have set up the spreadsheets giving their portion of the budget.

CHAPTER PERSPECTIVE
It is awkward to use a traditional two-dimensional spreadsheet for a large complex problem. As your business becomes more and more complicated, you will appreciate the ability to create multiple-page spreadsheets and link data from different spreadsheet files even more.

Networks and Electronic Data Interchange

CHAP 13

INTRODUCTION AND MAIN POINTS

Although computers make it much easier to process information, it can still be a big job to enter data into a computer by typing at a keyboard. One major improvement in computer design are information systems that minimize rekeying of information that has already been entered into the system. In order to accomplish this, computers must be able to share information.

In the 1970s, business computer users usually worked at terminals connected to mainframe computers, which could support many users at one time. Any authorized user had access to peripheral devices such as printers and to the data in the auxiliary storage (disks and tapes) that were connected to the computer. With the introduction of microcomputers, it became economical to provide workers with their own computers; however, completely isolated machines lose the ability to share information and hardware devices with other machines. To remedy this problem, computers in the same building can be linked together in a *local area network* (or LAN), and data can be transferred between computers at different companies at widely different locations by a process known as *electronic data interchange*.

After studying the material in this chapter:

▬ You will understand the purposes of a local area network system.

▬ You will know some of the steps that need to be taken to implement a local area network.

▬ You will understand why electronic data interchange is rapidly spreading throughout the business community.

OBJECTIVES OF LOCAL AREA NETWORKS

Local area networks can accomplish three objectives:

▬ They allow users to communicate with each other through electronic mail.

▬ They allow users to share data. Suppose you have several

people in the office who respond to customer queries; each needs to be able to look up data about the customer's account. One option is for each computer to have all of the data on its hard disk. This plan has two main disadvantages. First, because each data file will likely be large, each computer will need a large hard disk, which is expensive, and second, it is difficult to kept the data up to date on each hard disk. You might be able to copy the data onto a floppy disk at the end of each day and then carry that disk around to each computer to copy the data onto all of the hard disks. This process is cumbersome at best; it becomes much more complicated if the data file is too large to fit on a single floppy disk. Further, the computers will still not be current, since they will not have any changes made during any given day until after close of business.

The solution is for all updates to be made in one central computer and for all users to have access to that central computer.

▬ They allow different microcomputers to share hardware devices. Your business should have a laser printer for correspondence, but it is expensive to acquire a laser printer for every single desktop. If one laser printer is purchased and hooked up via a network to several microcomputers on the same floor, each user will be able to send files to the laser printer. You need to estimate your printing needs to determine how many microcomputers a single laser printer will be able to support without becoming too backlogged. (If you have a small number of computers to share one printer and you have no other need for a network, it is cheaper to wire each of the computers directly to the printer and obtain a switch that controls which computer is connected to the printer at the moment.) Other specialized devices besides printers can be shared. For example, a plotter (a device for high quality drawings) is probably too expensive for each desktop to have its own.

DESIGNING A LOCAL AREA NETWORK
To implement a local area network, there are several design choices you must make:

▬ Topology. The term topology refers to the pattern of connections in the network. There are several choices (see page 216).

- A ring network, in which each unit is connected to two adjacent units and the whole pattern of connections form a ring.

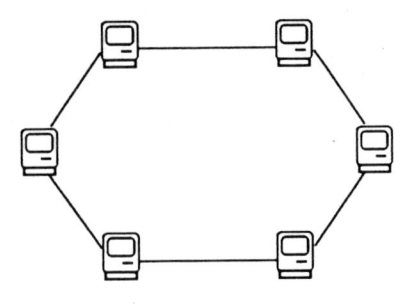

Ring network

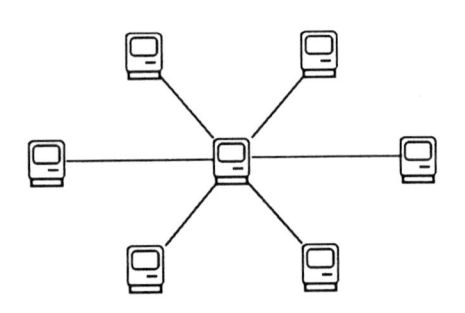

Star network

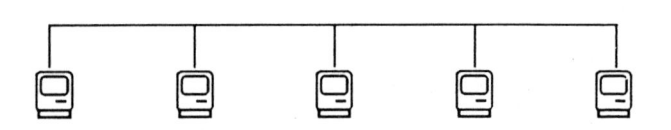

Bus network

- A star network, in which each unit is connected to a central unit.
- A bus network, in which each unit is connected to a main connecting wire along which data can travel back and forth like a shuttle bus. (The internal construction of the computer's CPU is also designed using the bus concept, with the bus connecting the registers in the CPU.)
- A hybrid network, using some combination of the above designs.

No particular network topology is always best; in each design each unit is connected to every other unit along some path. The physical characteristics of your location may dictate the choice; for example, you may need to use the bus design if there is only one feasible way to string the connecting wires between the machines. The ring design is often a good choice for relatively small networks; if the network is large, the wires often become too long and the signals start to fade (one solution is to connect several smaller rings together).

▬ Medium. You need to decide on the physical medium that will connect the machines. The choices include:
- Twisted pair wiring, which consists of two wires twisted together. This is the most economical choice, so it is a good choice for small networks. However, it is slow compared to other mediums (1 megabit per second) and is susceptible to interference from nearby electrical signals.
- Coaxial cable, consisting of four layers—a center conductor, an inner insulation layer, an outer conductor, and an outer insulation layer. Although more expensive than twisted pair wiring, it is better shielded from outside noise and can transmit data faster (up to 10 megabits per second).
- Fiber-optic cable. A fiber-optic cable provides a high-capacity, high-speed way to transmit data as pulses of light along plastic or glass fibers. Phone networks are being converted to fiber-optic systems. The physical process for transmitting messages (light pulses) is quite different from the physical process for transmitting messages through wires (electric currents). Fiber-optic cables are still more expensive than coaxial cables, but they are becoming more affordable. It is possible for a network to contain a mixture of fiber-optic cables for "highways" connecting smaller clusters of machines and coaxial cable or twisted pair wiring for the "local streets" within each cluster.
- Free space media. In cases where it is very difficult to connect

wires between the machines, there are other options that do not require wires: digital microwave radio or infrared light beam transmission.

You need to make other technical choices as well in order to establish a local area network—how the different machines will access the network (common choices include Ethernet, Token Ring, and ARCnet) and whether you need a higher capacity broadband system or a lower-capacity baseband system. Each computer needs a hardware device, called a network adaptor, placed in one of the expansion slots inside the machine and connected to the network cables. Advice from a trusted vendor can help you determine what is the best configuration for your specific location.

You also need to choose the software that will run the network. People using a microcomputer that is part of a network should be able to do everything they can do with a standalone computer, in addition to the added options provided by the network software. Two popular choices for network software are Novell NetWare and Microsoft LAN Manager; this chapter discusses some of the features of NetWare.

OPERATING A SMALL LOCAL AREA NETWORK

To implement a small network with a handful of personal computers using NetWare, one of the machines must be designated as the server—that is, the machine that will serve the needs of the other machines in the network. It is possible for the server to serve also as an ordinary computer; however, if the network is very busy it will be more efficient if the server is solely dedicated to that one task.

Each computer on the network needs to have a part of the network software copied onto its hard disk. This software (called the NetWare shell) takes over the function of the operating system that controls the actions of the computer. However, the users should think they are running their regular operating systems (such as DOS) as if the computer was by itself. The software should also provide a way for the user to connect to the data on the server machine.

At this point the computer in the network starts to behave differently from the standalone computer. NetWare assigns a particular drive letter to the file server. Because it is common in microcomputers for drive letters A and B to refer to floppy disk drives and C, D, and E to refer to hard disks, NetWare typically uses the letter F for the server. To access the server, the user needs to *login*—that is, establish a connection to the server. When you start a computer using MS-DOS you will probably see this prompt: c> (if C is your hard disk). Type F: to change the active disk drive to F, and then enter the command LOGIN. First, the server computer will want to know who you are (any multiuser system needs a way to identify different users). The prompt ENTER YOUR LOGIN NAME will be displayed on the screen. Enter your unique login name, and you're in. (If your network has more than one server, you also need to type the name of the server to which you wish to be connected.)

For security you may be required to give a password. The password requirement is designed to prevent other people from entering the system using your login name. It is tricky to choose a good password; it should be one that is not too difficult to remember but not easy to guess. Don't use your first name, for example. It is often recommended that you change your password on a regular basis.

If you have worked with a hard disk, you know that the number of files stored quickly becomes too large to manage without establishing different directories. (See Appendix 1.) Directories can be arranged in a hierarchy, with each directory containing additional subdirectories. The hard disk of the file server is also arranged in directories according to the purpose of the different files. Managing the hard disk of the file server is more complicated than managing the hard disk of a stand-alone machine because you need to determine the rules governing access to the data. When you use the hard disk of your personal stand-alone computer, you have the authority to do whatever you want, but you also must take responsibility for your actions. If you erase a file, then you are the only one who will know that it is gone; if you fill up the hard disk so there is no room for new files, you are the one who will suffer; if you type secret documents on your stand-alone computer, nobody else will be able to see them (provided, of course, that you have adequate physical security to prevent unauthorized persons from gaining access to the room containing the machine).

It is not wise to allow users with access to the hard disk of the file server machine to do whatever they wish to with it. You cannot let one user erase files that others will need, fill up so much hard disk space that they crowd out other users, or browse through confidential files from other users. A supervisor should control the allocation of rights to the network and assign any of

four general levels of access to particular directories:
- Unlimited access, meaning the user can read data from files in the directory and write new information to the directory.
- Modified write access, meaning the user has limited ability to make changes in some files.
- Read-only access, meaning the user can read data from files in the directory but cannot write any new information or change the existing files in any way.
- No access.

Each user may be given a subdirectory on the file server disk, with unlimited access to that directory. A user who needs to enter updates for data can be given the right to modify files in that directory; other users may have read-only access to the files containing the company data. Most users are also given read-only access to directories containing software such as Lotus 1-2-3, since you don't want individual users to be able to modify or erase valuable software or data. You can prevent users from gaining any access to directories with data from other departments, meaning they cannot even look at the list of files in that directory.

In order to send your printing to a network printer, use the NetWare Capture command to tell your computer to intercept output destined for the printer port and instead send it along the communications line to the network. The capture command, part of the NetWare shell, is designed so that your applications software doesn't realize that anything different is happening; it will generate the same codes that it would if it were sending output to a printer connected directly to the printer port of your computer. It should be possible to connect different systems together with little (or preferably no) modification to the way that the original application works; you should not have to adjust your word processing software to make it run on a network.

When the output from the printer command reaches the server, it is stored in a print queue—that is, a line of jobs waiting to be printed. You cannot expect the network printer to be always ready for you in the same manner that a printer connected to your own computer is. In general, the jobs are printed in the order received by the server, although the order can be modified if one job has a high priority or a large but less urgent job can be run during "off-peak" hours.

ELECTRONIC DATA INTERCHANGE
Businesses depend on the internal and external flow of information. Traditional information systems depend on paper being

marked correctly and transferred to the right place. However, paper-based information systems provide many opportunities for error since information must be copied from one form to another; in addition, paper-handling tasks absorb much worker time that could be spent on other functions. (You might wonder what would happen to the people who work at paper-handling jobs if these jobs were no longer needed. The best response to this concern is to point to the many times in the past when similar concerns were expressed—the introduction of automatic weaving equipment was resisted because of the loss of jobs for weavers, the introduction of automatic telephone dialing was resisted because of the loss of jobs for operators, and so on. Human living standards can be improved only with improvements in labor productivity, which means old jobs vanish but new jobs appear to take their place.)

Fax machines provide a solution to one disadvantage of paper-based information systems—the delays caused by transit. Instead of waiting for the mail carrier to deliver a document, thanks to the fax machine you can receive it almost instantaneously. However, fax machines do not solve the other disadvantages associated with paper-based systems—the information still needs to be copied manually to other forms.

It is possible for information to be transmitted in a machine-readable form, allowing future processing to occur automatically, via a local area network. In order to communicate with computers at widely spaced locations, it is necessary to establish a *wide-area network* such as travel agents use to book airline tickets. Other examples of wide area networks are ARPANET, established by the defense department to link researchers, and BITNET, which links universities world-wide. If you are connected to one network, you can contact someone connected to another network through a connection called a *gateway,* which links networks.

Networks allow people to communicate with each other through an electronic mail system in which you type your message at your computer and send it along the network. When the recipient connects to the network at some later time, the message can be retrieved. Electronic mail is faster than paper mail, and you can send the message directly from your desk without licking stamps or walking to the mailbox. The recipient (or the sender) can print a paper copy of the message if desired. Electronic mail is very convenient if you need to send the same message to more than one person.

A message sent via electronic mail arrives in machine-readable form. The concept of *electronic data interchange* carries the process one step further; it allows the data to be processed after they arrive, without any need for a person to reenter them. In order for this system to work, the sender and the recipient must agree on standard formats for the messages; the appropriate software can then process the data—for example, by automatically generating other messages.

Think of some of the paper forms that are commonly used in business: requisitions, purchase orders, order entries and acknowledgments, invoices, payment authorizations, and payments (i.e., checks). Now imagine the process that must be followed in a paper-based system when a department in a company wishes to purchase an item from a supplier. The department must fill out a requisition form and send it to another department for authorization. This results in a purchase order, copies of which are sent to the supplier, who responds with an order acknowledgement. Eventually the supplier sends the product along with an invoice. The receiving department sends a form acknowledging the receipt of the order, and payment authorization forms that allow a check to be written and mailed are completed. At each stage of the process, information must be copied to a new form, consuming worker time and opening possibilities for errors. (Even if computers are used to generate the forms, these disadvantages occur if people need to rekey the information for each form.)

In an electronic data interchange system, the general pattern of information flow is the same. However, instead of paper forms, electronic transmission using a standard format is used for each message. It is necessary for a person to type information at the start of the process, but once the information is entered into a computer, it does not need to be rekeyed. Thus, the requesting department calls up the software to generate a requisition, and then types in the information, such as the name of the vendor and the part number of the item. This information is transmitted electronically to the purchasing department. If the request is approved, a purchase order is generated automatically; nobody in the purchasing office needs to retype the data. The electronic purchase order is sent to the supplier; copies can be sent to other departments within the company. It is much easier to send copies of electronic documents than paper documents and they are easier to read. How many times have you been unable to read the last copy of a multicopy paper form because the writer did not press down hard enough when filling out the form?

The process continues as each subsequent document is generated automatically by the software designed to process the previous documents. At the final stage, the cost and delay of sending a paper check can be avoided by using an electronic funds transfer system. A check is not actually money but the instructions that direct the bank to transfer money; the actual transfer of money occurs when the bank subtracts from the payer's account and adds to the recipient's account. In the future these payment instructions will increasingly be sent electronically instead of on paper. Electronic funds transfer is now commonly used for direct deposit of social security checks, and it is becoming increasingly common for payroll checks. (The payer does benefit from the delay in sending a paper check, so vendors will probably have to offer favorable terms for companies using electronic funds transfer to compensate them for the fact that their account will be debited more quickly.)

Some disadvantages do exist with electronic data interchange system, but most likely these will be overcome. For example, invoice forms usually contain preprinted information on the terms of the contract; this information is missing from an electronic version, so the two parties involved need to find some other way of agreeing to the terms. In addition, the signature on a paper document is used as an indicator of acceptance; electronic documents contain no space for signatures. Electronic systems raise special concerns about security, so special effort must be made to guard the systems. If a message is confidential, it can be coded so that someone intercepting the electronic transmission will not be able to read it. Of course, paper systems have their own problems; signatures can be forged and documents counterfeited.

Because electronic data interchange involves the transfer of data between companies, it is necessary that connections be established between the companies and that document standards be agreed upon by all of the participants in the system. If your company has only a small number of trading partners, you can connect to them by calling them over the phone line, using your modem. This sytem requires both sender and receiver to agree on the time to make the call and on the communications protocol. If you have many trading partners, it is more convenient to connect your computer to a third-party network. You then send all your messages to the network which distributes them to your trading partners' electronic mailboxes, which are also connected to the network, or send them through gateways to other networks if some of your partners are not connected to your network. The recipients of the messages receive them when they call the network at their own convenience.

Standards for electronic data interchange have been developed in several industries, including the transportation industry (where shippers connect to the carriers), the automotive industry (where manufacturers connect to their suppliers), and the grocery industry. As of 1990, electronic data interchange represents a relatively small part of business information transfer, but there will probably be rapid expansion in this area during the early 1990s.

CHAPTER PERSPECTIVE

Computers are very valuable tools for processing information. The process of entering information into the computer is often the bottleneck that prevents realization of the full potential of computers. The solution is to make it possible for computers to share information so that data typed in one computer do not need to be retyped at another computer. Local area networks provide a way for several computers in the same location to be connected together. The process of electronic data interchange allows companies to communicate information automatically to other companies; that information can then be processed automatically without being re-entered.

REFERENCES

Emmelhainz, Margaret, *Electronic Data Interchange: A Total Management Guide* (New York: Van Nostrand Reinhold), 1990.

Florence, Donne, *Local Area Networks: Developing Systems for Business* (New York: John Wiley and Sons), 1989.

Lawrence, Bill, *Using Novell NetWare* (New York: Que Corp.), 1990.

Expert Systems

CHAPTER 14

INTRODUCTION AND MAIN POINTS
An expert system is a computer program that can process information in an area that calls for knowledge and judgment. Much progress has been made in developing systems that can be used for decision making.

After studying the material in this chapter:
- You will understand the nature of decision making in an expert system.
- You will know some examples of how to communicate with an expert system.
- You will be familiar with some of the tools that are used to create expert systems.

THE NATURE OF EXPERT SYSTEMS
An expert system resembles any other computer program in that it consists of step-by-step instructions that the computer executes exactly and very quickly. The expert system derives its special name from the fact that it performs competently in some area in which humans generally require special training before becoming competent.

Although you might think that calculators meet this definition, that is not really the case. Calculators do perform mathematical calculations at levels equaling or exceeding the level of a human expert, but they can perform only those operations they are told to on information they are given. In contrast, an expert system typically need only be given the information; it "figures out" what to do with it on its own.

A few years ago any program that performed complicated tasks was touted as being "artificially intelligent," "intelligently enhanced," or an "expert system" of some sort. Often the users of these programs were disappointed, for the products did not seem to be significantly different from conventional programs.

As a bank executive once asked me, "What is the difference between an expert system and a bunch of IF statements?"

No watertight test exists for identifying an expert system, and it would be a blearily philosophical task to try to develop one. There are, however, some guidelines. A conventional program generally relies only on information about how to perform a specific task, while an expert system usually contains ideas of how knowledge behaves in context and in general. These ideas are embodied in an inference engine. In addition, knowledge in an expert system is represented explicitly; in a conventional system knowledge is usually implicit in the procedures used.

Imagine that you are trying to write a computer program to help make inventory decisions. You begin by making a statistical model charting past inventory trends in various ways, perhaps even making a simulation; your manager, Jan Milyons, uses the graphs and numbers from the model to make purchasing decisions. This is the way things are usually done. But sometimes Jan does not purchase according to the model's prediction. Why?

The answer, of course, is that managers add a level of interpretation to the numbers that goes beyond the quantitative methods used in the models. For example, a manager may know that recent short-term trends were caused by unusual unrest in the Middle East and may give more or less weight to them than the computer's model does. Perhaps the manager may notice parallel occurrences in different models that affect one another; or something in the model may cast doubt on the efficacy of some rule of thumb.

The manager's ability to interpret data and analyze trends is expertise in action. It consists of several different skills—the ability to focus on the salient facts, eliminating erroneous possibilities without even considering them; the skill of knowing how to interpret those facts; the ability to understand how facts and trends impact one another; and, giving justification for steps in one's reasoning process are vitally important skills. If the computer program you want to write or buy requires them, it is probably an expert system.

INFERENCE ENGINES

Expert systems are often written as a collection of rules that take the form of "IF-THEN" statements in which some conditions follow the IF and a conclusion follows the THEN. In a conventional program, IF statements are tests that determine whether some instruction or set of instructions will be performed in the program; in an expert system, the IF is often a declaration of some conditions that must be true if the part following the THEN is to be true. The technical name for these IF–THEN rules is production rules. An example is:

IF Marge is married to Jim AND
    John is Marge's son
THEN
Jim is John's father.

In an expert system, the IF part of the statement may serve as the instruction or set of instructions and the portion that follows the THEN is the goal to be achieved. Just how the two parts of the statement are handled is determined by a "controller," called the inference engine. There are two basic kinds of inference engines for handling these kinds of IF–THEN rules—forward-chaining inference engines and backwards-chaining inference engines.

A forward-chaining inference engine begins with the IF side of the production rules and tries to fulfill the goal by investigating whether the conditions are true. It does this by treating each condition as a fact and looking into a special location in its memory to see if it contains a statement that the fact is currently true. This special memory location is called a blackboard. In the example above, the inference engine would see if the two statements "Marge is married to Jim" and "John is Marge's son" were on its blackboard. If they are, then it would conclude that the third statement, "Jim is John's father," is true and then write it on the blackboard. If one of the conditions is false, then the inference engine would simply go on to the next rule.

Backward-chaining inference engines begin with the THEN side of the rule—the conclusion—and investigate it, using the conditions in the IF side as new conclusions to research using other rules. In the example above, a backward-chaining system would look specifically for the goal "Jim is John's father" in the knowledge base and then, in an effort to decide if this conclusion is true, would try to find rules with the conclusions "Marge is married to Jim" and "John is Marge's son." In a backward-chaining inference system, everything cannot be a rule; if that were the case, the program might never stop reasoning about some goal because it would always have a new goal. For instance, consider the impact of having these rules in the knowledge base:

IF Marge is married to Jim THEN Jim is married to Marge.
IF Jim is married to Marge THEN Marge is married to Jim.

The program could never decide who is married to whom. In trying to establish that Jim is married to Marge, it will try to establish that Marge is married to Jim, which will make it try to establish that Jim is married to Marge, and so on ad infinitum. It will go around in circles.

Some bits of knowledge must be considered merely facts, true statements about the world.

Jim is married to Marge.
Marge is married to Jim.

These statements have no IF and no THEN; they are just straightforward assertions. No further goals are established, and computation can halt.

USING EXPERT SYSTEMS IN BUSINESS

Expert systems have been most effective in dealing with problems that are well defined and that require a great deal of routine work. Still, if your company is willing to make the investment, expert systems can help you make decisions in situations in which there is so much information that relationships between different factors become difficult to spot.

Perhaps your manufacturing process has grown very complicated, and decisions you used to make with accuracy are becoming more and more difficult because so many densely interwoven factors influence the decision that it is difficult to keep track of them all. Your database can keep track of the various factors; an expert system can help you make judgments about what is important. Here the system is an aid in the decision-making process and helps you and your company to focus your thinking.

Expert systems can also help articulate the expertise of employees who have been with the company for years and might some day move on. The expertise of such employees often exists as unconscious "rules of thumb" that has never been spelled out. But a knowledge engineer may be able to coax out this experience in the course of building the expert system and incorporate it in an effective program. There are three good arguments for doing this. First, the program, once written, can be copied like any other program to any place it might be needed, unlike a human being who can be in only one place at a time.

Second, the program will probably make your expert staff more effective by freeing them from worrying about details and enabling them use to their intellectual gifts for solving problems. Finally, having an expert system involved in the training process is like having a shock absorber to cushion the bumpy ride you may face if valued experts leave the company, taking their knowledge with them.

An expert system is not a panacea or miracle technology. It is just another helpful tool for handling information and making decisions in an uncertain environment. An expert system can not replace your human experts, nor can it make decisions reliably in areas outside of what it was designed for. Expert systems have notoriously brittle boundaries; inside those boundaries they often perform as well or better than most human experts, but outside of them they fail completely. Chess programs are a good example of this phenomenon. By and large, they play chess as well or better than most reasonably intelligent human beings, but they are lousy at checkers. Similarly, an accounting expert system will not necessarily be a good bookkeeper or financier— or even much of an accountant outside the narrow domain it was built for. Expert systems are an aid to people, not a replacement for them.

If your company's management information systems are at all complex, expert systems can probably enable you to do things that you are not presently doing. For example, your databases probably print out reports that your management uses to make recommendations and policy decisions. Generally, the relationships between data contained in such reports are useful but simple, while the conclusions your manager draws are abstract and complex. The difference is your manager's expertise, some of which can be encapsulated in an expert system. Probably you will find that once you create such a system, your manager will see new relationships that were previously overlooked. Studies suggest that employees who use expert systems make better and more consistent decisions than their peers who do not.

COMMUNICATING WITH AN EXPERT SYSTEM

There are four ways to communicate with an expert system. They are:

■ Natural language. For decades computer scientists and linguists have been trying to make computers understand natural languages such as English, French, and Japanese. While a comprehensive understanding of human languages is still in the future, effective techniques have been developed that can be used in limited areas.

The problem with getting computers to understand human language is the great amount of ambiguity in language. If the computer program can make some assumptions about which words are going to be used and how, they often achieve satisfactory results. Because expert systems, by design, deal with only a small subset of human experience, it is especially easy to program them to make such assumptions.

Natural language use by expert systems has its drawbacks. The two major problems are the expense of making the system and the fact that it may not be 100 percent reliable. In addition, although useful but relatively simple systems can sometimes be built by interpreting keywords without worrying about linguistics, there is a shortage of qualified programmers able to make more powerful natural language systems. Such programs require an unusual combination of skills, namely, programming expertise and some knowledge of linguistics. Some systems require such skills; for instance, weather reports in Canada are routinely translated from French into English by computer.

▬ Menus. A more familiar way of communicating with a computer is the use of menus. A menu is simply a list of options that the program has available for the user. At any given time a variety of menus with a variety of options may be available; the user picks the appropriate one. This kind of communication is used on many personal computers today. Figure 14-1 on page 231 is an example of a simple menu.

▬ Prompting the user for information. Even if the program uses natural language or menus, a great deal of its communications is probably going to consist of prompting the user for information via a question/answer format. A natural language system may simply ask what it wants to know and let the user type in the answer; most likely, though, the program will give the user a set of answers from which to choose. For example:

DID YOU HAVE DEFERRED INTEREST ON YOUR INVESTMENT? (Y/N)...
    CHOOSE: Y
    HOW MUCH?
    A) LESS THAN $1,000
    B) $1,000–4,999
    C) $5,000–9,999

D) $10,000 OR MORE
CHOOSE: B
IN WHAT STATE ARE YOU INCORPORATED?
>GOIRGIA
!! GOIRGIA IS NOT A STATE, PLEASE TYPE AGAIN.
>GEORGIA

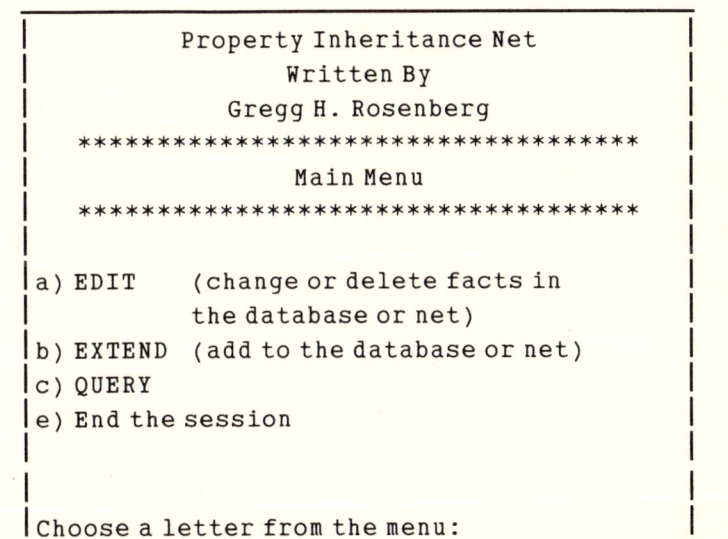

```
            Property Inheritance Net
                    Written By
                 Gregg H. Rosenberg
      ****************************************
                     Main Menu
      ****************************************

a) EDIT     (change or delete facts in
             the database or net)
b) EXTEND   (add to the database or net)
c) QUERY
e) End the session


Choose a letter from the menu:
```

Fig. 14-1

■ Interactive communication. Human beings usually have to use judgment in the areas often tackled by expert systems because in any given situation there is usually more than one possible conclusion. Consequently, expert systems generally go through a pseudo-reasoning process as they move from step to step. Several strategies have been developed by programmers to help systems choose among alternatives. Most of the strategies result in a ranking of alternatives in order of preference which is explored by the system in order until it reaches a desirable conclusion.

One way to augment the system's effectiveness in dealing with uncertainty is for it to rank the options at intermediate steps in the reasoning and then let the human expert choose among them. This method, called interactive communication, allows the expert system and the human expert to complement one another. The figure on page 233 is an example of an interactive interface for a medical diagnostic system. Diseases fall naturally into categories; this medical expert system ranks categories according to their likelihood and then shows the doctor its findings. The doctor then has a choice of following the most likely path or exploring some less likely possibility.

EXPERT SYSTEMS IN USE TODAY

The programming techniques necessary for making expert systems have been around for about a decade and a half, and hundreds were implemented in the 1980s in areas ranging from medicine and science to business and ethics. Following is a brief description of a few that have been used successfully in business.

Digital Equipment (DEC)'s expert system, XCON, is the key to its marketing strategy. DEC permits each customer to pick a unique configuration of hardware and software tailored to its needs. Since each order may have hundreds of components and hundreds of systems are configured each day, the strategy would not work unless it was automated. DEC was unsuccessful in its attempts to automate with conventional procedural programming, but was able to achieve satisfactory performance using a production rule language called OPS5.

Continental Airlines uses an expert system named the System One GateKeeper to improve gate scheduling. Airlines encounter incessant, complicated changes in airport gate schedules that can result in flight delays and problems with baggage routing. By using the System One GateKeeper, Continental expects to save $800,000 a year by reducing misrouting of baggage and passengers. The system also makes the job of the gate manager easier by accessing mainframe data on incoming and departing flight schedules.

Wendy's International, Inc., reports smoother operation, increased productivity, and more consistency in the Field Operations Support Center's problem-solving efforts since it began using an expert system to troubleshoot food ordering and cooking equipment problems. Before installation of the expert system, Wendy's relied on staff experience, some training, and lots of manuals to help store managers fix problems by phone. Now it uses Fusion, by 1st-Class Expert Systems, which runs on IBM Model 30 PS/2s. The system guides Wendy's personnel through the reasoning process step by step, asking pertinent questions and providing answers along the way. Users can also call up

EXPERT SYSTEMS

Symptoms Expl	Symptoms Not Expl	Test For	Medical Prototype
sniffles	runny nose	fever	
	coughing	aches	written by
	sneezing		
			Gregg H. Rosenberg

Enter Manifestations	Diseases by Rank	Instructions
sneezing	influenza	Use arrow keys to scroll
coughing	hepatitis	through diseases.
runny nose	megalomania	SE, SNE, and Test give info
sniffles	allergies	about the disease on the
	cancer	highlighted line.
		Press ENTER on the disease
		you want to search further.
		ESC for previous level,
		W moves to different window
		Q to Quit.

Messages

233

graphics that give details of particular machines.

Blue Cross of Western Pennsylvania has developed an expert medical claims evaluation system, Nurse Expert Review System (NERSys), based on the knowledge and experience of veteran nurses. The system, which can recognize the 12,000 diagnosis and 4,000 procedures accepted by the insurance industry, was built using in-depth interviews with nurses who review insurance claims and used their logic as the basis for accepting, rejecting, or requiring further information on claims processed by NERSys.

LANGUAGES FOR EXPERT SYSTEMS

Your systems experts will need to work with an experienced programmer in developing expert systems. There are generally two routes your company can go. The first is to build your system from scratch using a computer language; the second is to use an expert system shell.

LISP and Prolog

Several languages, LISP and Prolog chief among them, are especially useful for building expert systems. Object-oriented languages are often useful also. Your company's management information system department may balk at having to use one of these languages; generally, their arguments follow one of these lines of thought:

1. LISP and Prolog are too slow. Specifically, they are slower than language X (or C) which happens to be their favorite language at the moment.
2. All the programmers already know language X, but they do not know LISP or Prolog. Therefore, the learning curve will make it too expensive to use LISP or Prolog.

These arguments are usually spurious, for a number of reasons. Great improvements have been made in the execution speed of LISP and Prolog in recent years. Furthermore, because of special features in LISP and Prolog, it can be quicker, and thus less costly, to develop a system in one of them and then rewrite it in another language if necessary than to start in the other language.

The reason LISP and Prolog run slower than some conventional languages is that they have control features lacking in conventional languages. These features are usually necessary for an expert system to run correctly. Consequently, the programmers in your company would have to code these abilities in another language before they could get down to the nitty-gritty of encoding expertise; in essence, they would have to duplicate LISP or Prolog.

Expert system shells

An expert system shell is a pseudo-language specifically written for programming expert systems. It generally has very advanced capabilities, such as inference engine(s) and a builder's interface, that are not built into LISP and Prolog. Although Prolog does have a backward-chaining inference engine built in, it does not offer some of the more sophisticated and optimized features incorporated in the shells. In addition, the builder interfaces on some shells are so easy to use that sometimes even a person who is not a programmer can handle them effectively after some practice. Their drawbacks include high price, brittleness, and a limited range of effectiveness.

Expert system shells are built to accomplish specific kinds of tasks, such as entering rules or communicating with a database, tasks that are relatively easy. In addition, a shell whose capabilities are adequate for your beginning expert system may prove inadequate as the system grows. The moral is: Shop carefully before investing your time and money in an expert system shell. Be sure it is adequate both for your present and future needs.

Examples of expert system shells include Nexpert, Guru, and VP-Expert. Nexpert and Guru are systems of comparable ambitions; VP-Expert is a modestly-priced shell meant to facilitate building small expert systems. Nexpert is probably the best shell for complex medium or large expert systems, although it is a very comprehensive package and can be intimidating; Guru is a less coherent package that does not provide adequate mechanisms for controlling the hodgepodge of technologies it offers.

BUILDING AN EXPERT SYSTEM

There are several steps you should take to build an expert system. First, identify the area of expertise you want to encode. It should be in an area that is well defined, one in which most of the problem solving is routine and in which your company actually has an expert who can help. Then choose a knowledge engineer and decide together exactly what you want the system to do. This means identifying exactly what information you want the system to use and what kinds of conclusions you wish it to be able to draw. Be very meticulous and precise about this.

Whenever you work with computers, you should know ahead of time exactly what you want from them.

After you have your plan, identify the people in your company who have the expertise that you are looking for. Your effort will not succeed without the cooperation of the experts; make them enthusiastic about the project and then assemble a team to work with the experts in building the system.

Do not let your programmers talk you out of hiring a knowledge engineer—a person specially trained in building expert systems. Chances are that the programmers in your management information systems department have, or can learn, the programming skills necessary to program an expert system, and they will tell you this; however, there is a difference between programming an expert system and building one. Building an expert system involves more than just programming. Do not be lulled by the hubris of your programmers!

The knowledge engineer will encounter both technological and psychological difficulties as he or she works on developing your expert system. Building an expert system requires more than just programming in specifications for the solution to some problem; it also requires that the builder ferret out descriptions of deeply-buried intuitions from the experts and, just as important, translate them into a programming scheme. As the translation process proceeds, it will become clear that your expert is doing more than simply following the rules, and some corrections to the translation will be necessary. Promises are often made about expert systems that cannot be kept, and expectations raised to unrealistic levels. The best way to avoid being swept away by the hype is to become knowledgeable yourself. A reasonable test of whether you have a sufficient familiarity with a subject to make an informed judgment is often simply whether you can understand the jargon. If you are neither impressed nor put off by the jargon, you probably will not indulge in anything rash. It is also a good idea, if possible, to get the opinions of experts who do not have a stake in the project you are considering. In general, use common sense.

CHAPTER PERSPECTIVE

Human experts use a combination of knowledge and intuition in making decisions. In some cases it is possible to translate this expertise into a computer program—an expert system. As long as you do not expect too much from it, an expert system can be a valuable tool for decision making.

Problems

CHAPTER 15

INTRODUCTION AND MAIN POINTS
So far we have looked at many of the advantages provided by computers. However, as you are undoubtedly aware, there are some negative aspects to using computers. There is an old joke that asserts, "To err is human; to really wreck things up requires a computer." This is an exaggeration, but it contains some truth—Computers can make mistakes on a large scale. Actually, the computers themselves are often blameless; they are only following the orders they receive from their operators and programmers.

After studying the material in this chapter:

— You will understand ways in which computer data may be incorrect because of data entry mistakes or data damage, accidental or deliberate.

— You will know about software bugs.

— You will understand some of the concerns about the possible effects of computers on the quality of life.

DATA ENTRY ACCURACY
The data entry stage is often the main bottleneck that prevents computers from being used most effectively. Devices such as scanners and bar code readers can avoid the pitfalls of manual data entry. In addition, while there is no way to guarantee that data entry mistakes will not occur during manual data entry, there are steps that can minimize the damage. We have seen that one of the major goals of networks and electronic data interchange is to allow computers to share information with each other so that it is not necessary to retype the data for each machine, drastically reducing the possibility of error because there are fewer stages where manual data entry is required. In many cases, there are maximum and minimum possible values for each numerical data item that is entered; for example, the number of hours worked by an employee during a week can

never be less than zero or greater than 168 (168 is the total number of hours in a week; in practice, the limit can be set lower, such as 80). A data entry program can be designed to reject a value that falls outside this range and to ask the user to reenter the value. This is a useful way of catching certain types of errors, such as the entry of an extra zero. If you need to enter a long list of numbers in which it is very unlikely that two consecutive numbers are the same, the data entry program can ask the user to verify the result if two consecutive entered numbers are identical.

If you are working with a mainframe, you should have professional programmers available to design your data entry program. If you are entering data into a spreadsheet such as 1-2-3, you can write a macro to perform checks during the data entry process.

Other checks that the computer can perform at the time of data entry include:

■ making sure that the number of data items entered is correct (this means that you need an independent way of counting the items).

■ making sure that the data are of the correct type; for example in a field for sex, there are only two possibilities.

■ making sure that the appropriate fields are entered; for example, if an insurance customer has children, you might need to enter the ages of the children; if there are no children the data entry routine should skip that section.

If it is extremely important that the data be entered correctly, it may be worth the expense of having the data entered separately by two different people and then having a program check the two lists for any discrepancies. Assuming that it is unlikely that either program will make a mistake, it is even less likely that both will make a mistake on the same item (and still less likely that they will make the same mistake on the same item). After the computer identifies any discrepancies between the two lists, you can check the original data to identify the source of the error.

DAMAGED DATA

Another hazard is the possibility that data may be lost after being entered into a computer system. One basic rule minimizes this danger: Always maintain a backup copy of the data. The backup copy can be used to restore the data to the original system if necessary. Data on mainframe disk packs are backed up on magnetic tape; data on microcomputer hard disks are backed up on floppy disks or tape backup units.

It is costly to maintain backup data, so you need to evaluate these costs in comparison with the costs you would incur if the original data were damaged. The most reliable (and most costly) backup systems require backing up the original data frequently so that the most recent changes are backed up and then storing the backup data in a separate location. If the probability of the primary system failing is .01 and the probability of the backup system failing is .01, the probability that both systems will fail independently is .0001. However, this is true only if the two systems are truly independent—that is, there is negligible likelihood of one event destroying both systems. It is not appropriate to treat the systems as independent if they are located in the same building, because an event such as a fire would damage them both.

There is a trade-off involved in deciding how to back up data. If the backups are not done often enough, there is a risk of losing important data if a system failure occurs. On the other hand, frequent backups are costly.

In addition to keeping track of the processed data, you will often want to maintain a detailed log of the original source transactions that are entered. This allows you to trace changes in the data and makes it possible to restore your data in case of emergency.

Several types of events can damage data on microcomputers. They include:

- Power outages. The internal memory of a computer goes blank when the power is cut off. If you are working with a spreadsheet or word processing program, this means that you will lose all data entered since the last time you saved the data on a disk file. You should frequently save data to a disk in order to minimize the danger of losing data.

- Power surges. Occasionally a spike of unusually high voltage electricity may pass through your power lines. These surges can damage the integrated circuits in the computer. Relatively inexpensive surge protector devices are available to minimize this danger.

- Disk failure. The data stored on a floppy disk may be damaged due to physical mistreatment of the disk or by exposure to magnetic fields. One particular hazard is magnetized paper clips. If a paper clip has become magnetized and is placed on top of a floppy disk, its magnetic field will scramble the magnetic fields of the disk, losing the data that were stored there. To protect your disks, keep them in storage cases designed for that purpose. If you need to carry disks around, obtain carrying cases for the disks. Do not store disks on top of the computer or next to phone cords or other electrical cords. Also, remove all magnetic paper clip holders from your office, since they are often the reason that paper clips become magnetized.

■ Drive failure. The mechanical parts of a disk drive are subject to failure after repeated use. As with any machine, you need access to repair personnel, either inside or outside your own organization.

■ Accidental erasure. There is always the danger that a person may inadvertently cause the computer to erase valuable data, either through direct use of a command such as ERASE in DOS or through a copy command that overwrites an old version of the file. A well-designed program asks for verification before it executes a command that will overwrite existing data (for example, the 1-2-3 File Save command asks you to verify that you wish to replace the old version of the file before it saves the new version). The DOS Copy command does not require verification if you enter a command to copy over new data, so you need to be careful in its use. The DOS Erase command does ask for verification if you enter the command ERASE *.* that would erase all files in the current directory, but otherwise does not ask for verification. (Some programs allow you to undo your last action; for example, if you have accidentally deleted a paragraph while using a word processing program, you can use the undo command to get it back.)

If you do erase a file accidentally, you can sometimes retrieve it through the use of a utility program such as Norton Utilities. When the operating system erases a file, it does not literally search for every spot on the disk containing data for that file in order to scramble the information stored there. Instead, it erases the name for that file in the file directory for the disk, which has the effect of making it totally inaccessible for normal purposes. However, a utility program can sometimes find the data on the disk and restore the file if you have not waited so long that other files have been written to those locations.

■ Lack of space on the hard disk. As the capacity of commonly available hard disks has expanded considerably, it has become easier for people to find room for their data. However, the increased capacity has often led to increased usage, and users often find they can fill up a 40-megabyte hard disk once they have one available. If you need to save a large spreadsheet but do not have enough room on the disk, you will lose the changes you have made since the last save. You should constantly monitor the amount of available space on your hard disk so that you know when you are nearing capacity. One solution is to obtain an archive program that compresses the size of a file that needs to be stored but not used for a while; the compress command can be reversed when you need to restore the file to its normal situation.

- Transmission errors. When data are sent over phone lines, random noise may affect the signal. Recall that the data are sent as a sequence of bits, such as 1 0 1 1 0 0 1 1. If a transmission error causes one of these bits to be reversed, incorrect information will be received. One solution is to add an extra bit to each eight-bit byte. This extra bit (called the parity bit) is set so that the number of ones in the nine-bit group is always even (or odd, depending upon the standard agreed upon for the system). For example, the byte 1 0 1 1 0 0 1 1 contains an odd number of 1s, so the parity bit would be set to 1 in order to make the total number of 1s in the complete group an even number. The receiving computer then checks to make sure that each nine-bit group contains an even number of ones; otherwise it knows an error has occurred and therefore signals the sending computer to retransmit that group. This procedure will not pick up a problem if two bits have been reversed, but this is much less likely to occur.

DELIBERATE DAMAGE

Another hazard is posed by those who deliberately attempt to sabotage a computer system. It is a sad fact of human nature that resources must be spent to protect against this type of threat. There is a general tradeoff between better security and ease of use, and you need to make an intelligent compromise—you cannot expect perfect security and perfect ease of use.

Obviously, the physical security of a computer system is important, particularly with microcomputers that can be easily carried away. There are other hazards unique to the use of computers:

- Dial-up security. The power of computers increases dramatically when they share information with each other. Often, information is transmitted over ordinary phone lines. Once phone line access to the data is allowed, it is necessary to establish safeguards to prevent unauthorized users from dialing your computer and accessing (or, even worse, changing) your information. The first level of dial-up protection occurs with the use of passwords; each authorized user is assigned a password that must be typed to gain access to the system. However, no password system is foolproof. A password system provides more security if the passwords are long and meaningless, but these are harder to remember. If users need to keep a written copy of the password, there is a danger that the paper might fall into the wrong hands.

Safeguards should be taken to prevent an invading computer trying every possible password until it hits the right one. If a sequence of incorrect passwords is entered, the computer should alert a security official; ideally, the caller can be kept on the line until the phone call has been traced.

In another possible procedure, once the computer has received a call from a person who enters an authorized password, it hangs up and then dials the number of that user. In this way, the computer can make sure that only people using authorized phone numbers are allowed access to the system.

— Eavesdroppers. Another danger comes from those who try to steal your information by intercepting your electronic data transmissions. One solution is encryption—that is, sending your data in coded versions that will be decoded at the receiving location. This procedure is complicated, but the added protection is worthwhile if it would be very costly for the information to fall into the wrong hands.

— Inside jobs. Any organization runs the risk of damage caused by dishonest employees, against whom security efforts designed to screen outsiders will be ineffective. The best approach is to develop a system of checks and balances so that it is difficult for one individual to alter data and then conceal that fact; for example, a bank statement should be verified by someone other than the person who writes the checks. A particular danger comes from disgruntled former employees, who on occasion have attempted to sabotage organizations out of pure malice. You should take precautions to make sure that all accounts of former employees have been deactivated and their passwords invalidated.

VIRUSES

A virus is a biological organism that takes over part of a living cell and directs it to produce more copies of the virus. A computer virus does essentially the same thing: It takes over part of a computer system and directs it to produce more copies of itself.

Viruses are one example of malicious software—that is, software designed to cause damage deliberately. The term Trojan horse is generally applied to a program that creates the appearance of performing a useful task but in reality performs some damaging action when an unsuspecting user orders it to be executed.

Viruses, which are particularly dangerous because of their ability to spread and infect many systems, are created by people with a certain type of genius who seem to get a thrill out of the challenge. Most microcomputers need to read part of their operating system from a file on a hard disk or floppy disk whenever they are booted up (that is, started or reset). A virus program typically alters the operating system file so that the computer is directed to copy the altered operating system whenever it is booted up. In addition to providing for its own replication, a virus program provides for some form of action to take place when a specific condition is reached. Normally the virus does not execute this action immediately, since that would alert the user before the virus had a chance to spread. Instead, the virus may be designed to activate after a certain date or time or after a program has been executed a certain number of times. When the virus is activated, it may perform a destructive action such as erasing all files on your hard disk or it may simply display an annoying message that can be very disturbing to the user even if it causes no actual damage.

Because software has become so complicated, it is difficult or impossible to tell if a computer program might perform a harmful action. Defensive programs have been written to fight against viruses, but any type of software can be subverted by a clever enough virus. However, there are some steps that can be taken to reduce the danger.

First, attempt to cut viruses off at the source. If you never allow any external programs into your computer system it will be impossible for a virus to strike. It is usually impossible to keep your computer completely isolated, of course, but you can be careful about what programs you allow onto your system. As a general rule, you should buy software from reputable designers; software from a trusted designer taken directly from its shrink-wrap container is highly unlikely to contain a virus. (There have been cases where software from trusted designers has been infected, but most software designers now take extra precautions against such a danger.)

The threat of viruses is greater with software that comes from other sources, such as public domain shareware obtained from dial-up bulletin boards or by exchange of floppy disks. This is perhaps the most pernicious effect of the threat of computer viruses: They have disrupted the "free-exchange" culture that had developed in which many people helpfully offered software they had written for free to others through bulletin boards. The sad fact is that you must be very careful about using any software that comes from a source you are not sure about. If you run an office with several computers, one person should have the job of administering software; part of this job should be to check out new software before it is used on computers. Your business should establish a policy prohibiting individual users from putting unauthorized software on their own computers. Such a policy, which can succeed only if each user has received adequate education about the potential threat of viruses, is a real annoyance, but it is a sad fact of life that security measures can sometimes be nuisances.

Computers without hard disks require a floppy disk with the operating system files to be inserted into the disk drive whenever the computer is booted up. This provides a way for the virus to copy itself to all of the disks used to boot up the system, but there is an easy solution: Always boot up the system using one write-protected disk used solely for that purpose. A 5.25-inch disk can be write-protected by taping over the notch on the side, a 3.5-inch disk contains a small slide switch that can be set to write-protect the disk. The computer hardware cannot write any new information to a write-protected disk, thus preventing a virus from infecting the operating system files.

The ideal solution for computers with hard disks is similar. You should set aside the part of the hard disk that contains the operating system as write-protected. Write protection should be accomplished through hardware, since any software protection may be bypassed by a clever enough virus programmer. Unfortunately, most commonly used hard disks do not contain this protection (although it will probably become more common in the future).

When computers are connected to a local area network, it makes sense for most (or all) of the software to be kept on the file server machine, in a directory where no user other than the system supervisor is allowed write access. This allows users access to the software but does not allow them to infect it, either deliberately or accidentally. This system also has the advantage of making it easier to perform software upgrades for the company, since the upgrade can be made only on the server and not on each individual machine. It should be obvious that the server machine needs adequate physical security: If anybody can gain access to the server machine at night, there is a risk of tampering.

Computer users should be told to look for unusual activity that might indicate that some sort of malicious program is at work. A computer disk drive normally contains a light to indicate that the computer is reading or writing to the disk. Users should know when their programs should be using the disk so they will be alerted if disk access occurs at a point where it should not, such as if a virus is starting to erase or modify files. Users should also notice if some normal activity, such as booting up the computer, suddenly takes longer than normal. In these cases the computer supervisor should investigate.

Users also should be alert in case any of the files on their disk has suddenly changed—for example, if its creation date or size is altered. However, a clever virus programmer tries to avoid leaving any obvious clues, so the virus will normally reset the file's creation date to its original value and try to keep the file's size the same. There are programs available that can examine the files on a disk to see if they have been altered, although these programs are not foolproof.

No matter how careful your precautions, you should also have contingency plans in mind in case it is necessary to restore your data. The importance of backing up data has been discussed earlier. It is not a serious problem if the virus has infected the backup copies of files that contain only data, instead of computer programs. A data file, such as the list of your customers, does not contain any computer code for the machine to execute, so there is no place for a virus to hide; therefore, you may safely back up data files with your regular backup system. However, executable files (in DOS, usually those that have the file extension COM or EXE) run the risk of being contaminated by a virus, which can also infect any backup copies. Therefore, program software should be restored only by using the original manufacturer's disks. These original disks should be stored in a secure location so they do not run the risk of being tampered with.

Although the threat of virus is real, you should avoid being so preoccupied with it that you ignore other threats that are more likely to occur. One study found 65 percent of losses related to data security came from errors and omissions, 19 percent from dishonest or disgruntled employees, 8 percent from loss of infrastructure, such as power outages, 5 percent from water damage, and 3 percent from outsiders, including virus writers. (Source: Robert Courtney Inc., *Wall Street Journal, August 15, 1990, page B1.*)

SOFTWARE BUGS

A computer follows the instructions it has been given exactly. Unfortunately, these instructions often become so complicated that it is difficult to write them so that the computer will perform the task exactly as intended. Much of the time when the computer makes a mistake, the fault really lies with a software bug. Even if you do not program computers yourself, you should be aware of the possibilities of bugs so you will understand some of the limitations imposed by programs.

If your company is large enough to have its own programmers, you may have experience in working with them as they seek to debug programs. If you rely on software purchased from a vendor, you can usually assume that it has been thoroughly tested before it is released to the market. However, even well-tested software may contain unexpected bugs, so many software packages come with a disclaimer describing the inherent complexity of computer programming and stating that it is impossible to guarantee that the program will work in every conceivable circumstance. When you design a spreadsheet to customize the tasks needed by your business, your worksheet effectively becomes another layer of software with the possibility of bugs.

When people first began to write computer programs, little thought had been given to the issue of how to do it effectively. Since then, the subject has received considerable study, and many books have been written about computer programming concepts. Without going into too much detail, three general rules have been found to be effective guidelines for programmers:

1. Break a big program into a group of smaller parts (called modules). It is much easier to write and test a small module than it is to write a large program all at once. When you are designing the overall program you need to keep in mind what each module will do, but you do not need to think about exactly how it will work. This approach makes it much easier on the programmer because less detail must be kept in mind at one time.

2. Write comments that explain how the program works. Most programming languages provide for explanatory comments to be written as part of the program. These comments are ignored by the computer when it is exe-

cuting the program, but they are available to help people understand what is going on. Such comments are vital for a programmer who is attempting to modify a program written by another programmer.
3. Use mnemonic variable names that indicate the meaning of a quantity. We already saw how the use of the Name command in 1-2-3 makes it much easier to understand 1-2-3 formulas.

A program needs to be tested. If you are introducing a new system to perform a vital business task, you will need to test the system using artificial data before you begin to introduce real data. Typically you will need to run both the old system and the new system in parallel until the new system has been adequately verified under realistic conditions.

QUALITY OF LIFE AND PRIVACY

Some people have deep concerns that computers destroy privacy and lower the quality of life. Some of these concerns are serious, although others are exaggerated or misguided.

Computers do represent a potential threat to privacy, but not because of their ability to gather information. A computer can obtain only the information that is fed into it; if confidential information about individuals is made available to unauthorized sources, there is a potential for harm whether or not a computer is involved. Even worse, false information may be entered into a system; this can cause much harm, but again it is hardly the fault of the computer.

The privacy threat from computers comes from their ability to sort through data very quickly to look for specific information. Imagine that an evil crook had obtained personal information for each person in the United States, written on paper, one page per person. The crook would have great ability to cause harm, but the cumbersome nature of the form of the data would make it very difficult to search systematically through and harm people. However, if all these data were stored on a computer, the crook would suddenly have tremendous ability to search through the data to learn about people meeting any set of criteria. If the crook also had the ability to break into dial-up data bases and falsify information contained there, the potential for mischief would be magnified even more.

When your business obtains personal data about employees or customers, you should feel an ethical obligation to use that information only for the purpose for which it was obtained. In addition, you have certain legal obligations; in 1974 Congress passed the Privacy Act, which restricts the ability of government agencies to disclose personal information, and some states have passed additional privacy laws placing restrictions on businesses. The treatment of certain types of information is governed by additional laws, such as the Fair Credit Reporting Act and the Right to Financial Privacy Act. Privacy violations may also result in civil liability. Therefore, your business should be very careful with your treatment of personal information. Consult a lawyer to learn the specific laws that apply to your situation.

There is also much concern over the effect of excessive use of computers on workers. People who use computers for no more than a small number of hours per day usually find their productivity rises dramatically, and they also often enjoy their work. However, if a worker uses a computer for a full 40-hour work week or more, there can be undesirable effects. Too much repetitive wrist movement at the keyboard can cause wrist difficulties; staring at a computer all day can be hard on the eyes if the screen is not properly lit to minimize glare, and nonadjustable chairs and desks at uncomfortable heights can cause orthopedic problems.

One important solution to such concerns is to make sure that workers have enough breaks so that they can rest their eyes and wrists. If possible, part of each worker's job should not involve working at the keyboard. People tend to find a job that is too repetitive to be difficult no matter what they are doing.

Another fear is that computers will take over jobs now done by people, causing massive unemployment. Similar fears have been expressed many times in history when new inventions were introduced. Instead of causing mass unemployment, new inventions have always created totally new classes of jobs; and this has been the effect of computers. The good news is that many of these jobs are very challenging and interesting, which is good for the people with those jobs. The bad news is that there is a decreasing number of highly paid lower-skill jobs (such as assembly-line work), which will make it more difficult for people with less education to earn good livings. Unless improvements can be made in our educational systems, we run the risk of having a society with a significant and growing segment of illiterate people unable to find jobs paying adequate wages.

The worst fears are that computers may one day become so smart they take over and push us aside. We are a long way away from the time when a computer may have a mind of its own (if such a time ever comes), so these fears are exaggerated, at least for now. Still, it is sensible to take precautions. For example, we should not put the trigger for a major weapon system completely under the control of a machine. Because there is always a risk of computer malfunction, any vital system, such as air traffic control, that is under the control of a computer should also have manual backup systems.

CHAPTER PERSPECTIVE
You should be aware of the problems that can arise when using computers, such as erroneous data entry, data damage, deliberate data destruction, and software bugs.

REFERENCES
John Wack and Lisa Carnahan, *Computer Viruses and Related Threats: A Management Guide* (Washington, D.C.: U.S. Department of Commerce National Institute of Standards and Technology Special Publication 500-166).

Example: Collecting Past-due Accounts

CHAPTER 16

INTRODUCTION AND MAIN POINTS

The remaining chapters of the book describe examples of business tasks that can be performed on computers. Many examples could have been chosen; the purpose of these particular examples is to give you an idea of representative tasks for which computers can be helpful. As it is throughout this book, the focus is on the tasks themselves, with the computer seen as a tool to help perform the task.

Any business that makes sales on credit must worry about customers who do not pay their bills on time. The computer can be very valuable in providing information to the collector who phones these customers and diplomatically but firmly tries to obtain payment.

After studying the material in this chapter, you will know some ways in which a computer can help in the collection process.

COMPUTERS AS A HELP FOR A COLLECTOR

Computers can be used to organize the collection of past-due accounts in several ways: by flagging accounts as they become past due, generating delinquency notices automatically, displaying accounts for a human collector to process, allowing a collector to access the account history, and saving notes regarding contacts with the customer. Company-approved letters for most collection situations can be preprogrammed for collectors to use.

Systems can be programmed to put accounts into a special billing cycle as they become past due. Accounts that are only 30 days past due may not need the attention of a human collector; computer-generated notices can be sent as a reminder for people who have simply forgotten their payments. If an account becomes 60 days past due, the system can be programmed to flag it and assign it to a human collector. Accounts are displayed in sequence; as each is processed, any work done on it is noted, and the computer then displays the next account in the sequence. This system keeps the collector from working on the easier accounts first, since some action must be taken on each account before the next one can be displayed. The collector must have the ability to access accounts at will in order to be able to handle those occasions when the borrower initiates contact or returns the collector's call. The system can be programmed to assign accounts that have been in collections previously to the same collector who handled them in the past, saving the time it would take someone new to become familiar with the account.

A screen can be set to display information necessary to the collector, such as the customer's name, last known address, and any available phone numbers. This information can be entered into the system as accounts are opened and become part of each customer's permanent record.

It is helpful for the collector to have at least a 12-month payment history available. This allows the collector to see when the problem began and to be more specific when talking to the customer. If the customer missed one payment in January and one in June, the account would show 60 days past due, even though the customer has not missed two consecutive payments; the only contact would have been 6 months of computer-generated 30-day-late notices. It can be difficult for a collector to explain this to the customer without knowing the exact dates of missed payments.

A note field allows collectors to record their contacts with the customer and to review notes made by others who have worked the file. Collectors can note special payment arrangements the borrower has agreed to and any explanations the customer has offered for the delinquency, allowing the new collector to be sensitive to unusual circumstances in the customer's life. If the customer has been out of work, the collector knows that the first question to ask is, "Have you found a new job?" and not "Why haven't we received a payment?" If special payment arrangements have been made and are being kept, the collector can see this and may decide not to call the customer again. In the case of special-payment arrangements, it is helpful to be able to code the account to suppress the computer-generated late notices.

Frequently, customers cannot be contacted by phone. Prewritten letters that conform to all applicable laws and regulations regarding collection practices can save the collectors a great deal of time and can protect the company from possible lawsuits, since the letters can be reviewed by the legal department before they are sent.

A computerized collection department can save a company money, eliminating time spent sorting through accounts and deciding which ones need to be contacted. Accounts will not be missed, or ignored, because they must be worked in sequence; and notices can be generated for accounts that may not require the attention of an experienced collector. A collector can pick up a new file and become familiar with the background immediately, saving the time that otherwise would be spent repeating an earlier collector's work.

POINT-OF-SALE INFORMATION

Information from point-of-sale terminals can be used to make a store's customer service and billing inquiry departments much more efficient. All information regarding a transaction is in the computer system already; all that is needed is a program to organize it. If a customer in a store that is not computerized has a question regarding a purchase, the store has to pull the original sales ticket to see what was bought. With a computer system, the only time a sales ticket should need to be pulled is if there is a question regarding the customer's signature.

Most revolving retail account billings show only one item per transaction on the monthly statement. A customer who purchases three shirts and four pairs of socks may receive a monthly bill showing a $150 charge for socks if the first item entered at the point of sale was one of the pairs of socks. If the customer doesn't have a copy of the itemized receipt available, and doesn't have a clear memory of the transaction, he may well question the transaction. Prior to the use of computers, the only way to tell the customer what else was included in the purchase was to pull an actual copy of the sales ticket. For a large department store, such a system requires a great deal of employee time spent pulling and copying "media." If the sales ticket cannot be located and the customer doesn't remember the charge, the store may have to credit the customer's account, even if the purchase was actually made.

The computer can be programmed to store all information regarding purchases—what was purchased, where, and when. The customer service representative can access all purchase information by account number and date. In most normal borrower inquiries, once the customers are reminded of the purchase, they no longer question the bill; satisfying their inquiry has taken only a few minutes on the computer, instead of time spent pulling a sales ticket and either calling the customer back or mailing out a copy. A more elaborate system programs each item by stock number, instead of by department number. This allows the customer service representative to provide the customer with highly detailed information regarding the purchase. The primary reason to gather such sales information is to help the store's buyers target the preference of their market area and for the marketing department to target specific customers for specific advertisements, but it is useful to have the system set up so that customer service can also access the information.

Billing statements for purchases made on third party accounts, such as MasterCard, Visa, or American Express, show only the store and the date. Borrowers frequently do not remember those charges by the time they receive their billing statements. Even though a store has no account information regarding these customers, the point-of-sale terminal can be programmed to record the transaction by account number, allowing the customer service representative to access the same information as for a transaction on the store's own charge accounts. Again, this saves time otherwise spent pulling media to see what the items were and money that would have been lost if the third party accountholder were to "charge back" a transaction questioned by its customer.

Retail stores' computer systems already store a great deal of information, which can have many applications in addition to those originally contemplated. The more information that is accessible to a customer service representative when the customer first calls, the less time is required to solve the customer's problem.

CHAPTER PERSPECTIVE

It is very frustrating for customers to have to wait while a business representative finds information. Computers are valuable because they can make information available quickly, even in the middle of a phone call. Collecting overdue accounts, which can be a difficult process, can proceed much more smoothly if the necessary information is readily available.

Example: Mortgage Loans

CHAPTER

17

INTRODUCTION AND MAIN POINTS
Banks earn their profits by making loans; however, before they can lend money to potential borrowers, they must evaluate the risk that the loan will not be paid back. Mortgage loan underwriting is the evaluation of what constitutes an acceptable risk to the lender. By using statistical analysis, computers can be used to free human underwriters to spend their time on files that need their judgment and experience.

After studying the material in this chapter, you will know the type of information that is needed in the loan application process and how a computer can help with loan processing.

COMPUTERS IN MORTGAGE LOAN ORIGINATION AND PROCESSING
Computer processing of loan applications has several advantages over manual processing. The accuracy of the information on the documents is assured because data need be entered only once and checked, instead of being entered separately on each document with an increased risk of error. Errors in arithmetic and interest rate quotations can be eliminated. Each loan processor can handle a higher volume of files, because it is no longer necessary to spend time typing the same information on several forms. In addition, computers can be programmed to approve or deny files that meet specific criteria, allowing underwriters to concentrate their time reviewing only those files that require their experience and knowledge.

Many companies are aiming at computerizing their loan processing system from the time of application. A loan officer with a laptop computer and a modem would be able to access current rate information 24 hours a day, allowing the interest rate to be locked on the system at the time of application, even if it isn't during normal business hours, and enabling the company's secondary marketing department to forecast more accurately what loans will be available for future sale. Errors in quoting interest rates and fees can be eliminated by programming the system so that rates and fees entered must match a matrix of available programs. Although the system should be set up so that exceptions can be entered, it can be programmed to flag all exceptions for review by a supervisor or by the secondary marketing department.

In a fully computerized system, a loan officer handling an alternative, or reduced documentation, loan (typically one with a down payment of more than 20 percent), could use bank statements to verify the down payment and paystubs and W-2s to verify income, pull an infile credit report through the modem, send all available information to the mainframe, and, if the file matches predetermined criteria programmed into the main system, have immediate loan approval for the borrowers, conditional only on a satisfactory appraisal and a clear title report. If, to maintain quality control, a company does not want its loan officers to give approval in the field, a loan processor could follow the same procedures in the office, either giving all files to the underwriter for review or giving the underwriter only those files that were rejected by the computer.

The computer can save time for the processor when setting up files for higher risk loans and FHA and VA loans, which require full processing. The borrower's name, social security number, and address and information regarding bank accounts and employment need to be typed only once; this information can be used to print the final typed application and the verification of deposit and employment forms that are mailed to the banks and the borrower's employer. The system can be set up to require certain information before a file goes to underwriting, preventing details being overlooked. A system can be set to flag an item in several ways—it can highlight fields that require something to be entered, or generate reports of missing information. In the first design, operators often fill in the blank with random characters if the correct information is not available and then forget to go back and fill in the appropriate information when it is received.

Some companies with centralized underwriting offices are setting up systems in which the processor processes the file and then, when it is complete, types a code to send it to an underwriter; the underwriter then makes a decision based on the information in the computer and on the appraisal, which can be faxed to the underwriter for review. This system eliminates the time that would have been wasted sending the file from one office to another.

Computers make it easier to draw accurate closing papers. Names, addresses, and the legal description of the property need be entered and checked only once, ensuring the accuracy of all documents. The computer can accurately calculate the annual percentage rate for the truth-in-lending disclosure, based on the estimated closing date in the computer. Errors in arithmetic can be eliminated. The computer can be programmed to "know" which documents are required for specific programs and can display form numbers for the closer, so that the appropriate note, deed of trust, and any necessary riders are used. Once a loan is closed, the computer can be programmed to pick files randomly for audit, to pull files that meet the criteria for high risk loans, or to pull files that show a slow payment history in the first few months of the loan. By tracing problem files back to their source, errors can be identified and eliminated.

CHAPTER PERSPECTIVE

Almost any task where a large amount of information needs to be processed can be profitably done on a computer. Mortgage loan processing provides an example. The design of the complete system must specify not only the tasks of the computer but also the tasks of the people. Typically, the computer can handle routine tasks while it flags exceptional cases that require extra attention by a person.

Example: Purchase Order Maintenance System

CHAPTER

18

INTRODUCTION AND MAIN POINTS

Consider a department store chain that sells a multitude of different items obtained from many different vendors. The store's buyers decide what merchandise the chain should buy. Then the chain's information system generates purchase orders and other documents required to route the merchandise to the correct stores. In this chapter we consider a case study of a Purchase Order Maintenance system (hereafter referred to as POM) used by one retail department store chain. The purpose of the system is to track purchase orders as they are entered into the system, filled by the vendor, and distributed to the stores.

After studying the material in this chapter, you will understand how information flows in the purchase order system: the processes for initial data entry, updating, and receiving the items and directing them to the proper store location.

CONNECTING DIFFERENT COMPUTER SYSTEMS

The retail store chain has a central data processing center that uses an IBM mainframe. The central buying offices for the chain are located at the same site, and all purchase orders are entered here. The central warehouse for the chain, which has a Wang mini-computer, is responsible for receiving vendor shipments and distributing ordered items to the proper store. Most purchase order functions, such as updates to purchase orders and receipt of items, are performed on the Wang; the IBM mainframe is used for inquiry functions by the buyers. Two separate sets of purchase order files are maintained; in fact, there are separate files for general purchase order information, purchase order line item information, general purchase order receiving information, and receiving information for each line item.

The need for the separate systems arose from the POM software chosen. The chain's managers decided to use a POM system that is used by other divisions owned by the store chain's parent. This decision dictated the hardware selection (since the software is written specifically for the Wang). The software is written and maintained by the chain's own staff of professional programmers using COBOL, the language that is commonly used for data processing applications on large computers. The issues of compatibility between the two systems will be discussed in later sections.

Although this single system will be discussed as an isolated system, it is important to realize that it must interact with other systems. As ordered items are distributed, the merchandise inventory system is updated to reflect what items are stocked at each store. The system is also used to update files used to determine the number of items on order or backordered and to record the distribution of an item to each store. A key factor in allowing the interface to other systems is the use of an item number identifier which is consistent across systems. The item is identified by a department number (a department identifier used by the chain), a vendor number (an identifier assigned by the chain to identify each vendor), and a style number (the vendor-assigned identifier assigned to the item). The value of using the vendor's style number may not be obvious; however, because the number is used consistently throughout the tracking systems, it is an easy way to identify and is preferable to using an internal merchandise item number which must later be translated to a vendor specific item number.

PURCHASE ORDER ENTRY

The purchase order entry function is not an on-line function as you might expect. Because of the separate systems and the need to synchronize the purchase order files, purchase order entry is handled in a batch mode—the input is collected first in machine-readable form and then processed by the mainframe computer as a batch at a later time, typically at night (so that the batch-processing jobs do not tie up the computer's processing capability during the day when other on-line tasks can be performed and so that the computer's processing capability is not wasted at night).

The decisions about merchandise acquisitions are made by the chain's buyers, who submit purchase orders each day to the data entry department. The data entry clerks enter the data on a separate computer dedicated to this purpose. The programmers design the data entry screens for this computer so the clerks know what information to enter and so that a certain amount of entry validation is possible (for example, the screen can validate fields for specific data types). Information entered on this machine is stored on disk for later transmission to the mainframe. Once the information is on the mainframe, the software puts the purchase order entry information into the format expected by the Wang purchase order front-end program. In order to verify the accuracy of the data transmitted by the data entry equipment to the mainframe, control totals are produced on the mainframe and compared to the total generated by the data entry equipment at transmission time (typically, this total is the total number of records transmitted and received).

Once the totals are verified, the transmission of the purchase orders from the IBM to the Wang takes place. The data must be converted into a form that the Wang can understand. (The IBM and Wang use different internal representations of data—the Wang represents data internally in ASCII format, while the IBM uses the IBM-standard EBCDIC representation.) In addition to the control totals, a front-end edit program is used to check for completeness of data to ensure that portions of transmitted records, or entire records themselves, have not been lost during transmission and to edit the records for valid information before they are entered into the POM system. Any detected errors, which are usually the result of some human error, are written to an error report. For example, the buyer might have incorrectly calculated the total price of all the line items ordered, or the data entry clerk may have incorrectly entered purchase order detail information. Errors resulting from problems in the actual transmission of the data (from the data entry equipment to the mainframe, or from the mainframe to the minicomputer) are much more rare. Any errors that do exist are corrected on the Wang through the purchase order update process. Valid purchase order information is added to the Wang purchase order file and a log file (described later). At this point it is important to remember that the mainframe purchase order file has not been updated with the new purchase orders.

PURCHASE ORDER UPDATE
Throughout the working day purchase order information is updated at the request of the buyer writing the order. These updates frequently involve the correction of errors from the previous night's verification program or input of newly available information that was not available when the purchase order was

entered (for example, the distribution of items to specific stores or the actual shipping date). In these cases, standard default values have been established which pass the verification program but require correction before the file can be acted upon. An example is the distribution of items to stores. If, at the time of initial entry, the buyer has not specified a distribution, all received items are sent to the warehouse. If the merchandise is received before the distribution order, the items remain in the warehouse until the proper updates are made.

All updates are performed on the Wang system by personnel whose specific duties involve the updating and correcting of purchase order information. All purchase order update information is written to a log file, whose purpose is to record all changes made to the purchase order files throughout the day. Two important uses of the log file are to apply changes to the mainframe purchase order files and to permit the files to be restored if they are lost (for example, by a disk-drive failure).

The records in the log file, which are of variable length, correspond to particular records in one of the purchase order-related files. The entire updated record is written to the log file and an additional key area is used to identify the record type (for example, purchase order line item or receipt line item) and the action taken (updated or deleted). This log file is used to update the mainframe purchase order files—another batch job reads the log file, determines the file affected, and applies the correct update action to the file. In this way the separate sets of files are kept in sync.

PURCHASE ORDER RECEIVING

As purchase orders are filled, the purchase order receiving files are updated in a process similar to that used for general purchase order updates (log file records are written and applied to the mainframe files). The receiving process also drives another important process—the generation of price tags and labels.

As items are checked into the warehouse, they are matched to the original purchase order, which contains all of the information needed to create a price ticket, such as the retail price, department number, vendor number, style and color code, and store distribution. Based on the department number, the price tag or price label is generated in batches that exactly match the store distribution. If a particular store is to receive five of an item, only five tickets are produced for that store. This allows the person on the marking line to separate the items by store distribution quickly without having to count off the number of items for each store and prevents any tickets from floating around to be applied later to a similar but higher-priced item by unscrupulous employees.

The way in which these items are eventually sent to the correct loading dock is interesting, although not directly related to the purchase order system. Labels containing the eventual store destination are created and affixed to the boxes of items ready to be shipped. The boxes are put on the conveyor system and sent to the loading area; as the boxes reach the loading area, each label is scanned and automatically diverted to the appropriate loading bay.

Information from the purchase order system is also used as input into other systems. Because of this, the timing of these jobs is critical; it is imperative that the POM system complete the processing necessary to create the input into the other systems. Complicating the issue is the fact that the chain has stores in more than one time zone, shortening the nightly batch window (the time available at night to run batch jobs). To address this problem, the nightly processing of POM jobs starts at a certain time each day (4 P.M.). Once the processing starts, all purchase-order related files become unavailable for on-line use.

Another issue that must be addressed is the way in which separate POM files are kept in sync. Because the programs that handle the addition and update of purchase orders are not identical on the mainframe and the minicomputer, it is inevitable that the files will get out of sync as time goes on. To correct this situation, copies of the files on the minicomputer are periodically used to overlay the mainframe files.

CHAPTER PERSPECTIVE

Designing a system such as a purchase order system requires considering many different factors, including computer processing capacity. This chapter described how a minicomputer and a mainframe computer can work together in just one of the many information systems that must operate for a complex department store.

Example: Information Retrieval

CHAPTER
19

INTRODUCTION AND MAIN POINTS
Suppose you have just entered a large library looking for information on a particular topic. This task is practically impossible if you don't have access to an index telling you where to look; even with an index, the process of searching for the correct volumes is cumbersome and there is a risk that important sources may not be listed in the index. Could a computer be used to perform this type of search?

After studying the material in this chapter:

■ You will understand how computers can be used to retrieve information from indexes or from full-text databases.

■ You will understand how a law firm might use a computerized information retrieval service.

COMPUTERIZED LIBRARIES
In order for information stored on a computer to be readily accessible, the material must be available in machine-readable form. This requires storage capacity much larger than that of a microcomputer hard disk. One option is to put the data on CD-ROM (compact disk, read-only memory); microcomputers in the 1990s will increasingly be connected to CD readers as more and more CD information products become available (for example, the text of an encyclopedia can be placed on a CD-ROM, along with digitized versions of the illustrations and even sounds).

Another option is to connect to on-line data sources over phone lines. During the late 1980s many types of commercial on-line data bases became available. If one of these services is particularly important for your business, it will probably be worthwhile to subscribe to it. In addition, many of these sources are available at libraries; some offer indexes that allow you to determine the locations of information you require, and others contain full-text databases that allow you to search through the complete text of documents.

You also need a software system that retrieves documents in response to user queries. Even though computers process data at high rates of speed, they can take a noticeable amount of time to search through a large data base. The software should be designed to perform searches as efficiently as possible.

Many libraries are replacing card catalogs with computerized catalogs, which are easier to update, since it is not necessary to file separate cards for the author, title, and subject. Once the data for a book are entered into the system, the computer can automatically file the information in the right locations. In addition, library users can find information more quickly using a computer catalog, since they do not have to search physically through all of the cards. The big difficulty with establishing a computer card catalog is that it takes a long time to enter the data for the books already listed in the card catalog.

Suppose that you wish to obtain more information about on-line data bases and that you use a computer index to find articles about this subject. The example presented here uses a service called Academic Index, operated by Information Access Co. The service, which references articles in over 375 periodicals, is subscribed to by many libraries.

To start using the Academic Index, type in a key word describing your subject. Type the word ON-LINE. You will see:

ON-LINE.
-(periodical reviews)
ON-LINE APPLICATION SYSTEM INTERACTIVE SOFTWARE
(OPERATING SYSTEM)
see
THEOS (OPERATING SYSTEM)
ON-LINE BIBLIOGRAPHIC SEARCHING
see
On-line bibliographic searching
ON-LINE CATALOG NEWS.
-(periodical reviews)
THE ON-LINE CATALOGUE: DEVELOPMENT AND DIRECTIONS.
-(book reviews)

Move the highlight bar to the line that says "On-line bibliographic searching" to focus your search in this area. The screen will show more detailed topics that relate to this area:

ON-LINE BIBLIOGRAPHIC SEARCHING
see also
Data bases
-analysis
-anecdotes, satire, etc.
-books
-business use
-case studies
-computer programs
-conferences and meetings
-costs
-economic aspects
-educational use
-Europe
-evaluation
-fees
-finance
-innovations
-library applications
-management
-marketing
-periodicals
-personal narratives
-quality control
-services
-study and teaching
-technique
-training
-usage

Move the highlight bar to "management." The screen will now display information on six articles on this topic. You choose:

Searching full-text databases (column) by Carol Tenopir v113 Library Journal May 1 88 p60(2)

Now you need to go to the shelves to find this journal. The article itself is about how to search for information through a full-text database—that is, an on-line service that contains the complete texts of a set of documents, allowing you to search through any article for any particular word. This type of search can be a very powerful way to find information, but you must plan your search strategy carefully; if your search target is too broad, you will retrieve so many documents that it will be too much work to search through all of them yourself. On the other hand, if your search target is too narrow you run the risk of missing documents that would be helpful to you. In the next section we discuss the ways using a full-text database can be helpful for a law firm.

SEARCHING FOR LEGAL INFORMATION

A lawyer's job often involves searching for information and sometimes requires access to a complete library containing records of cases, statutes, and review articles. This material has been collected in machine-readable form and is available to law firms on a dial-up subscription basis from services such as LEXIS, operated by Mead Data Central.

Information in LEXIS is arranged in libraries; for example, there are libraries for corporate law, environmental law, and labor law. Within each library, information is arranged in files, and each file contains documents; for example, one file contains decisions by the U.S. Supreme Court, and the decision in each case represents a document.

Subscribers may connect to LEXIS by using their computer and a modem. The user enters a description of the information being searched for; for example, you can search for all documents that contain a specific word, such as "computer." There are several refinements built in to LEXIS to make it more likely that the results of the computer's search will match the user's intent; LEXIS automatically retrieves standard plural forms such as "computers" and standard possessive forms of proper names.

A broad search for a single word will probably retrieve too many documents. If you are interested in computer privacy, you might enter "computer privacy" as the search target. However, you will miss documents that contain sentences such as "computers are a potential threat to privacy." Entering "computer w/25 privacy" will find all documents in which the word "computer" appears within 25 words of the word "privacy."

You may connect two search targets with the word OR. Use this option carefully; the search "computer OR privacy" will retrieve any document which mentions either computers or privacy, which is likely to be far too many documents. The OR connector is particularly useful when the same item might be referred to in more than one way; for example, the search "Bankamericard or Visa" will retrieve all documents mentioning this credit card, regardless of which name is used.

You will often wish to add additional search targets to narrow your focus and reduce the number of documents retrieved. For example, you may be interested only in decisions issued after a certain date or in decisions given by a particular court. When you have identified the documents that you need to look at, you may have them printed.

CHAPTER PERSPECTIVE

In this book we have seen many ways in which computers can process information. As the hardware capability of computers improves in both storage capacity and processing speed, new horizons for information processing open up. One area likely to grow rapidly in the future is the use of computers to store and retrieve library information.

Appendix 1

This section is intended for readers without any experience with microcomputers.

The operating system is the software that controls the operation of the computer. First we discuss the operating system MS-DOS, which became the most widely used operating system on business microcomputers because of the popularity of IBM-PC's and compatibles. We then look at graphical user interfaces, used on newer operating systems such as that on the Apple Macintosh or Microsoft's OS/2.

Normally you find yourself in the operating system environment after you start a microcomputer. Under MS-DOS, the screen displays a prompt such as C) when you are in the operating system environment. (The C indicates that drive C is the current drive. Typically, drive C is your hard disk.) You then need to enter a command to cause your application program to begin; for example, typing 123 in response to the operating system prompt allows you to begin execution of Lotus 1-2-3.

Information stored on your disk is arranged in files. Each file consists of a name, followed by a period and a three-character file extension which indicates the type of file. A file with the extension .EXE or .COM is a program file containing machine language code that the computer can execute; a file with extension .WKS or .WK1 or .WKE is a Lotus 1-2-3 worksheet file; a file with extension .DOC could be a document file from a word processing program.

These are some basic commands that you should be familiar with if you work with MS-DOS:
DIR look at a directory of files on the disk in the current drive
DIR A: look at a directory of all files on the disk in drive A
DIR *.WK* look at a list of all files on the disk in the current drive with extension beginning with WK (i.e., look at Lotus 1-2-3 worksheet files). The asterisk, *, acts as a wild card that can represent any character or group of characters.

FORMAT A: used to format a new disk in drive A so that it will be ready for data to be stored on it.

COPY *source-filename target* copy from the specified source to the target file; examples include:

COPY BUDG1.WKS BUDG1B.WKS copy from the existing file BUDG1.WKS to the new file BUDG1B.WKS (both the original file and the copy file are on the current drive, since no drive designation is included)

COPY A:ARPT92.DOC C: copy the existing file ARPT92.DOC from drive A to drive C

COPY A:*.* C: copy all files on drive A to drive C

ERASE *filename* erase the specified file from the disk

A: change the current drive to drive A

C: change the current drive to drive C

When you work with a hard disk you will soon find you have so many files that using the complete directory of all files is unwieldy. Instead, you can organize your hard disk into different directories. You should group related files together. Use the MKDIR command to make a new directory; for example, the command MKDIR LETTERS will create a directory called LETTERS for you to store letters that you write with your word processing program. Use the command CD\LETTERS to change the current directory to the letters directory. Then, if you use the DIR command, you will see only the names of files in the letters directory, not all of the files on the whole hard disk. You can also create subdirectories below a given directory; for example, you can have a directory called LETTERS\APPLIC for letters to job applicants.

The Macintosh computer, introduced in 1984, provided a graphic user interface instead of the command line user interface used in MS-DOS. On the Macintosh, the user moves a pointer around the screen with the mouse. Pointing to the picture (or icon) representing a command on the screen and pressing the button on the mouse activates that command. The operating system communicates with the user by displaying dialog boxes offering choices on the screen; the user then points to the correct choice. A list of files then appears on the screen. The user moves the pointer to highlight the correct file and clicks the mouse. The Macintosh operating system is designed so that all application programs follow the same structure for giving commands, so that a user familiar with one application will not find it difficult to use other applications.

Microsoft's newer operating system, OS/2, contains many of

these same features in its user interface, Presentation Manager. OS/2 also includes other advanced features, such as the ability to run more than one program simultaneously. However, the fact that OS/2 requires a computer with a large memory and hard disk to run efficiently has slowed down its acceptance.

In 1990 Microsoft introduced Windows 3, which provided the advantage of the graphical user interface at a more economical price than OS/2. Windows 3 is a much improved version of the earlier program Windows, which allowed users to create applications that run in a section of the screen (called a window), making it possible to shift easily between applications. Windows 3 automatically senses the type of hardware installed (such as the type of microprocessor—80386, 80286, or 8088) so it can take full advantage of the available hardware. It can easily be added to machines that use traditional MS-DOS and allows MS-DOS applications to run just as they would have before. However, it also provides the ability to take advantage of much larger memory sizes and other hardware improvements. Because of these advantages Windows 3 achieved widespread popularity soon after it was introduced.

Appendix 2

This appendix briefly compares Lotus 1-2-3 and Microsoft's Excel. The essential features of Excel are similar to those of 1-2-3; it is a worksheet consisting of rows (labelled with numbers) and columns (labelled with letters) into which you may enter formulas that refer to other cells. (Putting an equal sign at the beginning of the formula lets Excel know that it is in fact a formula.) The arithmetic operations are the same as with other computer programs: +, addition; −, subtraction; *, multiplication; /, division; ^, exponentiation. Dollar signs are used to indicate absolute addresses, as in 1-2-3.

Many of the built-in functions are the same in Excel and 1-2-3, but there are slight differences in the way they are entered. For example, the function @SUM(A1..A10) in 1-2-3 is written =SUM(A1:A10) in Excel. The syntax of some other functions is slightly different; for example, in 1-2-3 the internal rate of return function is written @IRR(*initial guess, value range*); in Excel it is written =IRR(*value range, initial guess*).

If you need to transfer a worksheet file from 1-2-3 to Excel, or the other way around, Excel has a feature that allows it to read or write 1-2-3 worksheet files. This translation feature automatically translates formulas into the appropriate form. However, not every feature can be translated; for example, the formatting, graphing, and macro structures are different in the two programs. Also, if you are translating worksheets between Macintosh computers and IBM PCs, you need to translate the disk format either by using a machine that has an extra disk drive so that it can read both types of disks or by connecting the machines by direct wire or by phone and transmitting the file with a communications program.

Excel is a newer program, and it takes advantage of the user interface features of the Macintosh, such as the use of the mouse. If you are familiar with other programs that operate on the

Macintosh, you will find Excel easy to learn. For example, a list of menus appears at the top of the Excel screen:

() File Edit Formula Format Data Options Macro Window

Use the mouse to move the pointer to indicate one of these choices, click the mouse button, and the pulldown menu giving you the choices for that menu will appear on the screen.

Excel allows you to write powerful macros. Excel macros work very differently than those in 1-2-3 because the command structure of Excel is different. Macros are put on separate sheets, called macro worksheets. Excel macros allow you to create custom menus and dialog boxes, which can be very powerful tools for customizing your worksheet.

Glossary

ASCII standard coding system used on most microcomputers for representing letters and other characters as binary numbers

baud one bit per second; used to measure the speed of data transmission

binary number number expressed using a base-2 system in which the only digits are 0 and 1; for example, 1 0 0 1 in binary means $1 \times 2^3 + 0 \times 2^2 + 0 \times 2^1 + 1 \times 2^0 = 9$

bit binary digit; that is, a character that is either 0 or 1

bug an error in a computer program

byte the amount of memory needed to store one character, normally 8 bits

CAD computer-aided design; use of the computer in the design process, as in architecture

CAM computer-aided manufacturing; use of the computer in the manufacturing process

CD-ROM compact disk, read-only memory; a device for storing computer information similar to an audio compact disk

compiler software that translates a program written in a programming language (such as COBOL) into a machine language program

coprocessor a separate circuit that can help the main processor perform certain complicated tasks, such as mathematical calculations

CPU central processing unit; the part of the computer that decodes instructions and controls the operation of the computer

CRT cathode ray tube; television-like screen on which electron beams create visual images

cursor symbol on a computer terminal that shows where on the screen the next character you type will appear

data factual information (the singular form, datum, means a single fact)

desktop publishing the use of a personal computer to design and print typeset documents, allowing the user to arrange page layouts for text and illustrations

directory a list of the names of files on a disk or a subdivision of a disk containing related files

disk computer storage device; see *floppy disk* and *hard disk*

EBCDIC coding system used to represent characters on large IBM computers

electronic data interchange process of transmitting machine-readable data from one system to another so they can be directly processed by the destination system without retyping

electronic mail process of transmitting messages to other computer users, either over a local area network or across phone lines

expert system a computer program that can relate information to goals in an area where human beings must use knowledge and judgment

file the unit for organizing information on a computer storage device, such as a hard disk; an individual file may contain a computer program or data

floppy disk a storage device used on microcomputers consisting of magnetic coating on a small plastic disk, which is inserted into the disk drive of the computer

hard disk a storage device for microcomputers consisting of an aluminum disk coated with a magnetic surface that is built into the computer

hardware the physical components of a computer system; distinguished from *software*

K one kilobyte = 1,024 bytes

LAN local area network; a group of nearby computers connected so they may share data and hardware devices

LCD liquid crystal display; a type of display commonly used on laptop computers

MB one megabyte = 1,048,576 bytes

memory the part of the computer where information is stored; see *RAM*

menu a list of options for the user to choose from

microprocessor an electronic circuit that contains the complete central processing unit for a computer on a single integrated circuit (chip)

modem a device that allows a computer to transmit and receive data over a phone line

monitor a device, such as a CRT screen, for displaying computer output to the user

mouse a computer input device connected to the computer by a wire; the user rolls the mouse around the desktop to change the position of a pointer on the screen

MS-DOS Microsoft Disk Operating System; the operating system commonly used on IBM personal computers and compatibles

numeric keypad a keypad containing the numeric digits separate from the main alphabetic keypad, making it easier to enter numeric data

operating system the software that controls the operation of a computer

OS/2 operating system introduced by Microsoft for IBM PS/2 computers

RAM random-access memory; the main internal memory in a computer

ROM read-only memory; refers to a part of computer memory where data can be read from but not written to

software the instructions (programs) that govern the operation of a computer; distinguished from *hardware*

spreadsheet a format for arranging business data in rows and columns; paper spreadsheets were commonly used before computer spreadsheets became available

word processing the process of typing a document to be stored in machine-readable form so that changes can be made without requiring the document to be retyped

Index of Lotus 1-2-3 Commands

This index will help you find locations in the text where Lotus 1-2-3 commands and functions are described. @ designates functions; a brief description of the arguments for each function is included. / is used to call up the command menu. For each command the keystroke sequence needed to invoke the command is included. { designates macro commands.

Because this book focuses on business tasks, rather than the computer software itself, not all 1-2-3 commands have been described in this book. See your reference manual for more information.

Absolute address, 59
ALT key, for macros, 88
Arrow keys, 45

Backspace key, 45
{BEEP}, 115
{BRANCH *cell reference*}, 115–116

Column-width command, /WCS, 69
Control-break (interrupt macro execution), 116
Control page-up, 194
Control page-down, 194
Copy command /C, 56–59, 203
Criterion for selection, /DQC, 143–153

Data command, /D, 141–155
@DDB *(initial cost, salvage value, lifetime, current period)*, double declining balance depreciation, 174
Distribution command, /DD, 154
Dollar sign, 59, 166

Edit key, (F2), 65
Erase command, /RE, 123
Escape key, 65
Extract command, /DQE, 145

File command, /F, 67–68
File import command, /FI, 93
@FIND *(string to look for, string to look in, starting location)*, 151
Format command, /RF, 52–53
Formulas, 53
  distinguished from labels, 61
Formulas, printing, /PPOOC, 76

{GETLABEL *prompt string, location*}, 113
{GETNUMBER *prompt string, location*}, 113
GOTO key (F5), 94
Group command, /WGGE, 203–204

Help key (F1), 65, 93
@HLOOKUP *(item to find, range to look in, # of row to move down)*, 84

@IF *(condition, formula to use if true, formula to use if false)*, 109, 132
{IF *condition*} commands to be done if condition is true, 115
@INDEX *(range, column location, row location)*, 119, 124
Insert sheet, /WIS, 194, 200
@IRR *(initial guess, range)*, internal rate of return, 162
@ISERR *(cell reference)*, 115, 151

Label, 45, 61
{LET *location, value*}, 114
Linking files, 211

@MAX *(range)*, 65
Menu, 45, 92

Name command, /RN, 48–52
Name table, /RNT, 79
#NOT#, 152
@NOW, 125,
@NPV *(interest rate, range)*, present value, 160

INDEX OF LOTUS 1-2-3 COMMANDS

{PANELOFF}, 91, 113
@PMT *(principal amount of loan, interest rate, number of periods)*, mortgage payment, 163–164
Point, 57–58
Print file command, /PF, 68
Print printer command, /PP, 68
Protect command, /WGPE, 74
{PUT *range, column location, row location, new value*}, 122
@PV *(amount received each period, interest rate, number of periods)*, present value of annuity, 163

Query command, /DQ, 143
Quit command, /Q, 70
Quote mark, 45

Range command /R, 48–52
Relative address, 59
Retrieve command, /FR, 68

Save command, /FS, 67–68
@SLN *(initial cost, salvage value, lifetime)*, straight line depreciation, 174
Sort command, /DS, 141
STEP mode, for macros (ALT-F2), 91
Subroutine, in macro, 113
@SUM *(range)*, 63, 205
@SYD *(initial cost, salvage value, lifetime, current period)*, sum-of-years-digits depreciation, 176

Table command, /DT2, 166–169

Unprotect command, /RU, 74

Value command /RV, 116
@VLOOKUP *(item to find, range to look in, # of columns to move right)*, 83, 114

{WINDOWSOFF}, 91, 114
Worksheet command /W, 47–48

Index

Abacus, 27–29
Academic Index, 263
Accounts, chart of, 102–103, 106–107
Aiken, Howard, 31
Analytic engine, 29
Annuity, 163
APL, 36
Apple, 36–37 *(see also* Macintosh)
ASCII, 23, 93
Assembly language, 35
Atanasoff, John, 31

Babbage, Charles, 29
Backup data, 239, 245
Balance sheet, 97
Bar code, 13, 102
BASIC, 36
Blue Cross, 234
Budget, 72–86, 131–138, 177–191, 200–212
Bugs, 246
Bus network, 216–217
Byte, 10

C, 36
Carlson, Chester, 26
Cash register, 101
CD-ROM, 5, 262
Chart of accounts, 102–103, 106–107
Check writing, 101
Clock speed, 10
Coaxial cable, 217
COBOL, 35, 258
Collection of bills, 250–253
Commodore, 36
Commuting business, 72–81, 103–107, 116–118, 126–127, 131–135, 200–210
Compiler, 35
Computer aided design (CAD), 4
Computer aided manufacturing (CAM), 4
Continental Airlines, 232

Damaged data, 238–242
Data entry, 100–102, 237–238, 258
Datum, 139
De Forest, Lee, 31
Department stores, 71, 252, 257–261
Depreciation, 172–176
Desktop publishing, 4, 40
Dial-up security, 241–242
Digital Equipment, 9, 232

INDEX

Directories, 219, 268
Disk storage, 18, 239–240
Double declining balance, 174

Eavesdroppers, 242
Eckert, Presper, 31, 34
Electronic data interchange, 220–224
Electronic funds transfer, 101, 223
Electronic mail, 5, 214, 221–222
ENIAC, 31
Entry, *see* data entry
Excel, 42, 270–271
Expert system, 6, 225–236

Fax machines, 27, 221
Fiber optic cable, 217
Field, 139
File, 139, 267
File server, 218
Floppy disk, 18
FORTRAN, 35
Free space media, 217
Frequency distribution table, 154–155

Gateway, 221
Graphical user interface, 20, 267–269
Gutenberg, Johannes, 24

Hard disk, 18, 219, 268
Hardware, 2
Hierarchy, 104, 135, 219
Hollerith, Herman, 25
Hybrid network, 217

IBM, 19, 32, 34–40, 257
Ice cream shop, 44–65, 195–199
Income statement, 99
Inference engines, 226–228
Information Access Co., 263
Information system, 2
Integrated circuits, 32
Internal rate of return, 161–162

Jacquard, Joseph-Marie, 24
Jobs, Steve, 36
Journal, 98, 110–111, 117–118

Knowledge engineer, 236

Laptop computers, 11
Legal information, 265–266
LEXIS, 265
Library, 262–264

INDEX

LISP, 36, 234
Local area network (LAN), 214–220
Lotus Development Corp., 37

Machine language, 2
Machine readable, 8, 13–14, 24–27, 100, 221–222
Macintosh, 11, 12, 20, 39, 42, 268, 270
Mainframe computers, 9, 257–261
Mauchly, John, 31, 34
Mead Data Central, 265
Memory, 10
Menu, 47, 92, 230
Microcomputers, 9
Microprocessor, 11
Microsoft, 19, 38, 42, 267–271
Minicomputers, 9
Modem, 18
Monitor, 14
Morse, Samuel, 24
Mortgages, 163–171, 254–256
Mouse, 12, 39, 268, 270
MS-DOS, 19, 38, 219, 267–268
Multidimensional budget data, 182

Napier, John, 28
Natural language, 229–230
Net present value, 161, 199
NetWare, 218

Operating system, 19, 267–269
OS/2, 19, 268–269

Parity, 241
Pascal, Blaise, 28
Pascal (language), 36
Password, 242
Performance reports, 129–135
Personnel budget, 81–86, 206–212
PL/I, 36
Point of sale information, 252–253
Posting accounts, 116–123
Present value, 156–161, 199
Price/quantity relation, 46
Printers, 16, 220
Privacy, 247–248
Program, 2, 31, 35
Programming language, 34
Prolog, 36, 234
Punched cards, 25–26
Purchase order maintenance, 257–261

INDEX

Random access memory (RAM), 10
Record, 139
Relational data base, 139–140
Ring network, 215–216

Scanner, 14
Selection, from a data base, 143–152
Server, 218
Shipping service, 81–86, 206–212
Sholes, Christopher, 25
Slide rule, 28
Software, 2, 246
Sorting a data base, 141–143
Star network, 216–217
Straight line depreciation, 174
Sum-of-year's-digits, 174

Tandy, 36
Topology, 215
Transistors, 32
Twisted pair wiring, 217

U.S. government budget, 71, 178–182
UNIVAC, 34

Vacuum tubes, 31
Variance, 130
Viruses, 242–246
VisiCalc, 37
Von Neumann, John, 32

Wang, 257–259
Wendy's, 232
Wide area network, 221
Windows, 20, 39, 269
Word processing, 3, 8, 37
Wozniak, Steve, 36